an environmental
leader's tool kit

an environmental leader's tool kit

JEFFREY W. HUGHES

Comstock Publishing Associates
an imprint of
Cornell University Press
Ithaca and London

First published 2023 by Cornell University Press

Printed in the United States of America

Library of Congress Cataloging-in-Publication Data

Names: Hughes, Jeffrey W., author.
Title: An environmental leader's tool kit / Jeffrey W. Hughes.
Description: Ithaca : Comstock Publishing Associates, an imprint of Cornell University Press, 2023. | Includes bibliographical references and index.
Identifiers: LCCN 2022022095 (print) | LCCN 2022022096 (ebook) | ISBN 9781501768606 (paperback) | ISBN 9781501768613 (pdf) | ISBN 9781501768620 (epub)
Subjects: LCSH: Conservation leadership—Handbooks, manuals, etc. | Environmentalism—Handbooks, manuals, etc.
Classification: LCC S944.5.L42 H84 2023 (print) | LCC S944.5.L42 (ebook) | DDC 333.72—dc23/eng/20220722
LC record available at https://lccn.loc.gov/2022022095
LC ebook record available at https://lccn.loc.gov/2022022096

To those who prove every day that one person can make a difference.

contents

acknowledgments

Trying to execute environmental change is tough, uphill work. It would be far easier, of course, if you didn't need to deal with people—and if they didn't need to deal with you. But people are always part of *every* environmental equation—whether it is working with them, working against them, opening their minds to your side of things, opening your mind to their side of things, getting them to give you money, or any number of other challenges.

The most impactful people in writing this book have been those who have stood in my way. To make headway, I have needed to rethink how we environmentalists do business. For many of us, that means looking within and beyond ourselves, being willing to walk in another person's shoes.

The next most impactful people, and the ones I would most like to thank, are those who sacrifice their evenings and weekends serving on conservation commissions, planning boards, and other citizen groups. Without their selfless, learn-as-they-go efforts we would be facing a very grim future. I am hoping this book makes their efforts easier.

Dozens of known individuals, as well as a number of anonymous reviewers, have had a hand in making this book much, much better. I would like to thank them all by name, but I would go over the manuscript's word limit if I did, so I will limit the list to those who played especially outsized roles: Kate Baldwin, Sean Beckett, Nancy Bell, Alicia Daniel, Susan Drennan, Brett Engstrom, Glenn Etter, Charles Johnson, Dave Kaufman, Matt Kolan, Lisa Meyer, Doug Morin, Rick Paradis, Bryan Pfeiffer, Hannah Phillips, Walter Poleman, Jen Pontius, Peter Sterling, Emma Stuhl, Jacqulyn Teoh, Andy Wood, Kimberly Wallin, Deane Wang, and Justin Waskiewicz. I am also grateful to Ben Lemmond and Carolyn Loeb, who provided the illustrations, and (of course) Kitty Liu, acquisitions editor at Cornell University Press. Thank you all.

**an environmental
leader's tool kit**

Introduction

When a friend shared this story with me thirty years ago, I taped it to my desk as an everyday reminder that one person *can* make a difference, even when the odds are against you. As an environmental consultant, I lived that message 24-7 for a while, running myself ragged trying to make a difference here, there, and everywhere. But back then, most of the starfish I threw into the waves washed back to where I'd found them, no better off than when I had tossed them.

If I hadn't witnessed so many examples of one person moving the environmental needle against seemingly impossible odds, I would have stopped believing that one person *could* make a difference. To figure out what effective environmentalists were doing that I was not, I tore off my dunce cap and compared their successful approaches against mine. Over the years, and with the help of many along the way, I began figuring out which approaches worked, which didn't, and why, ultimately coming up with effective approaches of my own. And it's these approaches that I now share with you in this book—so you can make a difference too.

---

1. My thanks to Loren Eisley for this story.

What This Book Is About

An Environmental Leader's Tool Kit is a Cliff Notes-type training handbook of tools, techniques, approaches, and practical how-to skills for taking on place-based conservation and natural resource challenges and problems. It is for environmentally inclined people who want to make a difference—but lack the experience, knowledge, confidence, or skills to be effective. If you are a planner, consultant, activist, educator, or other environmental professional who needs help developing particular skills that you have not yet mastered, this book can give you the guidance you need. That said, this book is primarily for the unpaid heroes who wrestle with local problems because they care about what is happening in their backyard. *You* are the heroes who come from every political, ideological, religious, race, socio-economic stripe—from farmer to lawyer to teacher to mechanic. You are the ones who step forward to volunteer your time; you are the ones who show up for meetings when you could be home with your kids. You are the ones, through seemingly small actions, who make big things happen.

This book focuses on how to get things done at the local level, where so many meaningful environmental actions take place. Making headway on headline-grabbing environmental issues like climate change and social justice takes time—lots of time—and after years of trying you may not know if you have made any headway at all. Not knowing if your exhaustive efforts have made a difference is discouraging and probably explains why so many eager advocates for global causes lose hope and leave environmental advocacy altogether. Working at the local level is more gratifying because one person's efforts—*your* efforts—can have large, immediate, and lasting payoffs. Each success builds on the last one. Plus the tools, skills, approaches, and knowhow that you need to be effective on environmental matters at the local level are also needed to be effective at regional, national, and international levels. In fact, you will not be successful without them.

Now, the best way to learn real-world environmental skills is to seek guidance from experienced people who know things that you don't—masters who can take you under their wing and show you the way. Some real-world know-how can also be learned through trial and error, of course. And you can always seek advice from the countless books, journals, YouTube videos, Ted Talks, podcasts, advice columns, and online postings out there. But a master's wing rarely is handy when you need it most. Learning as you go doesn't work so well when time is limited and you cannot afford to make mistakes. And sorting through all the material out there to find a few useful gems takes time—lots of time—and it is hard to discern which advice is credible and time-tested, and which isn't. What then?

An Environmental Leader's Tool Kit is the place to turn when you do not have a master to show you the way, or when you do not have time to read a three-hundred-page treatise on a single, narrow topic, or when you cannot drop everything to spend hours searching for useful, practical, time-tested advice. In this book, you will find a broad array of practical, accessible, time-tested, how-to lessons from environmental practitioners like myself who have found what works. The book does not try to be the be-all-end-all source of wisdom on any single skill or tool. But it will show you what you need to know to get where you want to go so you can make a difference. And it may just help you do so before you're in the midst of a challenging situation and don't know what to do—after all, best intentions often go awry. Reflecting after the fact on what you could have done differently will make you more effective next time, but after-the-fact learning will not undo what went wrong. Knowing *ahead of time* what could go wrong—and what you could do to avoid it—works much better. The varied mix of skills, mindsets, and approaches in *An Environmental Leader's Tool Kit* will help you with that.

About the Tools in This Book

Environmental tools can take many different forms: from scientific gizmos having digital readouts to interpersonal strategies that bring people together and regulations that change human behavior. With so many different environmental problems and challenges out there, in so many different places, with so many different interested parties, you might wonder how it is possible for a tool to be universally useful.

Some environmental tools are useful in only one place or situation, of course. The tools chosen for this book, however, have broad application because they address needs that arise almost everywhere. For example, how do you get fence-sitters to join your environmental cause? How do you design a field study that yields the insights you seek? How do you secure funding for your nature center? How do you talk about phosphorus transport in a way that is more fun than a root canal? How do you make sense of unintelligible statistics? How do you chair a public meeting on land-use planning that promises to be hostile? How do you fight the good fight without burning out or sacrificing your own well-being?

Some of the questions in this book, as well as the tools used to answer them, may not at first glance seem especially environmental—they are more what you might find in a leadership or people skills book. That may not sit well with scientists and engineers who believe that environmental decision making and action should not be sullied by messy human perceptions, whims, and personalities. Being a scientist myself, I held those same views until recurring failures eventually convinced me—against my will—that getting meaningful things done in the real world was more important than scientific purity. That is when I really started taking the people factor seriously. Much too often, good intentions and hard work are nullified by insufficient understanding of, or respect for, people. Scientists achieve more when they accept the reality that science alone is never enough to move the environmental dial; in the end, people and their values ultimately decide what happens and what doesn't. The power of stepping out of one's lab coats and connecting with people as fellow human beings, in language laypeople understand, cannot be overstated. And regardless of whether you're a scientist, knowing how to work with people—especially those you disagree with or do not understand—is how you get meaningful things done in the real world. Understanding and showing respect for where others are coming from is the first step. In fact, when you feel certain that you are right and another person is wrong, listen hard to what that person is saying.

As it turns out, people are also your greatest resource for how-to knowledge. Some of the tools in *An Environmental Leader's Tool Kit* have their origins in published research, but much of what the book offers comes from what I have learned these last forty years working with conservationists, environmental advocates, governmental employees, environmental consultants, educators, graduate students, environmental planners, lawyers, and fellow scientists. Working with farmers, loggers, hunters, ranchers, and miners have added real-world perspectives; everyday people trying to make a difference have shown what works and what does not.

These individuals and organizations I've worked with also strongly influenced my decisions on which tools to include in this tool kit instructional guide. I was inspired by what they most often wanted, needed, or sought advice for. I myself sought advice from a dozen leaders and practitioners who have been especially effective at getting things done. I asked them the following three questions:

1. Which tools do they most wish that they'd had from the get-go?
2. Which tools are the most difficult or most painful to learn the hard way?
3. Why do they think so many well-intentioned efforts fall short?

Answers to the first two questions (which have been woven into the *Tool Kit*'s chapters) were quite varied. That was not the case with the third question, however. One reason topped everyone's list: many well-intentioned efforts fall short because people take action before they have accurately identified the exact problem that they want solved. When people jump on a bandwagon prematurely, they invariably choose the wrong tool for the job and come up with a "solution" that achieves nothing useful. Everyone feels the need to rush out and *do* something when crunched for time. But doing something makes sense only if you do the *right* thing.

Three Underlying Realities

This book teaches many science- and people-related skills, techniques, and approaches. Broadly, these are divided across the book's three parts into tools for making sure your actions match up with your desired outcome, tools for getting along with the people you'll encounter and work with, and tools for finding support for your cause and, importantly, for yourself. But none of these tools are of any use unless you internalize three realities.

The first reality is that a tool is a means to an end—not an end in itself. Stated another way: a tool has worth only if it changes a situation from where it is to where you want it to be.

Taking that simple truth to heart is challenging. When upset by a perceived wrong or need, the natural inclination is to get out there and *do something* right away, before you have carefully thought through whether the doing will deliver the outcome that you ultimately seek. That approach rarely ends well: in fact, as alluded to earlier, it accounts for many well-intentioned environmental efforts falling short.

The book's first chapter, "Don't Hammer Nails with a Saw: How to Problem-Solve Effectively," protects you from this fate by showing you how to make sure that what you do gives you what you need. The skills and mindset you will develop in this first chapter—the book's most important chapter—will help you select and use the right tool for the job.

The second reality is that humility makes you more effective. Stated another way: what you take to be the right way or the best way may, in fact, be neither.

When you believe that you are right and the other side is wrong, know this: those on the other side are equally convinced that *they* are right and *you* are wrong. They may have good reason to feel that way, too, and not because they are stupid or uninformed.

The third reality is that people complicate every environmental equation. Stated another way: solutions that lack buy-in have short life spans.

When you are anxious to get something done, it is tempting to skip over dealing with people who might slow your progress. That certainly seems like the path of least resistance, but know this: the people you skipped over will feel disrespected, and some are likely to fight back by sabotaging or undermining your efforts. In addition to making your life miserable, their spiteful actions may completely derail what you are trying to accomplish.

Of course, moving the environmental needle takes more than internalizing the three realities above, it also takes getting out there and actually doing something. *An Environmental Leader's Tool Kit* will help you figure out what those somethings are. Having a good sense of the problem you want to solve, and the research skills you need to achieve your desired end (Part I), is where we will begin.

part I

TOOLS FOR GETTING WHERE YOU WANT TO GO

Clarity on what you're fighting for is the cornerstone of any successful environmental action, but faulty assumptions will lead you astray and render your efforts ineffective. In these three chapters, you'll find tools for aligning your actions with your desired outcome: from determining exactly what it is that you ultimately hope to achieve (it's often not what you think) to conducting research that effectively guides how you proceed.

1

Don't Hammer Nails with a Saw

How to Problem-Solve Effectively

My Uncle Silas offered lots of unasked-for advice—some of it wise, some of it unwise, and some of it downright head-scratching. Among his favorites was this one:

Don't hammer nails with a saw!

As an eight-year-old kid, that advice seemed ridiculously evident to me. Who would be dumb enough to do such a thing? Fifty years later, I have the answer to that question: at some point, almost every one of us *will* try hammering nails with a saw, or try using some other tool that is completely wrong for the job. We are most likely to do that—grab the wrong tool for the job—when time is short, or we are at a loss about how to proceed, or we are overly anxious to get going and do something. Those of us who care deeply about the environment and want to make a difference are not a patient lot. Too often we act before we have really thought through our desired outcome.

This book presents many time-tested tools, but the value of any tool depends entirely on the situation in which it is used—whether it gives you the outcome you seek. That is because—and this was Uncle Silas's message—tools and techniques are possible means to an end, never the end itself. Said another way, tools and techniques can help get you where you want to go, but only if you are clear about your desired destination.

This chapter is about how to effectively tackle environmental challenges and problems by first identifying what you want to come out of your efforts—and why. It teaches you that your work starts by asking questions like *what is the desired end?* and *what change would constitute real success?*, not *what should I do?* and *how do I do it?* The foundational lessons of this chapter should be digested before turning to the specialized tools and techniques in later chapters.

Assessing Your Immediate Inclinations

To guard against going off half-cocked and *doing* something before I have really thought through what I want to come out of my efforts, I assess my immediate inclination by stepping back and answering three questions:

1. What situation do I really want to change?
2. If I had a magic wand that made my wish for change come true, exactly what would I wish for? What outcome would make me feel that my wish had come true?
3. If I go ahead and do what seems like a good thing to do, will the outcome align with the outcome that I am after? Will doing it yield the outcome that makes me feel that my wish came true?

If what seems like a good thing to do lines up with what I want to achieve, I know I am on the right track. If there is a disconnect between the outcome I am seeking and what the doing will achieve, however, the overly eager but chastened me returns to the drawing board to rethink what I should do to get where I want to go.

The following example shows how this back-and-forth might play out. Let's say that I'm very upset about the decline in songbird populations and I am determined to do something about it. As for what needs to happen (what I need to do), the answer seems obvious: educate people, raise awareness!

Before launching an awareness-raising campaign, however, I would press myself to answer the three questions above. My answer to the first question (What situation do I really want to change?) would be: I want the number of songbirds to stop declining.

My answer to the second question (If I had a magic wand that made my wish for change come true, exactly what would I wish for? What outcome would make me feel that my wish had come true?) would be: The number of songbirds is steady or increasing.

Moving on to the third question, I would then ask if my initial line of thinking about what to do (educate people about the problem, raise awareness!) would yield the outcome that I sought (for the number of songbirds to stabilize or increase). To help me think it through, I imagine a best-case scenario—that I implement the (imagined) awareness-raising campaign and it is 100 percent successful. Everyone is now aware of the songbird decline. That would be quite an achievement. But would it matter if the newly educated people just sat on their hands and did nothing? If they did not act on their newfound awareness, what would the doing have accomplished? Would having knowledgeable people do nothing make me feel that my wish for change had come true? Hardly.

A defensive reaction to that possibility might be that educating people would be just a first step to getting the result that I am ultimately after. That may be true, but why settle for a possibly useful first step when you could go for the outcome that you are ultimately after? If what you really want is *action* that stops songbird decline, then *that* should be what your doing focuses on.[1]

Thoughtfully answering the three questions above (and forecasting whether a seemingly good plan for doing will yield the outcome that you are really after) will hopefully make you less inclined to settle on a tool before you have thoroughly assessed whether it is the right tool for the job.

Tools That Look Good but Maybe Aren't

To guard against reinventing the wheel, we instinctively look to see how others have handled a similar situation. That makes lots of sense.

But here is what does not make sense: following someone else's lead (i.e., doing things his or her way) before you have really thought through whether *your* desired outcome exactly matches that person's desired outcome. Many, many times, it doesn't. For example, let's say that your organization or town just acquired a piece of land and your team is tasked with coming up with a stewardship plan for the property. Maybe your team has lots of experience doing this sort of thing, or maybe it doesn't. Either way, from seeing what others have done elsewhere, you know that certain things need to be done, such as:

1. You need to conduct a detailed inventory of the place to see what is there.
2. You need to map the property.
3. You need to establish fifty-foot buffer zones around vernal pools.
4. You need to rid the property of nonnative species.
5. You need to create interpretive brochures and signage.

---

1. That is not to say, of course, that educating people would necessarily be a worthless pursuit. But there is a world of difference between teaching people that a problem exists (raising awareness) and getting them to do something about it!

Those five doings (as well as a few others) have become standard operating procedure for groups tasked with developing a stewardship plan. But should you follow suit? Will those actions necessarily get *you* where you want to go with your property? Let's think each one through before rushing out to do it.

1. Do you really need a detailed inventory of the place? Is every plant, animal, and rock equally important or relevant to how you steward the property? Would it help you to know, for example, how many starlings or dandelions or pine trees the place has? What would you do with that information? How would it help you develop a useful stewardship plan?

2. Why do you need a map? What is it for? Who would use it? For what purpose? What would it show? Would third-graders, citizen scientists, and elderly residents all seek the same type of information? Would a map of natural communities, for example, help you identify where to locate the parking area? Would it point out patches of poison ivy to avoid?[2]

3. How do you decide what constitutes a vernal pool and what does not? Should every puddle or pool on the property be designated a vernal pool worthy of protection, even if amphibians do not use it for breeding? And why a fifty-foot buffer? If the terrain surrounding the vernal pool is steeply sloped (or flat as a pancake), does that matter? Would it affect how wide a buffer needs to be?

4. Why remove the nonnative species? Toward what end? On *your* property are they causing problems or likely to cause problems? Exactly which problems? If the nonnatives are not adversely affecting the species you care about, why bother trying to remove them? Would it be worth the effort of removing them if the surrounding landscape is loaded with nonnatives and is sure to populate your property with new recruits?

5. Why create signage and interpretive brochures? What are you seeking to achieve with them? Who would profit from them? In what way? If most visitors are locals, will they reference the signage and brochures more than once? Then what? Might frequent visitors prefer not having the property cluttered with signs and discarded brochures?

---

2. And don't forget that a good map does not include everything—it only includes what is useful to the user group. All distracting features are left out of the map.

The questions above are just a sampling of questions that you should address before blindly doing what everyone else does. That is not to say, of course, that another person's action plan will not work for your needs—some variation might. But as suggested by the uncomfortable questions asked above, someone else's generalized doings may not get you what you really need. Forecast the answers that will be needed for you to do the *right* thing, and adjust your doings accordingly.

Last, be leery of bandwagons, preconceived notions, accepted practices, and pat answers. To protect yourself from these facile temptations, and to ensure that *your* place or situation drives your actions, ask yourself this: would my actions have been the same if my place or situation had been different? If the truthful answer is that your actions would probably be the same no matter what, then you are taking the lazy, unthinking way out. That is not how you make a difference.

Ferreting Out What You Really Want

As the last section highlighted, the real, underlying problem (and an effective strategy for solving it) are rarely what you initially think they are. That is why trained problem solvers—including those who seek to solve environmental problems—spend excruciating hours or days defining the problem and desired outcome before they launch into actually doing something. Albert Einstein emphasized the importance of accurate problem definition this way: if he had only sixty minutes to solve a problem, he said he would spend fifty-five minutes figuring out the *real* problem that needed solving and spend the remaining five minutes figuring out the best strategy for solving it.

To see how easy it is not to follow Einstein's problem-solving approach, let's say that you are upset about the degraded state of Cowgirl Creek and are determined to fix the problem. The problem seems obvious (the creek is trashed), as does the desired outcome and the action that you need to take (clean it up). So, since (it seems) there is nothing to figure out, you don't waste time hashing over the obvious: you get out there and take action cleaning up the creek—you remove trash from the creek, mandate hundred-foot buffer strips along the creek to keep farming and livestock out, and restore native vegetation by planting trees along the creek. These tried and true solutions (tools) have been used many times in the past, so you are confident that they will work for you too.

Let's say that you successfully implemented the actions above. Would you *really* have solved the Cowgirl Creek problem? That depends on whether your actions addressed the real problem(s) that needed fixing. If your clean-up efforts (described earlier) made the creek look cleaner (less trash and less suspended sediment) but did not reduce *E. coli* to a safe swimming level, would you still judge your restoration effort to be a success?

Or how about high (but invisible) phosphate levels in Cowboy Creek creating dangerous algal blooms downstream in Salmon Lake—would you still feel good about your restoration accomplishment? Or if your restrictive hundred-foot buffer mandate drove some farmer friends out of business but failed to fix any of the creek's main problems—would you be okay with that? The answers to these hypotheticals depends, of course, on which outcomes you are after.

How can you be sure that the seemingly obvious outcomes that you seek are, in fact, the *right* outcomes? Many trained problem solvers and think-tank professionals use the repeat-why technique to push themselves to think beyond what seems obvious.

The Repeat-Why Technique

Being as specific as you possibly can, write down:

How you would like the problematic situation to be different:

(You should write down your answer so you can examine it critically.)

Now carefully analyze your answer and respond to the following questions: *Why* do you care about this? *Why* is it important? *Why* does it matter to you?

1. Why it matters:

(Think hard and record your answers so you can look them over.)

Now carefully examine your response (no. 1 above) by responding to the same set of why questions as before (Why do you care about this? Why is it important? Why does it matter?).

2. Why it matters:

(Again, think hard and record your specific responses.)

Now examine your last response (no. 2 above) and, once again, ask and answer the same set of why questions as before, recording your response(s).

3. Why it matters:

(If answering these questions is not pushing your mind into uncomfortable places, you are not thinking hard enough.)

Now consider your last response (no. 3 above) and again ask and answer the why questions from before. By now, the asking and answering of questions may seem to be leading you into pointless, existential realms. Do not abandon ship; digging deep is what is needed.

4. Why it matters:

Working through this repetitive but mind-bending exercise may make you feel like you are wasting time when you could be actually *doing* something. To show why it is worth hanging in there, let's take a look at one person's progression of thought about the Cowgirl Creek problem using the "repeat why" technique.

The person began by stating what seemed obvious:

- I want Cowgirl Creek to be clean and untrashed the way it used to be.

Her first why-question response (why she thinks that matters) was this:

- We used to swim in the creek and fish for trout but we can't do those things now.
- It's too trashed.

Her responses to the second set of why questions (*why* she thinks her answer above matters) were:

- It saddens me to lose such a special place.
- People shouldn't feel they have the right to trash a resource that's not theirs to trash.

Her responses to the third set of why questions were:

- Spending time beside a beautiful, clear creek grounds me and brings me joy.
- People shouldn't be so selfish, they should think about someone other than themselves.

Her responses to the fourth set of why questions were:

- I need a place to get away from my troubles when I'm having a rough time.
- A cleaned up creek won't stay that way if the selfish people keep acting that way. They'll just keep trashing the place.

She could continue asking and answering why questions, but two important and very different problems have already been clarified:

- Cowgirl Creek no longer provides an emotional refuge for this person.
- A cleaned up Cowgirl Creek won't stay that way unless people who trash the creek change their ways.
- Two very different *desired outcomes* have also been clarified:
- Restore the qualities of Cowgirl Creek that provide an emotional refuge for her.
- Get people to stop trashing the creek.

In the end, removing trash and cleaning up the creek would solve only half of the problem; if people continued to abuse the creek, her success would be short-lived and very unsatisfying. Going through the repeat-why exercise—before putting all her eggs in one basket and rushing off to do what seemed obvious (clean up the creek)—would alert her that she had two problems to solve, not one.

To summarize, it is all too easy to act before you think—to do whatever seems obvious before you have really thought through the problem and what you want to come from your actions. Many efforts fall short of the mark for that exact reason.

The Divide-and-Conquer Method

Ferreting out the real problem, and thinking through exactly which change would make you feel that you had succeeded, is the critical first step in problem solving. But then what? How do you translate your desired outcome into tangible, manageable actions?

If the problem is straightforward and manageable (a rarity in our line of work, unfortunately), solving the problem is relatively simple. In fact, a single tool may be all you need to get the job done. When the problem is more complex, however (e.g., raising money, leading a campaign, recalibrating the American psyche), knowing what to do, or even how to get started, can seem overwhelming—unless you divide and conquer.

To divide and conquer, break the complex problem, challenge, or issue into its component parts—the subset problems—and solve each of them separately, one at a time. This divide-and-conquer approach—solving the more manageable subset problems that collectively create the complex problem—always works better than looking for one do-everything megasolution.

Taking the Cowgirl Creek problem as an example, possible subset problems might include aesthetics, unsafe water for swimming, algal blooms, farmers' livelihoods, and attitudes of people who litter the banks with trash. Clearly, the outcomes that you would seek for these subset problems differ—that is why the subset problems and desired outcomes need to be treated separately and individually. No single, all-encompassing megasolution to the degraded creek problem would work.

Using SMART Objectives to Get Where You Want to Go

Once you have clarified the desired outcome for each subset problem, you can strategize manageable action steps to achieve each. Setting SMART objectives helps you do that. Most objectives, like the following, are neither SMART nor useful:

- Remove trash from Cowgirl Creek streambanks.
- Make Cowgirl Creek cleaner for swimming.
- Put up signs telling people not to litter.

To see how these weak objectives fall short, compare them to the strong SMART objectives below:

- On the section of Cowgirl Creek that flows between Routes 17 and 25, remove all visible streambank trash within twenty-five feet of the creek; complete removal by April 30, 2024.
- By July 15, 2025, reduce *E. coli* counts in surface water at Jenny's Crossing to less than xxx parts per million.
- By May 1, 2023, install a no-littering sign at the trailhead to Jenny's Crossing.

What makes these objectives SMARTER and so much better? Like crisp orders to a soldier, they leave little room for interpretation. They are:

- Specific (**S**) rather than general. You are clear about what you are after—your mission is straightforward and completely understandable.
- Measurable (**M**) rather than ambiguous. There is a clearly specified target against which you can assess your progress so you know when you have accomplished what you set out to do.
- Attainable and Reasonable (**A** and **R**) rather than pie-in-the-sky. What you are proposing is eminently doable.
- Timely (**T**) rather than open-ended. You establish a clear, unambiguous deadline for completion.

Weak objectives most often fall short on specificity, measurability, and timeliness. Study the un-SMART objectives (above) to see how they fall short.

Crafting SMART Objectives

To craft SMART objectives, begin by answering the following question: what collection of objectives, if achieved, would cause you to believe that you had achieved your overall desired outcome?

Record your answers on paper to avoid wandering off track, and be as specific and comprehensive as you can. Then, taking one objective at a time, review it critically to make sure that it:

- includes a verb (verbs force you to think about what you really want as outcomes)
- is measurable (how else can you know if you have completed it?)
- is attainable (if an objective cannot be met, it is not a useful target)
- is reasonable (considering time and resources at your disposal, will you really be able to meet this objective without compromising something else?)
- has a clear, reasonable target date for completion (deadlines force action)
- focuses on one single specific, desired outcome

Another way to assess whether a drafted objective is sufficiently strong (and SMART) follows:

- **Specificity**: If you asked a hundred people to do what the stated objective says to do, would all one hundred people do the same thing?
- **Measurable**: If you asked a hundred people how they would know when they had completed the job, would all one hundred give the same answer?
- **Attainable** and **Reasonable**: If you asked a hundred knowledgeable people about what you proposed to do, would eighty of them agree that it could be done by the stated completion date?
- **Timeliness**: If you asked a hundred people to identify when the stated objective needs to be completed, would everyone give the same answer?

Setting strong, SMART objectives is a key problem-solving skill that is too often given short shrift.[3] When feeling overwhelmed about how to proceed, step back, take a deep breath and approach the challenge in terms of how you can meet your final desired outcome through small, incremental action steps—in other words, divide and conquer.

The People Factor

Solving environmental problems would be infinitely easier if people were not part of the equation. But people and their doings *are* part of the equation.

---

3. Problem solving is, in fact, exactly what you are doing when you try to change a situation from where it is to where you want it to be.

Always. When seemingly great plans fall flat, lack of attention to people and their views is usually the underlying cause. The paragraphs below summarize a few realities that may not be on your everyday radar.

People (like every other organism out there) are inherently—and perhaps unfortunately—selfish, favoring their own self-interests over the greater good. Other organisms may not worry about whether that is honorable or not, but to keep from feeling guilty, we humans find clever ways to justify our selfish actions. For example, environmentally inclined people like me choose to live in the country (and drive cars and burn lots of carbon) when we could live in more carbon-friendly city apartments (and walk to work). We justify this selfish living preference by convincing ourselves that we *need* to live in a rural place to be happy. Convincing people to abandon their hard-wired, self-serving interests is a tough sell. But moderating their selfishness is easier.

When people fail to see things your way, do not assume that it is because they are stupid. Smart, reasonable people can have very different takes on whether or not something is a problem or concerning issue. A proposal to drain Bear Swamp that seems obviously wrong to you, for example, might seem like a great idea to nearby neighbors who hate mosquitoes. And people from afar may not care about the drainage proposal one way or another.

Also do not assume that people who fail to see things your way are uninformed. They may, in fact, be *very* informed—just informed about things that you are not. So before launching a campaign to educate them, educate yourself first. Exercise a little humility and find out (and try to understand) where they are coming from and why. Do not expect them to listen to what you have to say if you are unwilling to listen to what they have to say!

Also recognize that people follow their hearts more than their heads—beliefs, feelings, opinions, and values drive their actions much more than facts or reasoned argument. That accounts for why facts and data—no matter how compelling to you—are frustratingly ineffective at swaying someone else's version of reality. To have much chance of influencing someone's thinking, you need to work *with* the person's beliefs, values, feelings, and opinions. (See chapters 4 and 7 for more on this.)

Last but far from least, recognize that you do not need to reach everyone to be effective. Some people are more important than others when it comes to solving a particular problem or changing a particular mindset. Target those people first.[4]

---

4. "Stakeholder analysis" can help if you are unsure of who these people might be. (References for stakeholder analysis and other problem-solving tools can be found in the Recommended Reading section.)

Some Closing Thoughts

Every environmental effort—from sorting your recyclables to town zoning maps to international climate change accords—is a problem-solving effort because the goal in each case is to change a situation from where it is—the status quo—to a more desired state. The effectiveness of any proffered solution hinges on how well it addresses the exact situation that the problem solver wants changed.

Fixing an environmental problem would be infinitely easier if interested parties all held the exact same values and perspectives on it, but that never happens, even among seemingly like-minded environmentalists. So be careful about assuming that people around you see things the exact same way you do—there is a good chance that they do not. Even subtle differences in perceptions can lead to people trying to solve somewhat different problems, and coming up with solutions that may be at odds with one another. Also watch out for people—yourself included—pushing pet "solutions." Remember that *it is the desired outcome that matters*, not the tool or strategy you use to get there. As we will see in chapters 2 and 3, that applies to research and data collection as well as to connecting with future allies (chapter 4), getting the most out of your team (chapter 5), running a contentious meeting (chapter 6), mobilizing people to take action (chapter 7), raising money (chapter 8), and keeping yourself from going nuts and burning out (chapter 9).

2

Becoming an Ace Researcher

How to Find the Answers
You Need

The first chapter sought to recalibrate how you approach environmental challenges and problems. This second chapter shows how to use that approach when seeking information that you need but do not have.

When you need important information but do not have a lot of time to plan how to get it, the temptation is to get out there ASAP and start collecting data. We justify this knee-jerk approach by assuming that it is the best we can do given the circumstances. As it turns out, however, that assumption is very wrong. My experience trying to make sense of grizzly bear data from Alaska's Denali National Park bore that out in painful ways.

It was my first season as a park ranger, when the chief ranger—the one tasked with updating the park's bear management plan—asked me to analyze data that bear rangers had collected over the years. I didn't know what that entailed, but I was, of course, thrilled beyond imagination.

To get started, I asked the bear rangers what they were trying to learn about Denali Park's grizzly bears. "Everything," they answered. "We are collecting baseline data to guide management decisions."

To me, their open-ended approach to research was a refreshing, welcome break from the boringly narrow research found in scientific journals. Hallelujah! I thought as I sat down to pore over field notes recorded by various bear rangers over a twenty-year period.

The collection of data was incredibly rich and varied. Some rangers gave detailed descriptions of moose kills. Others described individual bears and their behaviors. The field notes also included reports of bears digging for ground squirrels, names of plants that bears seemed to be eating, human-bear interactions, bear-bear interactions, weather events, and musings on the appropriateness of live-trapping and relocating problem bears.

"So what should we do?" my boss asked me a few days later. "Should we close part of the Toklat Campground during the soapberry season?"

(Soapberry, a favorite food of grizzly bears, grew within spitting distance of some of the camping sites.)

The chief ranger needed an answer because the Toklat Campground had only a limited number of camping sites, and demand for those few sites already far exceeded supply. Campers were irate when they were turned away, so the chief ranger wanted to keep open as many camping sites as possible. He needed to balance that consideration, however, against the possibility that keeping sites open might lead to dangerous human-bear encounters.

The chief ranger was in a tough spot, so he turned to science (the bear data) and me for answers. Too bad the data—as abundant as they were—did not provide any answers.

My boss was not happy when I explained that I could not answer his questions. "Well, what *can* you tell me?" he wanted to know.

That question, like his first two, was certainly warranted. But I lacked an immediate answer. When I offered to get him a summary of findings in the morning, he left in a huff. In a panic, I extracted the following findings from the twenty-year data set:

- The rangers made many interesting observations.
- The rangers focused on different things (if they focused at all).
- The twenty years of field notes and collected data did not answer any of the boss's questions.

I sugar-coated those findings for my boss so he would not blow a gasket, but as expected, my report made him *very* unhappy. The boss sought a second opinion on what the data had to say. Unfortunately for him, the second assessment mirrored my own.

Three lessons came from this twenty-year debacle:

1. Research is about answering questions; it is not about collecting data.
2. Unstructured, freelance observations open the mind to new questions and lines of thinking, but they help little when you need clear answers to important questions.
3. Data collection that lacks a clearly defined purpose is usually a waste of time.

Making good decisions about conservation and stewardship matters is hard enough in its own right, but it is downright daunting when you have little information to work with. And the way to deal with this situation is simple in theory—go out and get the information you need. But, as this story with the bears shows, it is much less simple in practice. "Data" have no intrinsic value. They are nothing more than a *means* to an end (answering an important question), not an end in themselves. *Which* data are collected, and *how* they are collected, defines their usefulness. Useful and trustworthy information comes from careful planning and execution, not from hammering nails with a saw—or gathering everything and the kitchen sink about bear behaviors. That is what this chapter teaches.

The Allure of Baseline Data and Inventories

Collecting information on lots of things—often (and mistakenly) referred to as "baseline data"—seems like a can't-lose strategy when you know little about a given situation. And it can be a good strategy if you have really thought through which data to collect and how and why you would collect it. Unfortunately, good intentions notwithstanding, the allure of collecting baseline data often trumps careful consideration of the data collecting purpose.

For example, let's say that you wish to collect "baseline data" on forest health using this common protocol:

> In the center of each forest stand of each forest type, establish one circular sampling plot that is fifty feet in diameter. Within this plot, measure and record the diameter of all trees having diameters greater than four inches. Assess the average fullness of the leafed canopy in the plot by estimating overstory cover (i.e., the percentage of sky that is obscured by leaves). Also count and record the number of dead branches on the three largest trees in the plot. Resurvey twice each year.

At first glance, this widely adopted data collecting approach looks great: you build on earlier baseline data and develop the capability to detect worrisome trends in growth rates of trees (through diameter measurements), health of canopy foliage (through percent cover estimates), and dieback (through counts of dead branches).

At second glance, however—which usually does not occur until many years too late—the near worthlessness of the collected data becomes apparent. For example, because of the way percent cover estimates were made, almost half of the canopy leaves would need to be missing before those data would alert you to any problem. People looking out their car windows at fifty miles per hour would notice the forest health problem far earlier than that!

But the data shortcomings would not end there. Would the measured tree diameters be of any value if subsequent measurements were made at slightly different locations on the tree trunk? And how meaningful would the "baseline" count of dead branches on a tree be, given that all trees naturally sacrifice existing branches that are not earning their keep? And what is to be gained by surveying a plot three times a year? Wouldn't frequent surveys have unintended impacts themselves?

Numerous other assumptions, shortcomings, misperceptions, and expectations commonly come with collecting data before you have really thought through what you are hoping to get out of it. One expectation—a misplaced one—is held by far too many environmentalists: that the baseline data they collect today will be useful at a future date. Don't believe that. Baseline data that were collected without a clear guiding question almost always wind up in the dumpster.

Another strategy people tend to turn to when they don't know much about a given situation or a place is conducting an inventory or survey to see what is there. And it *might* make lots of sense *if* you rigorously think through what questions you seek to answer with the inventory *before* you start collecting data. The following example illustrates what typically happens when you do not put in that up-front effort. Let's say that an organization's stated mission is to protect critical wildlife habitat. A strip of undeveloped land along the Pleasant River has just come on the market, and a decision needs to be made soon about whether the organization should try to acquire it. People in the organization know virtually nothing about the property (not a desirable situation to be in when a million dollars are on the line and the organization does not have much cash in hand), but everyone is worried that the land will be developed into trophy homes if they do not acquire it.

The predictable, reactionary approach to this challenge is *Quick, we need to do something!*, with a frenzied, comprehensive, all-purpose inventory/survey launched to find out what is there. This approach is alluring because it is familiar, it produces lots of data in a hurry, it covers many bases, and it is commonly used by others. Those seemingly wonderful qualities notwithstanding, the inventory probably would not yield much of anything useful. Why? Because comprehensive, all-purpose inventories yield data rather than meaningful answers. For example, a comprehensive see-what's-there inventory of the Pleasant River property might tell you how many dandelions, red maples, earthworms, and robins are on the property. But so what? Would that information help the organization decide if it should spend a million dollars on the Pleasant River property? Wouldn't the organization rather have answers to more specific, relevant questions, such as:

- How much quality habitat for valued wildlife species x, y, and z is there on the Pleasant River property?
- To what extent are wildlife species x, y, and z using the Pleasant River property?
- Compared to other similarly priced properties, does the Pleasant River property have appreciably more quality habitat for valued wildlife species x, y, and z?

Figuring out exactly which question(s) you would most like answered—before you do anything else—ensures that you collect the *right* data.[1]

Scrutinizing Your Research Question and Data Needs

When your question and data needs seem obvious (which is how they usually appear), why waste time going over what you (think you) already know? Because your assumptions on what you need are not good enough when it comes to collecting the right data for the job. You can save yourself lots of future grief by holding off on data collection until you have subjected your presumed question and data needs to tough scrutiny. Here's a four-step way for how to do so:

1. Draft a research overview.
2. Set SMART objectives.
3. Create dummy graphs.
4. Play the three items above off against one another to make sure that they align.

The sections below go over each of these four steps; further questions to tighten up your research question and data needs follow.

The Research Overview

Always start by drafting a written overview of a research effort. This Research Overview, akin to an elevator talk or farmer's overview (chapter 7), explicitly

---

1. Defining the questions first also protects you from collecting data that you will not use. That may not seem like a big deal, but it is: the precious time that you waste collecting marginally useful data could have been spent collecting data that really could have helped you.

states the exact question or unknown that you are pursuing, with enough context, background, and explanation to make the overview interesting and meaningful to an outside party.

A good Research Overview explains succinctly and convincingly, using simple, jargon-free language, *why* my research undertaking is important. For example:

- *Research Overview of Project #1:* I am trying to figure out why the spruce-fir forest is in decline. That is a concern because the spruce-fir forest provides jobs and recreational opportunities for millions of New Englanders, and the forest also provides prime habitat for moose and bear. I am thinking the problem might be caused by harvested areas being so large that seeds cannot make it to many parts of the regrowing forest. That is why I am counting seedlings at increasing distances from the forest edge—to see if the number of seedlings declines as you get farther into the harvested area. If that is what I find, the solution might be as simple as making harvested areas smaller or narrower.
- *Research Overview of Project #2:* I am trying to figure out where pink lady slipper orchids grow best. If we can identify this rare flower's pre-ferred habitat, we can do a better job of managing landscapes to protect and increase its numbers. Some people think that lady slippers are found only on deep soils that are rich in nitrogen and organic matter. By monitoring the depth and nitrogen and organic content of soils where lady slippers are and are not found, I am hoping to settle this part of the lady slipper mystery.

Contrast the good Research Overviews (above) with the lousy ones below:

- *Bad Research Overview of Project #1:* I am quantifying fir and spruce seedlings (< 0.5m in height) in plots (1m x 1m each) on five-year-old clearcuts. We are sampling ten clearcuts, with the placement of plots (thirty per clearcut) stratified by distance to the forest edge. We will assess differences in density with a one-way analysis of variance. This will allow us to determine the density and size distribution of stems in these regrowing stands.
- *Bad Research Overview of Project #2:* I am measuring soil depth, organic content, and nitrogen mineralization at sites with and without *Cypripedium acaule*. I plan to sample twenty sites of each and compare them with a t-test. To measure soil depth, I will use a surveying pin and ruler;

to quantify organic content, I will ash samples in a muffle furnace; to measure mineralization, I will use the buried-bag method. Why am I studying *Cypripedium*? Because we know almost nothing about it.

Notice that the bad overviews fail to articulate the question or unknown behind the research. They also fail to provide context or background or any sort of explanation for why the research effort is important. Instead, they spew confusing collections of unconnected, jargon-filled details that would leave listeners wondering, "So what? Who cares?" or "What does this have to do with anything?" A Research Overview that prompts those types of questions is a warning sign that you may not really have thought through what you are doing, or why you are doing it.

To summarize, a good Research Overview:

- clearly and quickly captures the essence of the question that you hope to answer
- explains why your undertaking is interesting and important
- identifies specific data needs without going into unnecessary detail[2]
- is presented in simple, jargon-free language

SMART Research Objectives

A good Research Overview places your research question and data needs in context and highlights the new understandings that you hope to glean from your research. SMART objectives (introduced in chapter 1) partition this big picture overview into a collection of more manageable action steps—desired outcomes—that collectively cause you to believe that you have gotten the information that you really want or need.

As a reminder, SMART objectives are: Specific, Measurable, Attainable, Reasonable, and specify the Time (deadline) for completion. The following objectives have those qualities:

- Reduce maximum phosphate levels in Cowgirl Creek by at least 20 percent in each of the next ten years.
- Within two hours after five rainfall events this summer, determine if fecal coliform counts around Gull Island exceed state limits.

---

2. Specific details about how the study is being conducted are saved for later, if the listener is interested.

- For each of the next four years, compare survivorship of first-year opossums in town parks where dogs are, and are not, allowed to run free.
- Assess daytime use of the town beach on sunny and cloudy days this summer, from June 15 through August 30.

The research objectives above provide useful guidance because they are specific, measurable, attainable, and reasonable, and they have a timeline for completion. Objectives that lack these qualities leave much to be desired. The following examples of research objectives are far from being SMART:

- Improve the water quality of Cowgirl Creek.

  Weaknesses: This objective is so vague and open-ended that it provides no data collection guidance whatsoever. What does "water quality" mean? Is the problem beer bottles? Old tires? PCBs? What level of improvement are you seeking? How will you know if and when the water has become clean enough? If phosphate levels were reduced by one molecule per year, would that constitute success? Probably not. How about 100 milligrams/liter? Is that reduction attainable? Is it reasonable? As for timing, is there a point at which you'd judge the clean-up effort to be taking too long? If it took five thousand years to clean up Cowgirl Creek, would that be acceptable?
- Monitor pollution inputs around Gull Island.

  Weaknesses: This objective lacks specificity. Which pollutants? Which inputs? This objective also lacks measurability—how will you know if the monitoring was adequate? This objective also lacks a timetable—when should the monitoring take place? For how long?
- Compare health of opossums living in town parks.

  Weaknesses: This objective lacks specificity, a timeline, and measurability—an unambiguous way to know whether you have met this objective.
- Determine how much the town beach is being used.

  Weaknesses: Again, this objective lacks specificity, measurability, and a timeline.

Crafting SMART objectives for a research undertaking is hard work because it forces you to think hard about details and decisions that you are uncertain about or do not want to deal with.[3] Those research details and decisions must

---

3. Be sure that each objective includes a verb—verbs force you to think about what you *really* want as outcomes.

not be taken lightly, however, because they affect *which* data you collect, and *how* you go about collecting them.

Dummy Graphs

Sometimes it is hard to nail down SMART objectives, or to know which objectives are most important. Dummy graphs counter these difficulties by presenting your data needs visually.

To understand how dummy graphs can be used to clarify objectives, pretend that you are a reporter for *USA Today* and that you wish to convey to readers what you want your research to reveal. If you were instructed to tell your research story visually with only a few graphs or diagrams, exactly which graphs or diagrams would you produce? How would you present the bottom-line story in just a few graphs? The graphs that you produce—if they accurately capture what you are hoping to learn—would be visualizations of your SMART objectives.[4] If you replace a dummy graph's phony data with real data, you are assured of meeting the objective that your dummy graph portrays.[5]

Another way to think about dummy graphs and how to use them is to imagine that you have wrapped up your research and are putting together a PowerPoint presentation of just a few slides to report your most important findings. Which graphs would you include in your presentation? What collection of three PowerPoint slides would best tell the story that you wish to tell?

When creating dummy graphs, I personally prefer sketching them by hand so I am not distracted by the many formatting decisions that arise when using a computer application like Excel. Your preference notwithstanding—making crude dummy graphs by hand or polished ones by computer—be sure to label axes and specify units (e.g., kg, #/ha) completely and exactly. Also be sure to include a clear, complete, descriptive caption for each dummy graph. In the end, the litmus test for a good dummy graph is this: an unknowing passerby who picks the dummy graph off the floor should be able—without additional information, clarification, explanation, discussion, or narrative—to accurately recount the graph's intended take-home message.

---

4. In scientific writing, both graphs and diagrams are usually referred to as figures rather than as graphs or diagrams.

5. That works far better than the way most people do it (i.e., collecting data before figuring out what to do with it)!

The example below illustrates the relationship between objectives and dummy graphs, and how a dummy graph highlights the exact data that you need to collect:

Research Question: Why are there fewer Blue-Wing Teal in Bixby Marsh than there used to be?

Brief Research Overview: Over the past few years, duck hunters have been seeing many fewer Blue-Wing Teal in Bixby Marsh than they used to. Hunters have passed along their concerns to the Fish and Wildlife Service, and the staff scientists have decided they need to establish that the number of Blue-Wing Teal in Bixby Marsh is indeed declining.

Objective 1: To compare, by the end of the month, densities of Blue-Wing Teal in Bixby Marsh from at least three different Septembers.[6]

A dummy graph to tell that story might be figure 2.1.

Let's assume that you met this first objective and are now satisfied that the presumed pattern (that there are fewer Blue-Wing Teal in Bixby Marsh now than there used to be) is in fact true. With that reality established, you now can explore *why* there are fewer teal.

There are numerous possible reasons for why the teal population has declined, and any one of them could trigger a data collection effort. For example, if you chose to assess whether the decline is a function of fewer resident ducks living in Bixby Marsh or fewer ducks migrating in, your first cut at a research objective might be:

To determine if populations of both resident and migrant Blue-Wing Teal are declining.

This objective seems straightforward enough, and a cursory look at it leads you to believe that it is sufficiently specific, measurable, attainable, and realistic to be a useful target. I hope you will notice, however, that it is missing the time component, so you will make the necessary adjustment:

Objective 2: For the next three years, determine if populations of both resident and migrant Blue-Wing Teal are declining.

---

6. To simplify discussion, let's say that there have been periodic surveys and these data have been made available to you.

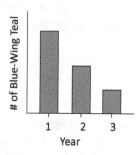

FIGURE 2.1.

With this second objective clarified, it seems that you need only decide how to inventory resident and migrant ducks. You check in with waterfowl experts to see how they would inventory resident and migrating ducks and then go forth and collect data. Since you are following the advice of experts, you are confident that you will get the data you need. And you *might* get the data you need. But you might not.

To see what could go wrong, let's fast forward to the end of your study and imagine that you are presenting your findings to concerned biologists and hunters. If you presented one of the following graphs (figs. 2.2a, b, and c), would you feel that your research effort was a success, that you came up with the answer? Would audience members feel that your research findings gave them what they needed to arrest the decline?

Maybe not. Let's say you found that the resident duck population is declining while the migrant population is not (fig. 2.2b). That is a good start

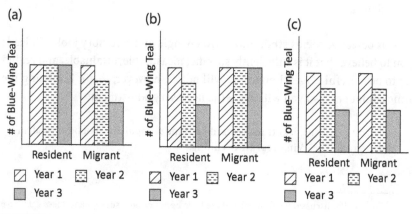

FIGURE 2.2.

because it directs you to focus future research efforts on resident ducks rather than migrants. But three years have passed, and you are really not much closer to stemming the decline than when you started. How satisfying is that?

You could have been much further along in solving the Bixby Marsh duck decline if you had used dummy graphs to identify the *exact* data you needed to collect. Consider figure 2.3, for example. Wouldn't it go much further in explaining what is going on than figure 2.2? How about figure 2.4? Doesn't it tell a more complete story than figure 2.2?

With a little forethought stimulated by dummy graphs, you could have identified and collected data that were more revealing and useful.

A dummy graph helps you visualize—before you start collecting data— exactly which stories you will be able to tell at the end of your study.

Here is another example of how dummy graphs could push you to identify those data that would help you most:

Research Question: How does rangeland vegetation change as distance from the creek increases?

Brief Research Overview: In the arid West, streamside zones are highly valued by both ranchers and environmentalists. Ranchers value streamside zones as producers of forage for livestock; environmentalists value streamside zones as hotspots for biological diversity. To guide future legislation on how stream sides should be managed and used, proposals are afoot to define the upland boundary of streamside zones.

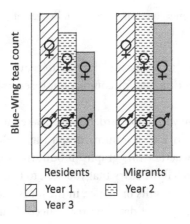

FIGURE 2.3.

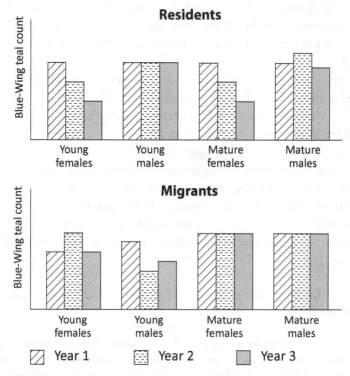

FIGURE 2.4.

One objective that, if met, would seem to answer the research question is the following:

> *Objective:* This summer, quantify the ground cover of plants from the creek bank to the dry uplands.

This objective appears to be specific, measurable, attainable, and reasonable, and it has a specified timeline for completion. It seems that you are ready to start collecting data.

Before strapping on your clipboard, however, take the precautionary step of displaying your objective as a dummy graph (fig. 2.5). You can then think futuristically about whether this graph—if built from real data—would give you what is needed to tell the story that you seek to tell.

Putting your desired results on paper, in the form of dummy graphs, helps you think about exactly what data you really need. It also protects you from wasting time collecting data that you really do not need. For example, looking

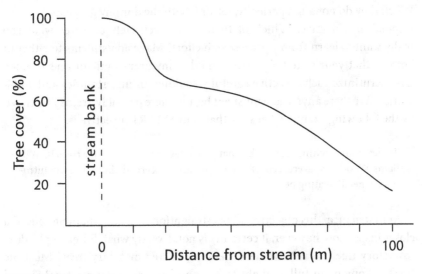

FIGURE 2.5.

over figure 2.5 alerted me to something that should have been obvious: that lumping all vegetation together into a single value of percent cover would tell me nothing about where individual species grow, or how their abundance changed as I got farther from the stream. Moreover, the dummy graph made me recognize that estimating percent cover would not reveal the presence of a rare wildflower that is growing in a grassy or brushy environment. A count of individuals would be much more revealing.

Many other realizations and wonderings were triggered by studying dummy graph 2.5. All were brought to the forefront by asking a simple question: if I were to collect the exact data needed to make this dummy graph real, would the resulting graph tell the take-home message? Would I have what I need to tell the story that I want to be able to tell? If the answer is yes, then the dummy graph has reinforced your notion about exactly which data you need to collect. If the answer is no, however, you need to rework your dummy graph until it *does* tell the story that you wish to tell. (Appendix 1 offers further tips on how to tell stories with graphs.)

Aligning Your Research Overview, SMART Objectives, and Dummy Graphs

When you are happy with your dummy graphs, check to make sure that they match your stated objectives. Usually, there is at least a minor disconnect.

When they do not align perfectly, rethink both the dummy graph and its corresponding objective. Which of them more accurately captures what you really want to learn from your research effort? Make adjustments to either or both so that your stated objectives and dummy graphs mirror one another. Last, scrutinize each objective carefully, looking for uncertainties and ambiguities. Are there any? There must not be, but there probably are, as illustrated by the following example. Let's say that your SMART objective is:

> To determine, within the week, what percentage of the overstory trees in Williams Woods are evergreen. (Perhaps you are concerned about a newly introduced, needle-eating pest.)

At first glance, this objective seems straightforward and unambiguous. On closer inspection, however, it certainly is not. Exactly what, for example, does "overstory tree" mean? Are dead trees considered overstory trees? Must the tree's canopy be in full sunlight to be considered an overstory tree? Should small trees growing in a forest opening be considered overstory trees if they are only five feet tall but all other stems are shorter? What does "this forest" mean? Should roadside edges of the forest be considered part of this forest? Should planted trees be included in the data set?

Most research questions, and many objectives, have ambiguities in them. These ambiguities must be clarified so that objectives are clear and completely unambiguous. Fuzzy objectives yield fuzzy data—the very thing you want to avoid.

Ambiguities in objectives can be corrected by defining, on paper, your intentions for each ambiguous phrasing. Record these clarifications directly beneath the objective. Using the objective above as an example (to determine, within the week, what percentage of the overstory trees in Williams Woods are evergreen), here are two possible clarifications:

- "Overstory trees" refers to all living trees not obviously planted that are more than fifty feet tall and whose canopies are in full sunlight.
- "Williams Woods" refers to all land within the marked boundaries of the property that is not obviously wetland and is not obviously recovering from recent forest management or fire.

A vigorous effort to remove ambiguity in objectives sometimes uncovers serious flaws or oversights in your study. Use these discoveries to strengthen your objectives and corresponding dummy graphs.

When developing a design for data collection, be sure to treat each objective as a study unto itself, with its own set of dummy graphs. If an objective is too broad to be represented by a single dummy graph, break it down into smaller, more manageable mini-objectives, and craft a dummy graph for each. Resist temptations to design one mega, do-everything data collection scheme. That approach always fails.

In isolation, mini-studies and mini-questions appear esoteric, unimportant, and uninteresting. Finding answers to a collection of small, focused questions, however, is usually the only way to answer a big, important question. But breaking a meaningful and important question into a set of more manageable mini-objectives and mini-studies can leave you and others wondering what happened to the question you were trying to answer in the first place. Research Overview to the rescue! Rereading your Research Overview will help you and others see the forest for the trees—how answers to the small, focused questions collectively answer the big, main question.

Some Further Questions to Ask Yourself

Once you feel confident that your questions and desired outcomes hit the mark, tighten them even further with these follow-up questions. Be sure to record your answers so that nothing falls through the cracks.

- How much time do you have to commit to the research effort? Do not overlook the reality that *collecting data* is only one part of a research effort, *processing and presenting the data* is the other. Expect data processing and presentation to take at least as much time as data collection.
- How exact does the answer to each question need to be? To be useful, the answer to a question must, of course, be sufficiently exact, precise, and reliable for your needs. *But it need not be better than your needs, and probably should not be.* If you wanted to know the density of fallen pine seeds and were counting seeds on the forest floor, for example, consider the resolution needed. Would you really need to know that exactly 637 seeds were found, or would a determination of 650 seeds/plot (+/– 25 seeds) be good enough? Would laboriously counting seeds one-by-one be worth the effort? Probably not.
- Might *when* you collect data—the season, time of day, recent or current weather—affect your results? Many animals use different habitats at different times of the year, are active at different times of day, or respond

noticeably to certain weather events. *When* you collect data can similarly tweak measurements of plants, soils, and water.

- Might you or someone else someday wish to duplicate your study in the exact same place? If so, permanently mark the sampling locations.

Developing a Tailored Data Collecting Plan

As suggested above, be leery of cookbook plans that claim to be the answer to your data collecting needs. There is no single right or best way to conduct research, because it is the *question* that dictates how a study is conducted, and which data need collecting. Someone else's approach, no matter how widely used, may not work for your question. Be discerning!

Most research efforts seek to answer more than a single question (you will know that you are seeking to answer multiple questions if you need more than one dummy graph to tell your story). To develop a data collecting plan that answers different questions, stay away from generalized, all-purpose, do-everything, one size-fits-all plans. Generalized plans do produce lots of data, but a lot of data is not what you need. What you need is the *right* data for each of your questions. All-purpose data collection plans will not give you that.

To develop a data collecting plan that is sure to give you what you need, divide and conquer (chapter 1) your research into smaller, more manageable units. Begin by developing a mini-plan for your first dummy graph, pretending that it is the only graph you need. Once you have developed a data collecting mini-plan for that first dummy graph, put it aside and move on to your second dummy graph. As with the first dummy graph, focus *solely* on developing a data collecting mini-plan for this second dummy graph. Continue this process of dividing and conquering your data needs and approaches until you have a mini-plan for each dummy graph. Taken together, the mini-plans become an effective, if not efficient, data collecting plan for your research undertaking. A trial run (pilot study) tightens the overall plan and makes it more efficient.

Launching a Pilot Study

Armchair preparation and planning will get you only so far in developing a good data collecting plan. You cannot know how well your seemingly great plan works until you troubleshoot by giving it a real-world try.

Before committing to full-scale implementation, always give your study plan a limited test run—a pilot study—to see what works and what doesn't.

Visit your field site or one very similar to it and collect data until you have enough to play with later. You will not include these data in your real study—they are just for practice—but you should proceed as though you are collecting them for keeps.

As you are collecting data in a pilot study, look for weaknesses, problems, glitches, and inefficiencies and take note of what is difficult, problematic, or especially time-consuming. If a better approach occurs to you, try it out and revise your plan as you go. Before departing the study area, draft an improved study plan, noting parts that need help or further consideration.

Your pilot study will suggest ways to fashion a data sheet that is efficient and easy to use in the field. That is fine, but remember that *collecting* the data is less than half the battle. Managing, transcribing, processing, and analyzing field data can be an absolute nightmare if the data are not arrayed properly on the data sheets when they are collected. Save yourself many hours of mind-numbing drudgery later—know exactly what you will do with your real data *before* you collect it!

It is near certain that you will need to enter your data into a computer spreadsheet or graphing program for analysis, so create data collection sheets that mirror the spreadsheet program that you will be using. Doing so makes data entry infinitely easier and reduces the likelihood of errors in transcription. Another option is to take a portable computer into the field and enter field data directly into the spreadsheet.

If you will be analyzing your data statistically (which you will for a monitoring study, see next chapter), seek advice from a statistician about how the data should be organized on the spreadsheet. Run a practice analysis using data you collected in your pilot study.

Having done all of the above, sit on your revised study plan for a bit, overnight if possible, so that your subconscious has time to chew over additional ways to improve it. Oftentimes the best improvements come after a little mental fermentation.

Getting Good Advice from Experts

When you don't know what to do or how to do it, seeking advice from experts seems a wise way to proceed. And it is wise—*if you know precisely what advice you are seeking.* Experts will not give you good advice, however, if you fail to present your needs clearly, or if you fail to ask the right questions.

To get off on the right foot with experts, introduce yourself and use your Research Overview to efficiently explain what you are up to. Briefly outline your needs and constraints—time, personnel, and financial. If experts challenge your assertions, all the better—take it as an invitation to explain your thinking to them. The better they understand what you're trying to do, the more helpful they can be.

Your Research Overview and statement of needs should not take more than a couple of minutes, so practice your spiel until you can give it in that short amount of time. Show experts the exact (written) questions that you are hoping to answer. Taking your questions one at a time, walk them through your dummy graphs and Power Point mock-up slides, asking: "These are the data that I think I need to answer the question—does that make sense?"

If experts agree that your proposed slides and graphs do make sense and will answer your question, ask how they would advise going about getting real data to replace the phony data on your dummy graphs. Listen carefully to their advice, take copious notes, and play back your understanding of what they tell you. If their suggestions confuse you or go against what makes sense to you, don't be timid—ask respectful questions until the advice makes sense.

Give careful consideration to expert advice, spoken or written, but do not mindlessly swallow it hook, line, and sinker. Experts naturally assume that *their* methods and techniques are the best methods. And they very well might be the best for the questions that *they* seek to answer. But recognize that the questions that *you* want answered may be somewhat different from theirs and you might need somewhat different information. Use your dummy graphs and your mock-up slides and your desired outcomes to articulate *your* exact needs. Be a little pushy (in a respectful way) by pointedly asking if *their* proposed methods and techniques will get you the data that *you* need.

Some Closing Thoughts

The purpose of some research is to affirm or support a position that you hold dear. That is all well and good, but how do you proceed when your findings contradict what your heart wants and expects to hear? Which carries greater weight: your deeply held beliefs and values, or the truths revealed by scientific data?

If you are sufficiently passionate about an issue—reintroduction of wolves or wilderness protection, for example—you will probably hold firm to your conviction, data be damned.[7] As for whether it is wrong to cling to

---

7. In that respect, you and your opposition have much in common!

convictions that are refuted by data, that is only marginally relevant, because strongly held values and beliefs are rarely spawned by rational, critical analysis. That reality, however, does not prevent most of us from treating them as absolute truths.

At some point, science will likely refute one of the environmental "truths" that you have held dear for a long time—for example, that selectively cutting trees is always better than clearcutting a forest. How you handle this discordance defines you in the minds of others. Once labeled, you are stuck. If you hope to work with people outside the choir, never pretend that your position is based on science and data when it is really an expression of a deeply held conviction. Nothing undermines your credibility faster or more completely than pretending that your position is based on science when it is not.

Honest admission helps others understand where you are coming from, and why you are not listening to reasoned argument. *Never massage data to support a deeply held conviction.* Stilted reporting may go unnoticed for a while, but the truth will catch up with you eventually. When you take the low road, you surrender your two strongest weapons—credibility and integrity.

The next chapter, "Things You Need to Know about Data Collection and Statistics," shows the inner workings of science and how researchers seek to promote objectivity over subjectivity in decision making. Two underpinnings of science, question asking and statistical analysis, guide how data are collected and how conclusions are reached with a known level of confidence. Chapter 3 may not make you a scientist but, hopefully, it will help you think like one.

3

Things You Need to Know about Data Collection and Statistics
How to Take Your Research Skills to the Next Level

The previous two chapters (I hope) have convinced you to challenge the counterproductive assumption that your question and data needs for a research effort are obvious. This chapter tackles other underpinnings of effective research—knowing what type of research question you're asking, hypothesis testing, and statistics (including why statistics is such a big deal in science). This chapter also teaches another critical but overlooked skill: describing your data collecting approach so that others understand exactly what you did and how you did it.

Identifying Your Research Question Type

The research question you seek to answer determines exactly which data you should collect, but it's the *type of question* you are asking which determines *how* you go about collecting and analyzing those data.

Research questions are of three types: **inventory/descriptive, comparative/ monitoring,** or **how/why**-oriented. You need to discern correctly which type of question you are asking; if you don't, your data collecting strategy will likely fall short of giving you what you need.

The three question types differ in the following ways:

- An **inventory/descriptive-type question** is a wondering about what something is, what something does, what is in a place, or how many of them there are. For example, how many moose live in Yellowstone National Park? What is today's *E. coli* level at Narragansett Beach? Where are the rare species in the Wenlock Management Area?
- A **comparative/monitoring-type question** is a wondering about whether one thing is different from another in a meaningful way, or whether a

thing changes meaningfully as time passes. For example, are nonnative worms expanding their range? Is a fifty-foot stream buffer more effective than a twenty-five-foot buffer? Has the number of calypso orchids in Oxford County changed over the last ten years?

- A **how/why-type question** is a wondering about *how* or *why* a particular event, trend, or situation is the way it is. For example, why do so many leopard frogs have deformed limbs? How do bears know what is good to eat?

Inventory/descriptive-type questions and comparative/monitoring are the bailiwick of environmental practitioners because the questions and answers have immediate, practical importance. How/why-type questions are more often pursued by PhD research scientists.[1]

Inventory/descriptive-type questions and comparative/monitoring-type questions may appear to be one and the same, but they are not. That matters because the data collecting approaches needed to answer the two types can be completely different: data collected to answer comparative/monitoring-type questions must be collected in a way that is statistically valid (more about statistics below). There is no such requirement for inventory/descriptive-type questions but—as with any research endeavor—the question dictates which data you collect, and how you collect them. Appendix 2 offers suggestions to help you with this.

To make the distinction between inventory/descriptive and comparative/monitoring-type questions clearer, here are some examples of comparative/monitoring-type questions that may be mistaken for inventory/descriptive-type questions:

- Are lady slippers substantially more common in some habitats than others? (This is a comparative/monitoring-type question because different habitats are being compared.)
- Has the number of lady slippers changed significantly over the last twenty years? (This is a comparative/monitoring-type question because the number of lady slippers from different years is being compared.)
- Are lady slippers responding in a meaningful way to management? (This is a comparative/monitoring-type question because managed and unmanaged places are being compared.)

---

1. Asking how/why questions is easy—five-year-olds excel at it. *Answering* how/why questions with any degree of certainty, however, is often exceedingly difficult.

The Importance of Hypothesis Testing

Hypothesis testing is not used much for inventory/descriptive-type questions but it is *the* method that scientists use to answer comparative/monitoring and how/why-type questions. Scientists embrace hypothesis testing method for these types of questions because:

- The method is transparent—everyone can see how you arrive at an answer.
- The answer (conclusion) is not influenced by your personality, preference, agenda, or bias.
- The answer (conclusion) is framed in terms of probability rather than by impression or subjective assessment—you therefore know how confident you should feel that your conclusion is correct.

Hypothesis testing works by evaluating whether the available evidence supports or refutes your best guess as to what is going on. That best guess is your hypothesis—a clear, straightforward prediction. Weather forecasters, for example, state their hypotheses as weather reports; gamblers express their hypotheses as bets. Fishermen hypothesize an effective strategy each time they select a fishing lure and try to catch fish with it. The accuracy of their hypotheses is tested by the results they get.

Since hypotheses are nothing more than predictions or possible explanations, getting them on paper is easy: simply write down, in present tense and as a complete, declarative sentence, what you think the correct explanation(s) to your question might be. Examples of hypotheses for some how/why and comparative/monitoring-type questions are shown below.

- Why are fewer than a third of the nesting terns laying eggs? (a how/why-type question)
- Possible hypotheses:
  - Many of the nesting terns are not yet of reproductive age.
  - Some nesting terns have not laid their eggs yet.
  - Some terns laid eggs but lost them to raccoons.
- Why does the town of Shelburne have more green space than the town of Winooski? (a how/why-type question)
- Possible hypotheses:
  - The town of Shelburne has more total acreage than the town of Winooski.
  - Shelburne's conservation commission purchases more land for green space than does Winooski's conservation commission.

- More Shelburne residents donate land to the town.
- Is Ted's Poultry Farm the main source of nitrate in our groundwater? (a comparative/ monitoring-type question)
- Possible hypotheses:
  - More than half of the nitrate in our groundwater comes from Ted's Poultry Farm.
  - Ted's Poultry Farm contributes more nitrate to groundwater than does any other source.
  - Ted's Poultry Farm contributes the same amount of nitrate to groundwater as do other sources.
- Has citizen participation in Earth Day activities declined since President X took office? (a comparative/monitoring-type question)
- Possible hypotheses:
  - Citizen participation in Earth Day activities has declined since President X took office.
  - Citizen participation in Earth Day activities has not changed since President X took office.
  - Citizen participation in Earth Day activities has grown since President X took office.

Notice that we generated a number of hypotheses for each question. You always should do likewise to protect yourself from tunnel vision. It is easy to lose objectivity when you put all of your eggs in the basket of a single, pet hypothesis!

If you use an appropriate data collection design to answer a comparative/ monitoring or how/why-type question, you can test your hypothesis statistically.[2] Statistical analysis has a powerful role in hypothesis testing and question answering (comparative/monitoring and how/why-type questions, less so with inventory/descriptive-type questions) because it forces objectivity. It does so by assessing the probability that your hypothesized pattern or process is real rather than imagined.

The Essentials of Statistics, Statistical Analysis, and Variability

My friend Mark (not his real name) landed a part-time job at a small, environmental consulting firm by knowing someone who knew someone who

---

2. See the Recommended Reading section for recommendations.

put in a good word for him. Like most entry-level consultancy workers, Mark spent most of his time running errands and doing other scut work. On occasion, though, he helped collect, transport, and prep water samples for analysis. It was not wildlife biology, which was Mark's passion, but collecting environmental data was real science, and he was proud to be doing it.

When the consulting firm landed a big new wetland contract, Mark went full-time as a wetland and data management specialist. He was thrilled. Over the next few months, Mark collected, processed, and stored hundreds of wetland samples. Mark became the firm's go-to data guy.

The day eventually came when the boss needed a summary of Mark's findings for a forthcoming hearing. Mark produced some graphs and bullet points from his data, but the boss did not have time to go over them with Mark until the day before the hearing. That is when Mark's Mount Vesuvius erupted.

After inviting Mark into his office and thanking him for his good work, the boss set to work with Mark, strategizing how they would present his findings. Mark got a real confidence boost when the boss told him that he wanted Mark to join him at the hearing. That confidence turned to sweat, however, when Mark learned that the opposing side would probably bring a statistician to the hearing to contest findings they did not like. "They will want to know everything about how, when, and where you collected, processed, and analyzed the data," the boss reported. "It is nothing to worry about though, we just need to be ready for them. Oh, and by the way, I didn't see your p-values or confidence intervals—we'll need those, of course!"

"So, Mark, let's run through some questions they're likely to ask," the boss continued. "First, tell us how you went about deciding where to collect the data." Mark assured the boss that he had surveyed all of the interesting wetland locations, but that he had focused most of his data collection where he had found the most plant species.

Mark's boss's ruddy face went white. "You did *what*?!" he screamed. He then tore into Mark's statistical cluelessness in language that would do any sailor proud. That is when Mark got the message that statistics is more than a bothersome course requirement in college—that it really *does* have a purpose in research and the real world.

After some serious moping over beers (which is when he told me about getting fired), Mark studied statistics with a vengeance. He started by digesting an elementary statistics book that gave him the basics as well as a newfound appreciation of the discipline. He then—because he wanted to!—took an upper-level college statistics class. Years later when Mark made hires for his own consulting firm, he made sure that every employee had a grasp of how statistics factor into study design and data collection.

Too few environmentalists grasp the fundamentals or power of statistical analysis, and this severely undermines their ability to think critically about issues. It also undermines their credibility and capacity to advance meaningful causes—scientists and decision makers tend to be dismissive of people whose claims are not supported by objective, unbiased analysis. To avoid becoming another Mark, study the following sections carefully. Understanding the relationship between data collection and statistical analysis will help you think more like a scientist and less like a Homer Simpson.

So What Exactly Is Statistics?

Statistics is a way to assess, with confidence, how similar or different things are or whether you have hypothesized correctly.[3] Statistics relies on measures of variability to determine the probability that Thing 1 really is different from Thing 2. (Statisticians use more intimidating, incomprehensible terminology and Greek symbols to denote "thing," of course, and that can throw you into a tizzy. Appendix 3 will calm your nerves, however, by translating terms and symbols that you are most likely to encounter.)

Within any collection of things, some individuals will be more or less similar. The blades of grass on your lawn, for example, may all look the same, but if you measured them carefully enough, you would find they varied in blade thickness. If you measured a number of grass blades, you could calculate an average blade thickness from your measurements and then see how close each individual blade comes to the average. You would find, of course, that the thickness of some blades was about the same as the average thickness, but you would also find that some blades were relatively thin or thick compared to the average blade. The more divergent the thicknesses, the more variable the grass blades would be.

If you carefully measured blade thickness on different lawns, or at different times during the summer, the average thicknesses would probably be somewhat different. But would the *measured* grass blades accurately

---

3. Technically, you will be testing your null hypothesis—the exact opposite of what you have hypothesized. The reason for this statistical oddity is that you never prove something true, you only can prove it false. Proving that the null hypothesis is incorrect is as close as you can get to proving that your actual hypothesis is true. It may sound weird, but it works.

represent the *unmeasured* grass blades around them? Could it be that you just happened to measure grass blades that were uncharacteristically thin or uncharacteristically thick? If you had selected a different bunch of blades to measure, do you feel confident that your earlier findings and conclusions would stay the same? Short of measuring every single blade of grass, how could you know the answer to that question with any level of certainty? You could not know—unless you randomly selected the blades you measured. Statistics could then tell you how much confidence you should place in your conclusion.

"Randomly selected" does not necessarily mean what you may think. Here is what it does mean: that *every object or location in your study area has an equal chance of being selected or not selected.* Random selection (more commonly referred to as random sampling) does *not* therefore mean that sampling is spread evenly over all parts of a study area or study population. Random sampling, in fact, can result in clustered data collection, with some locations or objects sampled heavily while other locations or objects are not sampled at all. When this occurs, there is an instinctual urge to make the sampling more equitable throughout. Reject this urge to make it right—you will only make it wrong! To sample randomly, you *must* rely on a random number generator.[4] Do not believe that you can decide what is random—you cannot!

Note that inventory/descriptive-type questions do not (usually) require random sampling. In fact, random sampling may be inappropriate. How/why and comparative/monitoring-type questions, in contrast, *require* random sampling.[5]

More on Statistical Analysis

Statistical analysis is about determining the amount of variability within and between the things that you are trying to compare. To illustrate what this means, let's say that you wish to answer the following comparative/monitoring-type question:

Are nonnative honeysuckles more abundant along logging roads than in the surrounding interior forest?

---

4. Your computer, calculator, or cell phone can generate these for you.
5. The one exception to this is repeat sampling, where you remeasure *the exact same item(s)* (e.g., the exact same tree, the exact same blades of grass) at different times to determine if those exact items change.

Three outcomes are possible, each of which represents an (alternative) hypothesis:

- Nonnative honeysuckles are more abundant along logging roads than in the surrounding interior forest.
- Nonnative honeysuckles are less abundant along logging roads than in the surrounding interior forest.
- Nonnative honeysuckles are equally abundant along logging roads and in the surrounding interior forest.

Let's say that the first hypothesis articulates your prediction best, so that is the one you want to test. (The purpose of testing your hypothesis is to evaluate—objectively—if you are right.) Let's also say that your data collecting effort yielded the following results:

DATA SET 1

- You found 30 nonnative honeysuckles along one representative 5m x 100m stretch of logging road (the total area you sampled was 500m²).
- You found 25 nonnative honeysuckles within one representative 5m x 100m plot of interior forest (the total area you sampled was 500m²).

From the above data, what would you conclude? Is thirty honeysuckles appreciably more than twenty-five? Would these data convince you that nonnative honeysuckles *are* more abundant along logging roads than in the surrounding interior forest? Maybe yes, and maybe no.

Now let's say that you conducted the study differently, in that you counted honeysuckles in *five* bands of roadside (instead of just one), and that you did likewise in *five* bands of interior forest:

DATA SET 2

- You sampled five randomly selected stretches of logging road instead of just one, with each stretch being 5m x 20m. The number of honeysuckles on the five stretches was 6, 6, 7, 5, 6. In the end, you therefore sampled the same area as before (500m²), and you counted the same total number of honeysuckles (30).
- You sampled five randomly selected plots of interior forest instead of just one, with each plot being 5m x 20m. The number of honeysuckles on the five plots was 5, 4, 5, 6, 5. In the end, you therefore sampled the same area as before (500m²), and you counted the same total number of honeysuckles (25).

Notice that both sampling schemes (Data Sets 1 and 2) sampled the same land area, and both schemes yielded the same number of honeysuckles. You might therefore assume that the two sampling schemes are equally informative. They are not.

Data Set 2 can be analyzed statistically; Data Set 1 cannot. Data Set 2 can be used to test your hypothesis, and answer your question, with a known level of confidence; Data Set 1 cannot. That's because Data Set 2 contains information about the extent to which honeysuckle abundance varies within the sampling area—from one sampling location to the next. Data Set 1 provides no such assessment of variability-within because only one single (large) area was sampled in each habitat type. Without some measure of variability-within, you can't draw a definitive or objective conclusion about whether twenty-five honeysuckles is meaningfully different from thirty honeysuckles. About all you can do is speculate on whether the difference in number has any real meaning in nature—not an impressive return for your data collection effort!

More on Variability-Within

Let's now look at another aspect of variability. Let's imagine that the results from the study design of Data Set 2 yielded somewhat different results:

DATA SET 3
- The number of honeysuckles along five stretches of logging road (each stretch 5m x 20m) was 0, 0, 27, 0, 3.
- The number of honeysuckles within five plots of interior forest (each plot 5m x 20m) was 21, 0, 0, 0, 4.

Studying Data Sets 1, 2, and 3 carefully, some comparisons are worth noting: all three data collection efforts sampled the same land area ($500m^2$), and all three efforts sampled the same total number of honeysuckles (thirty along the road, twenty-five in the interior forest). The intensity of sampling was therefore identical in all three data collection efforts.

Now notice something else: the *average* number of honeysuckles in Data Sets 2 and 3 are identical (both data sets average 6 along the road and 5 in the forest). Also notice that the *individual* abundances of honeysuckle in each sampling location are very different. In Data Set 2, every individual value is close to, or identical to, the average value (6 or 5, respectively); in Data Set 3, every individual value is far from the average value:

	ROADSIDE	INTERIOR FOREST
Data Set 2	6, 6, 7, 5, 6	5, 4, 5, 6, 5
Data Set 3	0, 0, 27, 0, 3	21, 0, 0, 0, 4

Looking over these two data sets, does one seem to tell a less ambiguous, more convincing story than the other? Most people say that Data Set 2 is much more revealing than Data Set 3; they also say that Data Set 2 suggests that roadsides do have more honeysuckles than do interior forest tracts, even though there are not many more. When asked about Data Set 3, most people shrug and say they do not know what to think.

Statisticians are quick to tell you not to trust first impressions, but in this case, first impressions are on target. If Data Set 2 were subjected to statistical analysis, a statistician would report that she is 90 percent sure that the perceived difference in honeysuckle abundance in forests and along roads is in fact real. The statistician would draw no such inference from Data Set 3.

The driving force behind every critical analysis of data for comparative and how/why-type questions is variability-within. For Data Set 2, the within-habitat variability is very low; for Data Set 3, the within-habitat variability is very high.

If the within-variability is sufficiently small, even slight differences in things being compared may prove meaningful. If within-variability is very high, however, even very large differences in things being compared may prove inconsequential. The following example illustrates this. Let's say that you're comparing two things (to answer a comparative-type question) and the following measurements make up your data set:

DATA SET 4
- Thing 1: 23.11, 23.12, 23.11, 23.11, 23.11, 23.11, 23.11, 23.1
- (average value = 23.11)
- Thing 2: 23.15, 23.14, 23.15, 23.15, 23.15, 23.15, 23.16, 23.15
- (average value = 23.15)

The spread between the two averages (23.11 and 23.15) is very small in numerical terms (only 0.04), but based on calculations of probability, a statistician would conclude that Thing 1 really is smaller than Thing 2. In fact, the statistician would tell you just *how* confident she is in making that proclamation (e.g., if the truth were to be known, there is only one chance in a thousand that Thing 1 is *not* really smaller than Thing 2). Knowing the level of confidence that is placed in a proclamation contributes greatly to the power of statistical analysis.

Now let's look at a data set where the variability-within is very high:

DATA SET 5

- Thing 3: 23.15, 15.62, 0.03, 65.99, 78.96, 7.53, 14.60, 2.81, 9.00
- (average value = 24.19)
- Thing 4: 43.21, 8.16, 77.77, 59.63, 24.57, 117.2, 2.12, 10.1, 51.3
- (average value = 43.78)

The spread between the two averages above (24.19 and 43.78) is very high in numerical terms (19.59), but based on calculations of probability, a statistician would not conclude that Thing 3 is necessarily smaller than Thing 4. In fact, the conclusion instead would be more along the lines of, "if the truth were to be known, there is only a 50 percent chance that Thing 3 really is smaller than Thing 4." *A sizable difference between averages does not mean much if the variability-within is high.*

Without getting into the mathematics of statistical analysis and variability calculations, low variability-within (Data Sets 2 and 4) indicates high predictability—it means you would have a good chance of accurately predicting values if you were to conduct additional sampling. That is not the case with Data Sets 3 and 5: high variability-within indicates low predictability—it means you would have little chance, for example, of accurately predicting the abundance of honeysuckle if you were to sample additional stretches along the road or additional plots in the interior forest. The next band you sample might have twenty-plus honeysuckles, or it might have zero honeysuckles, or it might have any abundance in-between. It is hard to say.

To show what this has to do with testing your hypothesis (that nonnative honeysuckles are more abundant along logging roads than in the surrounding interior forest), let's say that you decide to increase your sample size for Data Set 3 by counting honeysuckles in five additional, randomly placed stretches along the road, and in five additional randomly placed plots in the forest. Let's say that your expanded data set now looks like Data Set 3b (with the new data are in bold):

DATA SET 3B

- The number of honeysuckles in ten randomly selected 5m x 20m stretches of roadside = 0, 0, 27, 0, 3, **0, 0, 1, 0, 0**. (The average number of honeysuckles per band was 3.1.)

- The number of honeysuckles in ten randomly selected 5m x 20m plots of interior forest = 21, 0, 0, 0, 4, **24, 27, 41, 26, 35**. (The average number of honeysuckles per band was 17.8.)

How would you interpret these data? What would be your conclusion? Based on the new averages, the take-home message would seem to be that honeysuckles are much *less* abundant along roads than in interior forest—a complete reversal of your earlier conclusion from Data Set 3! Notice also that, had you sampled six or seven stretches (instead of five or ten), your conclusion probably would have been different still. You probably would have concluded that there really was not any meaningful difference in honeysuckle abundance along roads versus in the forest.

Statistical analysis is about determining the probability that one thing really is different from another, or that one thing really is related to or caused by another. Statistical analysis is an objective way to draw inferences because conclusions are based on probability rather than on whim or impression. Knowing the variability-within is essential.

It is worth noting that, as variability-within increases, the probability of statistical analysis detecting differences or relationships is reduced. Conversely, as the variability-within is reduced, the likelihood of detecting differences or relationships (if there are any) is heightened. The main way to reduce variability within a data set is to increase the number of samples you take on a thing. That is why scientists typically collect lots of data on just a few things rather than collecting just a few data on lots of things.

A Look Back

Looking back on Data Set 1, it is obvious that the single count of honeysuckles in one large roadside plot and the single count of honeysuckles in one large interior forest plot give no insight on variability-within. Without a measure of variability-within, statistical analysis is not an option, hypothesis testing is meaningless, and drawing inferences is impossible. Data Set 1 was a well-intentioned but wasted effort: we do not know any more than when we started about whether honeysuckle *really is* more abundant along roads than in interior forest. The only thing we learned from Data Set 1 is that one roadside location has thirty honeysuckles, and one interior forest location has twenty-five honeysuckles. That is it—end of story.

So watch out for data collecting efforts for *comparative-type* questions that, like Data Set 1, do not measure variability-within. Also watch out for nonrandom sampling. Well-intentioned environmentalists take these dead-end roads much too often.

How to Randomly Sample a Place

To illustrate how you could sample a study area randomly, let's say that you wish to answer a comparative-type question of whether the abundance of a rare species is lower on polluted sites than on unpolluted sites. To begin, you would first need to make some conceptual decisions about where it is appropriate to collect data. Certainly you would want to sample some places that *are* polluted and some that *are not* polluted, but you would also want to hold some variables constant so that the comparison is meaningful. For example, to minimize unnecessary variability in the data, you might choose to sample polluted and unpolluted sites that have similar climate, topography, ecosystem type, soil, hydrology, geology, successional stage, and land use.

Let's say, for illustration, that you have identified an acceptable study area—a rectangle of 100m x 200m for the polluted site—and that you need to place five plots randomly within it. One way you could do that is presented below (see the Recommended Reading section for other teachings for other ways).

Using the random number generator on your computer, calculator or cell phone, generate a series of two-digit numbers, making each number a percentage. For example:

11%, 83%, 27%, 26%, 35%, 02%, 99%, 87%, 06%, 44%, 86%, 22%, 71%, 81%, 09%, 38%.

Taking these numbers in pairs, create coordinate pairs:

(11%, 83%) (27%, 26%) (35%, 02%) (99%, 87%) (06%, 44%) (86%, 22%) (71%, 81%) (09%, 38%).

The first (two-digit) percentage number in each coordinate pair—the x-coordinate—can be used to represent the percentage distance along the study area length; the second (two-digit) number—the y-coordinate—can be used to represent the percentage distance along the study area width.

To identify where the first random plot should be placed within the study area, multiply the long side (200m) of the rectangular study area by the x-value (11%), and multiply the width (100m) of your rectangular study area by the y-value (83%):

(11% x 200m, 83% x 100m) = (22m, 83m), the location of your first random plot.

Now proceed similarly with the second coordinate pair (27%, 26%):

(27% x 200m, 26% x 100m) = (54m, 26m), the location of your second random plot.

And the third (35%, 02%):

(35% x 200m, 02% x 100m) = (70m, 2m).

And the fourth (99%, 87%):

(99% x 200m, 87% x 100m) = (198m, 87m).

And the fifth (06%, 44%):

(06% x 200m, 44% x 100m) = (12m, 44m).

Starting at any corner of the (100m x 200m) rectangular plot that is easily accessed, use the calculated coordinates to locate the five randomly selected plots (fig. 3.1).

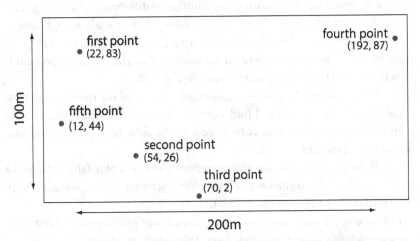

FIGURE 3.1. Five randomly selected points, with locations determined from random number coordinates (x, y) that were treated as percentages of the side and length distances of the sampling area. In this example, the lower left corner was used as the starting point, but starting from any other corner would have been equally valid.

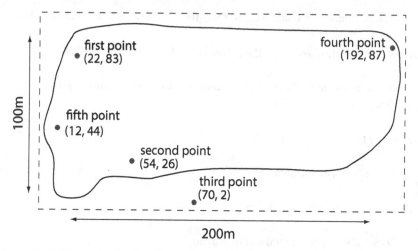

FIGURE 3.2. Five randomly selected points in an oddly shaped sampling area (the region demarcated by the solid line). The broken line is an imaginary 200m x 100m sampling area that was created to facilitate placement of points. Note that the third point (70, 2) falls outside the true sampling area and would not be sampled; a new, randomly selected coordinate pair that falls within the true sampling area would replace the rejected point.

Each two-digit coordinate was used as a percentage of the length (first coordinate) and the width (second coordinate) of the study area from a predetermined corner of the study area.

In this example, situating the sampling locations was easy because the study area was a rectangle with easily multiplied dimensions. Situating sample locations is no more difficult with an oddly shaped study area, however: simply convert your oddly shaped study area into an imaginary rectangle by conceptually extending borders on all sides so that the oddly shaped study area is enclosed by the imaginary rectangle (fig. 3.2).

As above, you would choose a convenient corner of the (imaginary) rectangle as a starting point, and find sampling locations by measuring out the x and y distances from this corner. You would then have located five randomly placed plots to sample.

But there is a problem: the third randomly selected plot falls outside the study area (fig. 3.2), so you cannot use it. You therefore need to replace it with your sixth coordinate pair (86%, 22%).

Falling outside your designated study area is one justification for not sampling a randomly chosen location. Two other justifications are:

1. The location duplicates, overlaps with, or somehow is affected by an earlier sampling effort (e.g., the location you are about to sample was trampled when you sampled a nearby plot).

2. The location falls in a place that is not at all relevant to the question that you are trying to answer (e.g., the location lands on a road, in a river, or on a spot where someone recently had a campfire). If sampling a location makes no sense, replace it with a newly created (random) location.

Two reasons that *never* justify discarding a randomly selected location are:

1. Large parts of the study area are not represented.
2. It is obvious to you that the randomly selected locations do not capture the full diversity of the site—that the study area is more heterogeneous than the randomly selected locations suggest.

As cautioned earlier, *never try to improve random sampling when the selections go against your sense of what's right.* Random means *random*—that every place within the study area has an equal chance of being selected. If all of the locations wind up being side-by-side, that is the way it goes.[6]

Creating a Compartment Map

The sections above help you decide exactly which data you need and how you will get them, and they show you how to sample randomly if you are seeking to answer a comparative/monitoring-type question. But *where* you collect data—*and where you don't*—is also a critically important part of any data collecting plan. Compartmentalizing your study area into meaningful, manageable units on a map helps you with this. The map gives you something tangible to work with as you decide how, when, and where to collect (or not collect) data.

Many off-site resources can help you create a preliminary map of compartments before you ever step foot in a place. Topographic maps, geology maps, soil surveys, historical documents, aerial photographs, and the Geographic Information System (GIS) are especially useful. To locate these and other possibly useful resources for a study, one option is to contact the maps and documents department of your state university's library and ask for help. You will be amazed at the resources they will find for you.

---

6. When using random numbers to determine where or what you will sample, use the randomly selected numbers in the order generated, do not skip around. Generate more coordinate pairs than anticipated so that you will have replacements if you need to reject one or more of your randomly chosen locations.

No single best resource exists for creating a useful compartment map—the best is always defined by the question that you seek to answer. If, for example, your question is *which locations have prime agricultural soils?*, you would probably rely on the county soil survey to map appropriate locations. If you seek to answer the question *are there any deer yards on the property?*, you would probably study wintertime aerial photographs and draw polygons around large blocks of evergreen trees.

Some questions, such as *where on this property are the biological hotspots?*, are hard to compartmentalize from a single resource. To identify likely hotspots, you would probably seek clues from a combination of resources such as topographic maps, aerial photos, geology maps, and soil surveys. Collectively, they would help you locate rich soils, rocky cliffs, wet places, limestone, and other promising places that may harbor unusual suites of species.

Creating a spatial map of compartments from off-site resources does not mean, of course, that the compartment map you create will accurately portray what you find on the ground. To be sure that your compartment map reflects reality, you need to ground-truth it and adjust the polygon lines as needed.

Describing Your Data Collecting Methods

Data provide answers to questions, but are those answers the *right* answers? To assess that, people need to know where, when, and how the data were collected. That is why researchers always describe their data collecting process— their methods—in great detail.

Best intentions notwithstanding, descriptions of data collecting methods usually leave out key details that stay unnoticed until someone tries unsuccessfully to interpret your data or duplicate your study. The following methods description, written by a diligent, conscientious data collector, illustrates this:

> The study plot was located on a floodplain at the mouth of Little Otter Creek in North Ferrisburgh, Vermont. The site was bounded on one side by river, the opposite side by road, and either end by woods. Entering from the road where the painted trees began, the road was 2° NE and the path to point zero was NW295°. Point zero was at river's edge in the SE corner of our 100m x 100m site. The baseline ran NW °25 and 5 transects at 17m, 32m, 52m, 67m, and 89m were set going 75° NW. Plot points were marked with a 0.6m PVC post (~ 1.5cm diameter). 5m x 10m plots were laid out using a 5m rope from post along

transect line 5m. A permanent flag marked the corners and 10m were measured perpendicular to the flag 345° NE. A permanent flag marked these corners and 5m were measured parallel to the transect lines 75° NW. The last
corner flags were set there. 1m x 2m plots were nested inside the 5m x 10m plots
using the NE corners, long sides along the 10m lines. These were our herb plots,
the larger our tree plots.

This seems to be a pretty thorough description of methods, doesn't it? To con-
firm your impression, draw a schematic picture of the data collection effort.
Pretend that you are conducting a follow-up monitoring study and you must
repeat the data collecting effort exactly. Do not read further until you have
created this sketch in the space below.

Translating the written description of methods into a picture was frustrating because elements of the description were unclear, incomplete, or
contradictory. Certainly you would have done better (at least that is what
you think)!

Think again. It is exceedingly difficult to step outside yourself and recognize that what is obvious to you may not be at all obvious to others. In the
case of the Little Otter Creek study above, we are fortunate to have methods
write-ups from two other members of the research team. Carefully study
their descriptions (below) to fill in gaps in the first methods write-up. Revise
your sketch as you go, until you are confident that you have the data
collection method right.

We established a baseline (330°) along the bank of the creek. The zero point was
located 10m from the marsh (southern extent of the proposed clearcut). We
established five transects at 60°, no less than 15m apart. Five sampling plots

were established along each transect at 5, 15, 25, 50, and 100 meters. A PVC pipe (1.5cm in diameter) was used to mark the bottom right corner of each plot. One plot (50m rectangle) was established at each point by following 330° for 10m, followed by 5m at 60° (corners marked with red flags). A second plot (2m rectangle) was established at each plot inside the 50m plot. The longer 2m edge of this smaller plot also followed 330° from each PVC stake.

Our five transect lines ran 100m in length through the portion of Little Otter Creek floodplain marked for logging. Point 0 was at the water's edge and transects followed a bearing of NE 75°. There were 5 sampling points (each with a PVC marker pole) along each transect at: 5m, 10m, 15m, 25m, 50m, and 100m from point 0. Several sampling methods were employed. First, trees were sampled in a 5m x 10m area at each point. This sampling area was at a 90° angle to the transects, with the marker pole representing the bottom corner. Next, herbaceous and shrub species were sampled in a 1m x 2m area at each point. This $2m^2$ area was bounded by a 2m PVC range pole at a 90° angle to the left of the marker pole, and a meter stick parallel to the transect.

How did the sketching go? Not so well? That is odd because all three data collectors take pride in their work, and all three assured me that they had carefully reviewed their write-ups multiple times for accuracy and completeness. They *knew* that their methods descriptions were first rate. But they weren't— their seemingly great write-ups were incomplete and inconsistent.

It is very, very hard to judge the adequacy of your own methods write-up. The only way to test its adequacy is to have someone who is unfamiliar with your project examine it critically. If the reviewer cannot *sketch* your data collecting methods accurately, your methods write-up is not good enough.

A Better Way to Describe Your Methods

Use pictures to support your methods descriptions. The methods write-up below (for the same Little Otter Creek study) illustrates their value.

STUDY SITE

The study site was along Little Otter Creek, North Ferrisburgh, Vermont. The eastern edge of the study area (marked by an orange PVC pole driven into the stream bank) lies approximately 50m west of the bridge that passes over Little Otter Creek on Route 7 (fig. 3.3).

Monitoring sites were positioned (and data were collected) from July 10 to August 2, 2018, along five parallel transects that started at the stream bank (0 meters) and ran away from the stream at a bearing of 223° from magnetic north. The easternmost transect was marked by the orange pole. The other four (more westerly) transects were chosen randomly, and were positioned at distances of 38m, 62m, 85m, and 143m from the orange pole.

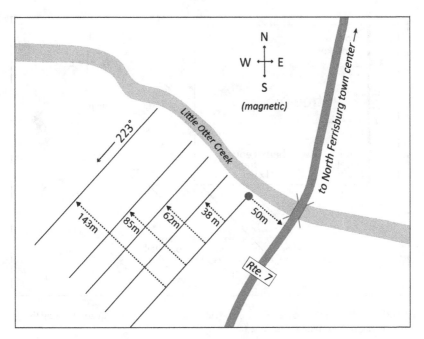

FIGURE 3.3. Location of sampling transects in the Little Otter Creek study area.

Along each transect, data were collected at distances of 0m, 5m, 15m, 25m, 50m, and 100m from the stream bank (fig. 3.4). Tagged white PVC marker poles (0.5m above-ground) were driven into the ground at each of the above distances along each transect; Global Positioning System (GPS) coordinates for each sampled location can be found in the appendix.

Each white marker pole functioned as the northwest corner of a plot (5m along the transect x 10m perpendicular to the transect) to sample trees (woody stems > 2cm diameter-at-breast height). Within the southwestern corner of each of these plots, shrubs (woody stems < 2cm diameter-at-breast height) were sampled in a nested subplot (1m along the transect x 2m perpendicular to the transect; fig. 3.4). Herbaceous plants (non-woody stems) were sampled in four nested "quadrats" (1m x 1m each) that were placed in the corner of each tree plot (fig. 3.4).

Whenever possible, use diagrams, sketches and schematics to supplement narrative descriptions of how, when, and where you collected the data.

What to Include When You Describe Your Methods

Some details of data collection do not matter, such as whether data were recorded with a pen or pencil, and should not clutter your methods

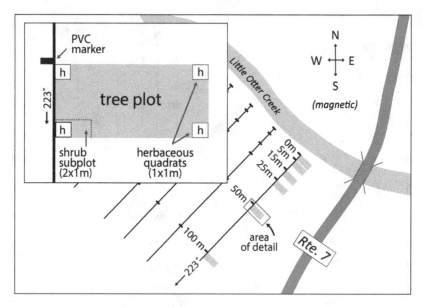

FIGURE 3.4. Positioning of tree plots, shrub subplots, and herbaceous quadrats along the Little Otter Creek sampling transects.

description. The following details, however, are almost always relevant and should be included:

- A detailed map of the study area (include obvious, unambiguous reference points). Include a small inset map to show where the study area is located within the state or region.
- Compass directions on maps, including the north arrow. Indicate whether declination has been accounted for, and whether the north arrow refers to magnetic north or true north.
- A scale on each map. If a map is not drawn to scale, say so.
- A sketch of the sampling design (e.g., plot locations).
- The sampling period, including the year.
- Consistent terminology throughout. For example, if you refer to your 1m x 1m sampling area as a "plot," use only that designation throughout. Do not refer to the plot elsewhere as a quadrat, subplot, or the like—synonyms cause confusion.
- The number of samples or measurements taken.
- Dimensions of plots and all other sampling units.
- Consistent units throughout, either all metric or all American standard. For example, do not describe one part of your methods in feet but another in meters.

Those are details that you always should include, but before assuming that your written description of methods is adequate, have someone scrutinize it mercilessly. Seek out readers who are unfamiliar with your project. The litmus test for completeness of a methods write-up is this: can an unknowing reader duplicate exactly what you did and how you did it without asking clarifying questions?

In sum, think of your description of methods as a recipe for data collection. If you disappeared tomorrow, would others be able to understand, find, use, or correctly interpret the data that you collected and managed? Would they know where the data came from and when they were collected? Would they understand the data's meaning and possible use? Would they be able to duplicate your study? Only an outsider can make those assessments.

A Few Data Collecting Suggestions and Reminders

Lab scientists typically record their data in bound notebooks, but field scientists are better off collecting data on loose data sheets. If a bound notebook is taken into the field and lost or damaged, you lose days, weeks, or months of work; if a data sheet goes missing, you lose only a single day's data at most. Loose data sheets are also easier to organize, and they are easier to run through a copier for archiving. Making backup copies of your data sheets, and storing them in a separate location from the originals, is a good insurance policy.

What makes for a good data sheet? That depends on what information you are collecting and what you will do with the data afterward. That said, I have found the following protocol useful for any study:

- At the top of each data sheet, record a descriptive project title (e.g., Endangered Orchids), date of collection (including year), data collector's name, and where the data were collected.
- Use the back of data sheets to describe site features that are interesting, unusual, or prominent. (Sketches, even if drawn poorly, add greatly to any description, and you will greatly value them later on when you are trying to remember a place.)
- Leave wide margins on data sheets for explanatory notes and clarifications.
- Do not assume that what is obvious to you will be obvious to others, and do not trust your memory. Write down—in excruciating detail—even seemingly obvious details.
- Remember to have an outsider review your data sheets painstakingly— before the research day ends—to identify ambiguities and numbers that

need to be clarified. *The best data checkers are those who know nothing about what you are doing and who take nothing for granted*; the worst reviewers are those who check their own data.

- To foster greater responsibility and accountability, have data sheet checkers write their name at the top of data sheets they have reviewed and found completely understandable.

Other data collecting suggestions and challenges—and what to watch out for—can be found in appendix 4.

Some Closing Thoughts

Research is about answering questions, it is not about collecting data. So do not concern yourself with a data collection strategy—or any of the tools, methods, gizmos, or techniques that you might employ—until you have identified the exact question that you wish to answer.

Sometimes curiosity, not exigency, frames the research question; this commonly occurs when you conserve a property and plan to leave it as is. With no pressing management decision on the horizon—but lots of interest in getting to know the place—questions typically center on what makes the place tick or how the place came to be the way it is. No approach works better at tackling these wonderings (or is more fun) than donning your detective garb and taking a slow, sleuthing walk through the property in search of site clues and indicators. Appendix 5 teaches some of the basics; other "reading the landscape" teachings can be found in the Recommended Reading section.

Good question asking begets good science, which increases the likelihood that a research effort will yield clear answers. But understanding how science operates has a less obvious benefit also: it confers respect. The views of scientifically literate environmentalists are taken more seriously, by a wider range of people, than are the views of environmentalists who operate on passion alone.

Being respected and taken seriously matters a great deal when trying to connect with people who may not see things your way. The next section, "Tools for Working with People," teaches ways to engage and team up with these people.

part II

TOOLS FOR WORKING WITH PEOPLE

The cause that you're fighting for, and the outcome that you seek, dictate how you proceed, but the *people factor* ultimately decides whether your effort succeeds. This section presents ways to work effectively with people (including people you dislike or disagree with), and to do so with grace, equanimity, and minimal stomach churning.

4

Do You See What I See?
How to Connect with Future Allies

I wanted to scream for the ten billionth time. What is wrong with these people?! How can they be so clueless?! How can they not get it?!

We had laid out the scientific facts about climate change in black and white. But it did not move these people in the least. When I asked them why, they said they did not trust what the scientists were telling them.

What is behind what we trust and believe? Many of our notions come from what we learn growing up. My mother, for example, taught me early on that if I touch a bird's eggs, the mother bird will not return to the nest. My ornithologist colleagues have since taught me that the egg touching story is pure malarkey, but I still catch myself telling kids not to touch a bird's eggs or the mother will not return. Why do I do that? I think it is because the knowledge I gained growing up still somehow defines my inner mindset. Unless I am actively working to evaluate its correctness, my default mindset automatically takes over as the accepted way for how things are or should be—even if I trust and believe what my colleagues are saying.

Part of the work of being an effective environmentalist is getting people to trust and believe you. And we tend to think of that work as education—educating people about an issue or cause you care about. It certainly is frustrating to get nowhere when you try to educate someone who just doesn't get it. When you are feeling that frustration, however, be honest with yourself: is educating the person your *real* design, or is your real aim to bring the person over to your side? It may be that when you say you need to *educate* someone, you are really saying that their view is wrong and needs to be changed. But to be intellectually honest about it, educating someone is about opening the person's eyes to a full range of possibilities, with no ulterior motive. Bringing someone over to your side, in contrast, is about advocating a position that you hold dear. If someone's eyes are opened but the person chooses *not* to side with you, you have successfully educated the person but unsuccessfully advocated your position.

This chapter offers tools for successfully connecting with people—whether to educate them, in the truest sense of the term, or to advocate your position so that they become your allies. How do you make headway with complete strangers? Or with people who firmly believe that they know what they are talking about and are unwilling to hear or consider what you have to say? This chapter teaches ways to counter all of these obstacles, starting with understanding where everyone is coming from—yourself included.

Getting Past the Us versus Them Dynamic

To connect with someone who does not see things your way, understanding the person's default mindset—and the forces behind it—is key. But understanding *your own* default mindset and the forces behind it is at least as important. That means coming to terms with your own assumptions and preconceived notions.

Typecasting people is one example of assumptions and preconceived notions at work. Many of us typecast people as good guys and bad guys, buying into the us-versus-them syndrome. Anti-environmental talk show hosts, for instance, love to flame the us (environmentalists) vs. them (anti-environmentalists) dynamic by painting us as privileged, arrogant, judgmental, antihunting, antilogging, out-of-touch city liberals who do not know much of anything about the land and do not need to worry about feeding and clothing our kids. At the same time, we environmentalists also tend to paint those who oppose us with an equally broad brush. Whether we admit it or not, many of us reflexively dismiss anti-environmentalists as clueless.

Blindly accepting this holier-than-thou viewpoint—where you know what is right and they don't—simply makes the situation worse. What would make the situation better, though, is being willing to consider that maybe—just maybe—these other folks have good reason for seeing things the way they do. Take, for example, the story of the Spotted Owl movement vs. Oregon loggers.

In the mid-1980s, environmental groups pressured the US Fish and Wildlife Service to list the Spotted Owl as an "endangered species." The campaign succeeded, and vast tracts of old-growth forest were rendered off-limits to logging.

Oregon loggers vigorously opposed the listing, not because they hated wilderness or Spotted Owls but because protecting the land would mean losing their jobs and how they feed their families. Environmentalists, in their eagerness to protect wilderness, waited too long to concern themselves with where the loggers were coming from. In so doing, they painted themselves as privileged "enviros" who cared more about owls than working people.

Even though the Spotted Owl movement was many decades ago, "environmentalist" remains a bad word in many Oregon communities. But this story precisely illustrates how people do not randomly or arbitrarily choose their feelings. Just as you have a reason for feeling the way you do about an issue, so do others. In fact, just as past events and experiences have shaped how you think and see the world, so have other people's past events and experiences shaped how they see things. That is worth keeping in mind when you decide that someone is clueless or ignores the truth. It might just be that *you* are the one who is ignoring some truths, or that some of *your* truths are not really truths at all. Maybe your "truths" are just value-laden notions.

About the only truth that you can count on is this: when someone seems clueless or is just not getting it, what is really going on is that the other person is not seeing things *your* way. Hidden beneath your perception of cluelessness is an assumed truth that your way is the one and only *right* way, and that the other person's way is the *wrong* way. That mindset unknowingly creeps into how you talk with people and comes across as patronizing. No one responds well to that.

To move beyond this impasse of us vs. them, a little humility always works better. Humility comes easiest if you recognize that some people who do not seem to get it do, in fact, get it. They just get it differently from you—often for legitimate reasons that are beyond your immediate knowing. Connecting with these folks takes understanding *why* they see things differently. That takes effortfully learning about—and honestly caring about—what is important to *them*, what motivates them, what they love, what they worry about, and what they envision as the right path forward.

Connecting with People through Indirect Approaches

Openly advocating a position is how we typically try to change the views of people who do not see things our way. For those who hold hardened views that we seek to change, however, *direct* advocacy does not work very well—an *indirect* approach almost always works better. Indirect approaches work because they get people talking with and listening to one another through connecting over something they all care about—no matter their individual viewpoints—such as their home place. Some indirect approaches that have proved effective are described below.

The PLACE Program

Walter Poleman's PLACE Program (Place-Based Landscape Analysis and Community Engagement) is remarkably effective at getting people from different political and socio-economic groups talking with, listening to, learning from, and respecting one another.[1] It works through shared learning about their shared home place.

PLACE helps local residents explore the natural and cultural history of their local landscape by working directly with local schools, town commissions, historical societies, and conservation organizations to develop an integrated series of presentations, field trips, and workshops that honor the town's natural and cultural heritage. Residents become landscape sleuths who study and interpret what makes their place the way it is—the hills, rocks, soils, water, climate, plants, animals, people, land use, and history (see appendix 5 for sleuthing clues and tips).

PLACE helps community members look at a place they care about with fresh eyes by emphasizing the interrelationships between natural and cultural history. The integrated, inclusive effort fosters a sense of community and a shared sense of place and leads to a more informed and creative town planning process. PLACE does not tell residents what to think, and there is no agenda or proselytizing. The program works because it gives community members new eyes to see the place they most value—their home. It helps people understand and appreciate a place's specialness by tapping into what they care about.

Community Celebrations

Community celebrations of a place also tap into what matters to people by providing a forum for community members to come together to share what they value and love about their community. To orchestrate a community or watershed celebration, partner with a community group that has the community's well-being at heart. Advertise the get-together broadly using direct mail flyers, notices in the town newspaper, and posters placed where people congregate. Ask clergy to announce the celebration in their services.

Community celebrations should be relaxed, fun, neighborly get-togethers; sharing food helps set the tone. Potlucks are collegial sharing events, but community members who do not have time or money to prepare something must

---

1. More information about the PLACE program can be found at http://www.uvm.edu/place/.

not feel guilty if they are not able to contribute. However you organize food, be sure there will be enough on hand (and don't forget to have extra plates, cups, napkins, and utensils).

A two-hour celebration in the early evening generally works best, but weekend events work well too. Before settling on a date and time, however, always check with schools, libraries, community centers, and the town office for possible conflicts. Do not force parents to choose between their kids' ballgame and your community celebration!

To prompt discussion and interaction in the event, set up several separate stations, each of which prominently displays an upbeat, agenda-free question. These questions can help you understand where people are coming from, as well as what is behind their opposition to an environmental initiative that you favor. Three good questions to get people talking are:

- What do you especially love or value about your community/town/ watershed? What makes it a special place?
- Are you liking how your community/town/watershed is changing? What are your concerns?
- What are your hopes and ideas for your community/town/watershed's future?

Post large flip-chart sheets on the wall at each station. Encourage participants to write comments directly on the sheets, but also place an upbeat scribe at each station to capture spoken comments so they are not lost. When the celebration ends and you have thanked everyone for a wonderful get-together, collect the flip-chart sheets and explain how you will share the results once you have organized them into meaningful groupings. Suggest possible next steps for those who are interested.

Remember—from start to finish—that these get-togethers are *not* about setting people straight. Community celebrations *are* about getting to know people and developing mutual trust and understanding. That should be your sole agenda.

Site Visits and Field Outings

Field outings and site visits provide low-key opportunities for hands-on learning, schmoozing, fundraising, recruiting new supporters, and mending strained group dynamics. Outings also work magic at building enthusiasm and trust, even among adversaries. In fact, when you do not know what else to do, try spending time in the field together.

Outings to the field also make issues, challenges, and opportunities real. *Seeing* what is going on, or how special a place is, touches the psyche in ways that discussion in a sterile meeting room does not.

Spending time in the field together is also friendlier and less threatening than sitting in a lifeless room, staring at one another across a table. The unexpected discoveries that always surface when you spend time in the field—an animal sighting, an unusual flower, a weird-shaped tree—get people talking with one another as fellow humans rather than as good guy-bad guy antagonists. Hardened positions invariably soften.

There are two golden rules to leading a field outing: make everyone feel welcome, and make sure that everyone is physically comfortable. View yourself as the host and act like one.

As host of your outing, you need to protect group members from hunger, thirst, sunburn, insect bites, itchy plants, and wet body parts. Bring snacks, drinks, sun lotion, insect repellent, and plastic bags to sit on. An unexpected cup of hot coffee late in the day will make you a hero, even among enemies. And do not forget people's bathroom needs: full bladders make for inattentive audiences. Figure out (and explain to group participants) how their bathroom needs will be met. Do this before you head into the field.

Always prepare for rain, snow, cold, heat, sun, and wind. You cannot change the weather, but you can change the comfort level of group members by being prepared. Pack a windbreaker and a couple of extra hats for the ill-prepared. You may think that is going beyond the call of duty (which it maybe is), but that is not the point. Good outings do not happen when people are miserable. If you are bothering to lead the outing at all, you should do whatever you can to ensure that everyone is comfortable. That is how they, and you, get the most out of it.

All of the suggestions and guidelines offered later in this chapter apply to site visits and other field outings. One detail that is often overlooked, however, is where you—the speaker—position yourself relative to the sun. Everyone naturally shies away from looking into the sun so, unless you are consciously thinking about it, you will stand with your back to the sun. Doing so means, however, that everyone else is looking *into* the sun. That is not what you want.

Another common oversight is sharing information when people are so spread out that some will not be able to hear what you are saying. People typically walk single file behind the leader, making it hard for people near the back to hear you. To speak with the group as a whole, select a good stopping place and then walk a few yards beyond it before stopping. Wait for the group to catch up to you. Now double-back until you are facing the middle of your group (fig. 4.1). And remember to position yourself so the sun is in *your* eyes, not in the eyes of your audience.

If you have a theme for your outing (discussed a bit later), and if you follow the suggestions presented later in this chapter, your outing will go famously. Here are a few other suggestions that will add frosting to the cake:

- Promote discussion, minimize lecturing.
- Save meaty discussions for stops where everyone can participate.
- Turn unexpected discoveries into teachable moments. Special finds or observations will grab your audience's attention whether you want them to or not, so don't fight the unexpected punches; roll with them.
- Keep short your stay at a stop. Move to the next discussion spot before group members become chilled, drowsy, or antsy.
- Big groups always take longer to mobilize than small groups. The larger the group, the fewer the stops. Ask someone, ahead of time, to bring up the rear and keep slowpokes moving.
- End your outing definitively, reviewing high points and thanking participants for joining you.

The paragraphs above cover the *mechanics* of hosting a field outing. That is all well and good if you know lots about the place that you will be visiting and have engaging insights to share. But what if you don't? Then what?

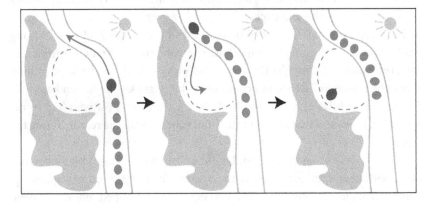

FIGURE 4.1. Technique for addressing the group as a whole when you are leading a group that is spread out and walking single file. Select an appropriate stopping place, walk a bit beyond it, and then stop. Wait for stragglers to catch up so the group is tightly lined up behind you, then circle back so you're facing the middle of the compact group rather than just the individuals immediately behind you. When presenting, always position yourself so that *you*, not group members, are facing the sun.

The good news is that you can lead extremely engaging field outings without knowing a great deal about the places you are visiting. The key is knowing what to look for—the *landscape clues* that tell a place's story. Appendix 5, a primer on landscape sleuthing, teaches many landscape clues and what they indicate. For example, what does rock size in a stonewall tell you about past land use? Why did a past landowner attach barbed wire to one side of the post rather than the other? What does that tell you about the person's intentions?

Such landscape clues can tell you much about a place and how it came to be, but those clues are just the tip of the iceberg. *Every* landscape has scores of clues just waiting to be seen and interpreted by you and others. Invite outing participants to become landscape detectives with you to share *their* discoveries, insights, and wonderings with you and the rest of the group. This collective storytelling makes any place come alive and brings people together better than any information-rich lecture. Give it a try.

Connecting with People through Presentations

Field outings, community celebrations, and the PLACE program can be enormously effective at engaging community members who do not necessarily share your views, but these initiatives take a fair amount of advance planning and coordination. When time is short, an in-person presentation works well at connecting you to people—*if the presentation is more story than information dump.* Presentations that go the other way are counterproductive—they separate you from the audience.

Take, for example, this story of Dr. Jones's presentation at our training workshop on environmental impact assessment.[2] For the first few minutes of his presentation, I thought Dr. Jones was playing with us: he kept pulling down the projection screen but could not get it to stick—the screen kept rolling up. It was hilarious. Eventually Professor Geel, the host who had introduced Dr. Jones and was seated in the front row, came to the rescue, fixing the screen.

Even once the screen was fixed, Dr. Jones kept us hanging a bit longer, fiddling with computer connections and waiting for the projector to warm up. After a couple of long minutes, his PowerPoint popped on the screen. Dr. Jones certainly gave us our money's worth—every PowerPoint slide was packed with information, all of which Dr. Jones dutifully read. I had a hard

---

2. This really happened—I swear it (Dr. Jones is not his real name).

time concentrating on his presentation, however, because my caffeine level had faded and I had not gotten enough sleep the night before. Looking around the room, I realized I was not the only one suffering.

A sudden, loud crash at the front of the room woke up everyone. There—sprawled on the floor under his tipped-over desk—was a recently awakened, discombobulated Professor Geel. A mangled version of his eyeglasses lay several feet away. Hastily, I retrieved the eyeglasses for him and helped him right the desk. He sat back down, much embarrassed for flipping over the desk when he fell asleep.

Dr. Jones, thankfully, never lost sight of his mission. He had lots of material to get through, and he got through it all. All in all, it was a highly informative and memorable presentation.

But not for the reasons Dr. Jones intended. Like too many specialists, Dr. Jones failed to recognize the importance of connecting with the audience—of meeting them where *they* are. Dumping a bunch of facts and knowledge on them is not enough; your job goes far beyond delivering accurate information. To be effective, a presentation needs to resonate with audience members' emotions, faith, interests, or values. Unless audience members are exactly like you, with the exact same interests and background (a rare occurrence), you need to *help* audience members be interested in what you are presenting.

So take stock of where your audience is coming from when planning a presentation. Who are the audience members likely to be? What will they know? What won't they know? What will they want to know? What will you want them to know? Record on paper your answers to these questions and refer to them as you prepare your presentation.

Figuring out your audience ahead of time helps you prepare efficiently and wisely. For example, if you were presenting to farmers about the problem of phosphorus runoff from agricultural fields, you would want to spend some time learning about federal, state, and municipal laws and regulations that might affect farmers. You also would want to learn about farming practices that have proved effective elsewhere and how much they cost to implement. Other phosphorus-related issues, such as runoff's effect on trout spawning habitat, may be more important to you than how runoff affects farmer livelihoods, but when talking with farmers, *your* interest needs to take a backseat to theirs. So align your presentation with the interests of the audience. Do not forget that *you* are not the audience that you are seeking to engage![3]

---

3. If you were presenting to an audience of Trout Unlimited members, for example, you would shift your presentation to how phosphorus runoff affects spawning habitat.

Zeroing In on Your Presentation's Theme

Effective presentations are presented as stories that are built around themes rather than around subjects. The theme of a presentation is your message or purpose—your presentation's bottom line. The theme holds your presentation together by providing context and meaning; it keeps audience members from wondering, *So what?* or *Who cares?*

Here are some examples of what a theme might look like:

- Conservation easements are our best hope for protecting land from development.
- Starting a land trust to promote conservation easements is easy.
- Conservation easements make good financial sense.
- Biodiversity does not mean what most people think it means.
- Biodiversity is a fad that will pass.
- Biodiversity is the most important issue we face today.

Notice that themes are much more informative and focused than topics or subjects. Themes help you prepare engaging presentations because they provide roadmaps of where you want to go.

Here is a simple, step-wise approach to clarifying your theme (just fill in the blanks).[4]

1. Generally, my presentation is about

   Examples:
   - Generally, my presentation is about community and sense of place.
   - Generally, my presentation is about land-use planning.

   Now state more specifically what you want to tell the audience by completing the following sentence:
2. Specifically, I want to talk with my audience about

   Examples:
   - Specifically, I want to talk with my audience about how one goes about building a community.
   - Specifically, I want to talk with my audience about the importance of land-use planning.

---

4. Adapted from Sam Ham (see Recommended Reading).

Now clarify the purpose of your presentation (the theme). Do this by completing the following sentence:

- After hearing my presentation, I want audience members to understand/believe that

Examples:

- After hearing my presentation, I want audience members to understand and believe that building a community takes work, but it can be done with the right kind of effort.
- After hearing my presentation, I want audience members to understand/believe that land-use planning is an environmental issue that every individual must become involved in.

Notice that well-stated themes can stand alone as complete sentences. If your theme cannot do that, your theme is not as clear as it needs to be.

Telling a Story

The theme identifies your take-home message—what you want audience members to think, feel, or understand when they walk out the door after your presentation. With your destination established, you now can strategize how to get there.

Everyone likes a well-told story; no one likes an avalanche of disconnected facts. *Facts do not change hearts or minds, but an engaging story might.* That is as true for PhDs, business people, and politicians as it is for children.

Good stories have plots or story lines (themes) that hold the story together and provide a purpose for the story. Great storytellers package pieces of the story in a way that is engaging, understandable, and relevant to the audience. They do this by attending to four key elements:

1. An awareness and interest in audience members—who they are, where they are coming from, what they are interested in, what they know, what they feel strongly about, and why they have chosen to listen to you.
2. A lead-in to the story that is engaging and personalized, where listeners are quickly transported outside themselves.
3. A body to the story that is easy to follow, where elements of the story build on one another.
4. A wrap-up to the story that ties together loose ends and provides closure.

Untrained speakers typically spend more than 95 percent of their preparation time dithering over facts and information—the body of the presentation.

Most trained speakers prepare very differently, spending only 60–65 percent of their available time on the body of the presentation and the other 35–40 percent on the bookends—the lead-in and the wrap-up—and they typically develop the bookends of their presentation *before* working on the body. Clarifying the *theme* of your presentation (described earlier) helps with this by identifying a story that is worth telling.

Starting with an Effective Lead-In

A good lead-in engages the audience by convincing them that they are in for an interesting story. A good lead-in also relaxes you so that your presentation is more like a relaxed conversation rather than an uptight lecture. That is more enjoyable for everyone.

Always allocate *at least two minutes* of any presentation for a gripping lead-in, even when your presentation is only ten minutes long. Never cut the lead-in short—you and the audience both need that much time to feel comfortable with one another, to relax, and to get on the same page. When you find yourself tensing up during the body of a presentation, it is because you did not spend enough time preparing yourself and the audience through your lead-in.

A good lead-in is entertaining and personal, but it also sets up the story that you will be telling. There are many ways to create a strong lead-in to a presentation, but the easiest, surest way is to share an interesting, personal, two-minute story about yourself that links you to your theme. This mini-story works wonders for jumpy nerves because it always works. The audience is always attentive, and since you are the world's authority on yourself, you can talk without notes for a few minutes in a conversational, relaxed way. That sets the mood for the rest of your presentation.

To illustrate an effective lead-in, here is how one speaker began a presentation about the importance of land-use planning:[5]

> Good evening and thank you for coming. I'm Sally Shelton and I'm here to share some thoughts with you about the importance of land-use planning. If land-use planning weren't so important, you'd never find me up in front of you all—public speaking is not what I do for fun. But it's too important an issue for me to stand on the sidelines, even on a Tuesday evening like this when I'm missing my favorite TV show.

---

5. Not her real name. To further protect her identity, I disguised her beginning a bit also.

As you may know, I grew up on a ranch and saw how tough it is to make a living, even in the best of times. So when people from away started making noise about how the streamside zones need to be protected from overgrazing, you can imagine how I felt about that. Like all of you who live on and work the land, I don't need an outsider telling me how to protect the environment.

But then I saw—first hand, when I was a Peace Corps Volunteer—what can happen, and it scared me. It would scare you too.

I'd like to tell you that we have nothing to worry about here in south Texas because south Texas is not West Africa. Other than being hot, dry, and dusty, the two places don't seem to have anything in common. But then my Peace Corps assignment ended and I came back home to south Texas. Here's what I saw . . .

The speaker used this as a lead-in to what is happening in south Texas, and why people should be concerned. She then went on to make specific recommendations about what should be done, and how audience members could make a difference.

This lead-in was effective because it established a common bond between the speaker and the audience, many of whom were from ranching families themselves. By helping audience members see her as one of them, the speaker convinced audience members that she understood where they were coming from. In so doing, she erased doubts about whether or not her presentation was relevant to them.

Her lead-in also served as an introduction to the story that she was telling— a story about herself and her changing perspectives on land-use planning. Last and perhaps most importantly, the casual, personal beginning calmed her nerves. By the time she launched into talking about what she saw, the tone and delivery of her presentation were conversational.

Sally's lead-in (above) appeared to be unplanned, and this contributed to the presentation's effectiveness. It was, however, highly scripted. Like most great speakers, Sally labored incessantly over the first three minutes of her presentation. She composed, edited, re-edited, and fine-tuned the beginning of her presentation on paper until she was satisfied with every last detail. She then practiced the lead-in aloud, again and again, until she was happy with it and could do it without notes. She then memorized the first few sentences of her lead-in so that she could deliver them effortlessly when she knew she would be most nervous. The scripted start got her going, and it was smooth sailing from that point on. She was herself, talking as she would talk with neighbors.

Leave nothing to chance when orchestrating the lead-in. Always ask yourself: Where will the audience be seated? Where will you stand? What will you do with your hands? If you are going to move about during the first few minutes (usually a good idea), plan your route so that you do it without thinking.

Now critique your rehearsed lead-in. Is it relaxed? Fun? Provocative? Will the audience enjoy it? Will you enjoy it? Is your theme clearly introduced? Will the lead-in launch you into the body of your presentation? Will listeners know why they should care? Will they feel your presentation is relevant? If you are unsure, keep challenging yourself with "So what? Who cares?" questions until you are able to see the bigger picture and articulate it.

Never shortchange the effort you put into planning your lead-in, even when you are freaking out over how little time you have to prepare. You do not need to be an authority to give a great presentation, but you do need to talk *with* the audience rather than *at* them. A good lead-in helps you do that.

Keeping Your Audience Engaged

With a clear theme in place, and a friendly, engaging lead-in behind you, you have already started to tell your story. If your lead-in was good, you are relaxed and you are talking as you would with friends. You are enjoying yourself and looking forward to telling your story.

Good presentations and stories are conversational in style, even though you are the only one talking. When you organize your presentation as a story, the body of your presentation flows smoothly. A few key words on a note card or a few visual aids are all you need to stay on track and feel secure.

After twenty or thirty minutes of talking, your presentation may start bogging down; this most often occurs when you stop telling a story and revert to talking at people. When an audience's interest starts flagging, you will feel it, and your anxiety will grow correspondingly. Plan remedial action: have a personal vignette or aside that is related to your story at the ready, and inject it into your presentation. Adding a personal connection to what you are talking about always grabs an audience's attention. Sensing their renewed interest will calm your nerves.

You can also jump-start a flagging audience's attention anytime by stopping in mid-sentence, hesitating for a moment, and then asking aloud what many have started wondering themselves: "So what? Who cares? Why does any of it matter?"

Asking those questions aloud, and letting the questions sink in while you collect your thoughts and frame meaningful responses, will shock audience members out of their dormancy and rekindle their interest. The reset will also put your nerves back on track.

Tips for an Effective Wrap-Up

The last two minutes of a presentation are critical, just as are the first two minutes. Together, the four bookend minutes will make or break your presentation.[6]

An effective wrap-up pulls together disparate parts, fills in missing pieces, clarifies connections, and reinforces your take-home message. It also provides closure to the story you are telling. Every presentation, be it emotion filled or data rich, needs a discernible, conclusive, memorable wrap-up. The wrap-up is what people are most likely to remember because it distills your presentation's message to the basics; it is also the last thing they hear.

Here are two wrap-up details that should not be overlooked:

1. Let the audience know when you are wrapping up your presentation. Preface your ending by saying "in conclusion" or "to summarize." Those words will focus everyone's attention on your wrap-up.
2. Never end a presentation with a mealy mouthed "I guess that's all." When you are done, use a simple "thank you" or "thank you, are there any questions?"

Managing Your Terror

A carefully orchestrated, inviting, friendly, personal, and relaxed lead-in will keep you from freaking out during your presentation. As noted earlier, if you're jittery during a presentation, it is because you shortchanged the first couple of minutes—your lead-in.

Being nervous beforehand is another matter: it comes from worrying that you will look stupid, which comes from worrying that you will not meet the audience's expectations. To neutralize this worry, make the audience's expectations commensurate with your level of knowledge. Great speakers can give powerful presentations on most anything, even things they know little about. They do this by taking listeners on a journey, not by spewing encyclopedic knowledge on them.

If guiding the audience rather than wowing it with erudite commentary sounds like making an excuse for superficiality, reflect for a moment on presentations that have been especially memorable for you. Did the speaker just

---

6. Many accomplished speakers figure out their wrap-up ending before they do anything else. Settling on a desired final destination helps them plan a presentation that gets them there.

dump tons of information on you, or did she lead you on an exploration where you made discoveries yourself? The presentations that have engaged me the most were guided explorations where the speaker took me to a place where I could discover things on my own. The approach is akin to showing someone how and where to search for arrowheads so that she can find one herself. To me, that is far more exciting than being handed someone else's arrowhead.

So use the lead-in of your presentation to establish that you're a guide, not a talking head. Establishing this expectation at the outset draws people in as fellow discoverers and frees you from feeling that you need to know everything about everything. For example:

> Hi, I'm Jeffrey Hughes from Organization X, thank you for coming. I'm going to talk with you tonight about the appearance and spread of a rock slime in the Connecticut River and why I think we should be concerned. I'm certainly not an authority on this weird slime known as rock snot[7] —far from it—but it's become sort of a personal crusade for me to understand what's going on. By talking it through with you, I'm hoping we can demystify some of the unknowns.
>
> I first met rock snot last July when I was trying to catch a few trout for dinner. I was wading along, minding my own business (but not catching any trout) when my feet went out from under me and I suddenly was drinking half the river. That's when rock snot really got my attention. Here's what I've been able to piece together since then . . .

Adjusting expectations for your presentation to make them realistically achievable should calm your pre-presentation nerves considerably. Here are some other ways you can manage pre-presentation anxiety.

- Chat with audience members before your presentation. Chatting keeps your mind off your anxiety and helps establish a rapport with the audience before the presentation begins.
- Hide out in a quiet, private place the few minutes preceding your presentation. Listen to soothing music or a relaxation tape to calm your nerves.
- Take several slow, deep breaths. After inhaling through your nose, hold your breath for a count of eight, then exhale slowly through your mouth.

---

7. Known to scientists as didymo.

- Gnaw on an apple before speaking. Eating an apple keeps jaw muscles busy, the mind occupied, and the mouth moist. The relaxed nature of eating an apple is somehow comforting.

Taking the spotlight off yourself before the presentation officially begins also helps. You can do this by providing an interactive activity for audience members such as giving a fun quiz or having them introduce themselves to someone they do not know.

Reminders for Getting the Most Out of Your Presentation

Giving presentations does get easier and more enjoyable if you:

- carefully script and practice the first two-minute lead-in and the last two-minute wrap-up before spending tons of time on the body of your talk
- talk *with* people rather than *at* them
- take listeners on a journey, present information as a "story" that *you* would enjoy listening to
- watch TED talks and reflect on what makes them engaging
- tell people *why* they should care about what you are talking about

Last, learn from each experience and build on it. Focus not only on what you could have done better, but also on what you did well. After every presentation, while the experience is still fresh in your mind, answer these few questions:

- Did you enjoy yourself? (If yes, the audience enjoyed it also.) What did you do to make it enjoyable?
- What parts of the presentation didn't you enjoy? Why? What didn't you like? What could you have done to make them more enjoyable?
- Did your lead-in relax you and get you talking comfortably and conversationally? If yes, how did you create that dynamic? If the lead-in did not accomplish those things, why? What could you have done to create a better dynamic?
- What worked well—what did you feel good about?
- What lessons do you want to apply next time?

It is wise to record these thoughts so you don't lose them!

Some Closing Thoughts

I used to think that the best way to get people onboard is to educate them. I still believe that. But watching effective environmental leaders in action over these last forty years has taught me that effective education is a two-way street.

When we care deeply about an environmental matter, or when we (*think* we) know what needs to be done to address an environmental wrong, we too often assume that those who do not see things our way are ill-informed. That assumption might be warranted, of course, but there are many other reasons why a person may not see things your way. Until you understand and respect what those reasons are—until you *connect* with the person—your impassioned efforts to "educate" them will fall on deaf or patronized ears. But when you successfully connect with these people, you'll find yourself with new allies.

This chapter's focus on *connecting* with people is also the focus of the next chapter, "Becoming an Ace Leader." Connecting with fellow environmentalists would seem to be far easier than connecting with people who do not see things your way. And it is, of course, at first. But working with people over an extended time period gives everyone's minor annoyances time to fester and degrade the team's effectiveness. The next chapter teaches ways to manage yourself, as well as others, so that does not happen to you.

5

Becoming an Ace Leader
How to Get the Most Out of Your Team

Effective problem solving resembles a well-played symphony: individuals with different strengths work together for a shared purpose. But how do the players know—and keep track of—what that exact shared purpose is? How do they know which note to play, or when to play it? How does the conductor get the most out of individual strengths? How does she coordinate them all? This chapter describes how conductors and other effective leaders do these things—how they orchestrate and manage the different energies, talents, and opinions that characterize any assembled group.

As emphasized in the first chapter, the actions you take and the tools you employ need to be driven by an accurately defined problem and desired outcome. That is challenging enough if you alone are the problem solver; it is orders of magnitude more challenging when other people are part of the problem-solving effort.

If everyone in the group agreed on the exact nature of the problem and what constituted an acceptable outcome, the group could move on to seeking viable solutions. But *does* everyone agree? Usually not. It has been my experience that people assume that others see things his or her way when, in fact, they do not. That misguided assumption creates all kinds of unnecessary difficulties, many of which are interpersonal.

Most of us blindly trust our own view of things, especially when—in *our* mind—the problem and the way to solve it seems obvious. This blind trust can lead to group members pushing their individual solutions with almost religious fervor. Rather than everyone working together to achieve a desired outcome through whatever means possible, the mindset shifts to people pushing their own, independently derived solution over others. That dynamic can split a group into antagonistic, uncooperative factions.

How do you get group members to respect and value approaches different from their own? How do effective leaders manage disparate personalities and strengths to get fellow campaigners to pull in the same direction? How do they succeed when others do not? This chapter teaches some ways.

Personality Traits That Get Your Teeth Grinding

Personality differences can—but should not—wreak havoc in a group. Take, for example, Joe, Owen, and Jed, founding members of the Friends of the Preserve citizen group. Joe, Owen, and Jed were all committed to the Preserve, but they were very different people. Joe was a methodical, detail-oriented engineer; Owen was a free-thinking, big-picture artist; Jed was a practical, handyman sort who put a premium on experience and common sense.

The three tolerated one another at first, but that tolerance dissipated as they started working together. Before long, their personality differences and lack of respect for one another took center stage and splintered the group—some members quit, some took sides, and some just ignored the others and did their own thing.

Since we all firmly believe that *our* way is the *best* way, it is not surprising that we devalue those who see things differently than we do. If you were a Joe-type, for example, someone like Owen—a hairball of disconnected ideas—would probably set your teeth grinding; someone like Jed—a set-in-his ways traditionalist who valued experience over established rules—would drive you nuts too. And if you were mainly an Owen-type, why would you *ever* willingly work with a boring, regimented Joe or a stick-in-the-mud Jed? And if you were a Jed sort, why would you *ever* want to subject yourself to the lockstep mentality of a Joe or the off-the-wall ideas of an Owen? What would they bring to the table that you would not?

We naturally try to stock our groups with people who approach things the way we do, and forming groups that way—all Joes, all Owens, or all Jeds—does make for smoother interpersonal sailing. But one-dimensional thinking is not what you need when tackling tough environmental problems. The people factor (introduced in chapter 1) is one reason for this. Another reason is that different skill sets are needed at different stages of problem solving—a one-dimensional, my-way-or-the-highway approach just does not work. For example, Joe's analytical skills would be just what you need to point everyone in the same direction. And Owen's unfettered mind would be key when you are stuck in a rut. And when it is time to implement messy strategies and get things done, Jed would be just the person you would want for the job. Differences in approach are a strength, but only if the differences are valued and shepherded.

The personality traits of a Joe, Owen, or Jed will set your teeth grinding if you treat them as character flaws rather than as potential strengths. The same can be said of procrastination. Some procrastinators are lazy or uncaring, of course, but that does not accurately describe many folks who wait until the nth hour to do something. Many of these late-finishers, in fact, are extremely hardworking and intensely responsible—they just need the stress of a rapidly approaching deadline to be energized into action. Like skydivers, bungee jumpers, and downhill racers, these late-finishers have a high stress threshold and are easily bored until pushed to the edge. Once they get going, however, they pull their weight and do quality work.

Just as early-finishers cannot understand what is wrong with procrastinators, late-finishers cannot understand what is wrong with early-finishers. Why are they so uptight? Why do they get so bent out of shape over distant deadlines? Why can't they just chill? The short answer is that early-finishers have lower stress thresholds than procrastinators. That is why putting things off until the last moment upsets them so.

Having everyone openly admit their early or late finishing tendencies (and their level of commitment to the project) *before* a project gets rolling helps people understand where everyone on the team is coming from and makes for a better working arrangement. If there are both early- and late-finishers in your group, early-finishers can shoulder the work that comes first. When it comes to crunch time, late-finishers are the ones for the job. Taking on tasks in this way allows early- and late-finishers to work within their natural comfort zones, where they are most productive.

Learning to tolerate annoying personality traits is all well and good in theory, but if you're anything like me (the way I used to be, that is), part of you is wondering why you should bother. Why not go it alone? Going it alone *might be* simpler and less stressful in the short term, but it is much less likely to yield the environmental outcome that you ultimately seek. Internal strife in a group—what you'll foster if you go it alone—poisons the cause. Before you know it, group dynamics will take center stage, replacing the environmental cause you were working on together.

Why Meetings Make People Scream

Much dysfunction in teams could be avoided if members were up-front about their hard-wired tendencies. Even more dysfunction could be avoided if the prospect of attending a meeting did not make people want to scream.

There are many reasons why people hate meetings, but here are the top suspects—my worst of the worst:

- I do not have a clue *why* we are meeting or *what* the meeting is really about.
- Nothing gets done. The same old stuff is rehashed again, and again, and again.
- We meet for an hour when ten minutes would have been more than enough.
- Windbag Chuck drones on endlessly about nothing.

More often than not, the root cause of painful meetings is the first reason above—a lack of clarity around the meeting's purpose. Here's an example. Let's say that you are holding a meeting to deal with people being chronically late. The meeting's purpose and desired outcome may seem obvious to you (e.g., to find out *why* people are chronically late), but if *your* exact purpose is not stated explicitly, some attendees will assume a different purpose for the meeting, such as to scold or threaten latecomers or to announce a new lateness policy. In this situation, attendees may end up talking lots but accomplishing little—all because they entered the meeting without knowing what exactly its purpose is.

Making a meeting worthwhile takes more than just getting people together to talk. Meeting participants need to know the exact purpose of the meeting—what it is about and what it is seeking to achieve—for the meeting to have a chance of succeeding. In fact, meetings work best when they are approached as problem-solving efforts rather than as group get-togethers. The *reason* for holding a meeting *should be* to move a problematic situation from where it is (e.g., infighting, uninformed people, decisions not made, tasks not completed) to where you want it to be (e.g., group harmony, informed people, decisions made, tasks completed). A meeting is a means to an end, not the end itself.

Running an Effective Meeting

If there are meetings in heaven and I make it through the pearly gates to participate in them, they will:

- be short and infrequent
- have an explicitly stated purpose, and the intended outcome will be clear

- stick to an agenda and start and end on time
- specify exactly who is doing what and by when
- enforce limits as to how long windbags are allowed to carry on
- not be interrupted to bring latecomers up to speed

Appendix 6 shows other wishes on my prayer list. In the end though, none of them matter if your *reason* for meeting—exactly what you hope to achieve in the meeting—isn't crystal clear to you and everyone else.

Figuring Out Just Exactly Why You're Meeting

Holding a meeting is just one of many possible ways to change a situation from where it is to where you want it to be. Always consider other strategies; oftentimes a telephone call, memo, note, email message, or chat in the hall works better. Once you've determined that a meeting is absolutely necessary, ensure that you've really thought through what you are hoping to come out of the meeting before putting it on everyone's calendars. Is your meeting:

- to inform people about something?
- to assign tasks?
- to generate ideas?
- to develop a plan?
- to give people a chance to be heard or let off steam?
- to identify, assess, or uncover the strengths and weaknesses of various options?
- to marshal support for or against an action?
- to select the best alternative/reach a decision?
- to forecast what could go wrong or not work during implementation?
- to build community?

Being clear about the meeting's purpose—*why* the meeting is being held—leads to your *desired outcome* for the meeting, exactly what you want to come out of the meeting. Answers to the following three questions should help you tease this out:

1. Exactly which outcome would make you feel that the meeting was a giant success?

2. Once the meeting is concluded, what do you want to have happened?

3. When people walk out the door after the meeting, what do you want them to be thinking?

With the meeting's purpose and desired outcome established (be sure to write them down so you do not stray from them), you can now turn to planning the meeting—what you will do, how you will do it, and with whom.

Deciding Who Participates

Deciding who should participate in a meeting and who should not is mighty important, so make selections carefully. Including the wrong participants or leaving out the right ones can create very unpleasant problems for you. So play it safe: ask trusted colleagues to review your tentative list of participants before committing to it.

As for who *should* come to your meeting, that depends on what you are hoping to get out of the meeting. If you are looking for ideas, pick upbeat, freethinkers who have a devil-may-care attitude; stay away from critics, naysayers, and wet blankets. If you are aiming to uncover weaknesses and flaws in a proposed action, invite the naysayers and critics who find fault in everything. If your goal is to validate the concerns of minority opinions, invite people whose voices have not been heard.

Choosing to invite some people but not others to a meeting can create hard feelings unless you capitalize on people's natural disdain for meetings. A way to do this is to explain that, to reduce the time everyone spends sitting through uninteresting meetings, you want to try splitting up meetings so that not everyone needs to go to every meeting—whereas some people will go to some meetings, others will go to others. To reassure everyone that they will be kept in every loop, promise that a written record of every meeting (the minutes) will be distributed broadly. This fewer-meetings strategy lets you handpick who attends which meetings.

There will probably be some meetings, however, that everyone will want to attend, whether you want them to or not. If leaving out people will cause hard feelings, consider holding a couple of small meetings rather than a single, large, free-for-all meeting. Sell the idea by explaining that holding a couple of smaller meetings gives everyone a chance to contribute more fully. To the extent possible, stock one small meeting with the people you want; stock the other meeting with everyone else. In the end, everyone's need to meet will be satisfied, and those for whom the meeting really is intended will be shielded from those who should not be there. If this strategy of dividing and conquering is not an option, all you can do is be extra clear about the meeting's purpose and how the meeting will be run. Clear ground rules protect the facilitator/ chair from appearing to take sides when someone needs to be reined in.

Meeting participants are easily sidetracked by hidden agendas, power struggles, closed-mindedness, strong-mindedness, compulsive talking, hostile personalities, lateness, absenteeism, lack of preparation, status differences, and residual frustrations held over from prior meetings or interactions. Advance planning helps you neutralize these forces before they destroy or delay what you are hoping to accomplish—before they drain whatever spirit you still have. Setting a clear agenda (and following it) is your best weapon.

Setting the Agenda

Once you have concluded that holding a meeting is your best option, clarified your desired outcome(s), and decided whom to invite, communicate the desired outcome to meeting participants in the form of a written agenda. The agenda is a road map or preview of coming attractions that explains the purpose of the meeting, the desired outcomes of the meeting, and the order in which items will be covered. Logistical details such as the day, time, and location of the meeting are also included, as is the contact information (name, telephone number, email address) of whoever is running the meeting. Appendix 7 shows what an effective agenda looks like.

An effective, crisply packaged agenda frames the meeting, sets the tone for how the meeting will be run, keeps everyone on task, and deters aimless discussion. Meetings that are run without that structural foundation create as many problems as they solve. That is as true for small committee meetings as it is for larger, more formal meetings.

Each item on the agenda must be specific, straightforward, and unambiguous. When a meeting is going nowhere, it is usually because the agenda items are vague or ill-defined. Some common ones that invite trouble are "to work on X," "to talk about X," and "to discuss X." Participants will interpret these ambiguous phrases differently, and they will act accordingly. Just based on these examples, participants may end up either generating ideas, evaluating options, articulating concerns, deciding on a course of action, assigning tasks, or sharing information. When participants take off in different directions, frustration is the only certain outcome. Crafting (and following) a detailed agenda keeps that from happening.

Getting Things Done Efficiently

The agenda provides an efficient roadmap of how the meeting will proceed; the minutes—an efficient written record of what actually transpired in the meeting—completes the circle (see appendix 8 for an example). The agenda and minutes make it clear that the meeting has purpose—that it is more than just a pointless gab session.

Participants should *always* walk away feeling that the meeting was worthwhile. That will be the take-home perception if you run the meeting efficiently by following a thoughtfully prepared agenda, ending on time, summarizing (before adjourning) the meeting's key points—including which person is going to do what, and by when—and reviewing what happens next.

It is tough to accomplish much in a large group, so consider breaking the group into smaller, task-specific committees. Try to stock each committee with at least a couple of individuals who have a genuine interest in what the committee is tasked with working on. More will be achieved, and faster, that way.

Generating New Ideas at Meetings

One reason people schedule meetings is to brainstorm new ideas. Brainstorming *can be* an effective idea-generating technique *if* the technique's principles are followed. But those principles are almost never followed.[1] Several studies have shown that the version of brainstorming that is most commonly employed does not work very well at generating new ideas. In fact, some studies have shown that people often produce *more* ideas, and *better* ideas, when they brainstorm on their own rather than with others.

In groups where there is a hierarchy, or a boss, more junior team members may be especially disinclined to offer imaginative ideas because they worry about looking stupid or saying something the boss won't like. To get people in a hierarchized group to share their ideas and perspectives openly, those concerns must be brought under control. Bosses can encourage subordinates to

---

1. Because people do not know what the principles are, or that they even exist.

say anything they wish—pretend I'm not in the room!—but that works about as well as telling a mouse to ignore the cat. A more effective way to squeeze imaginative ideas out of timid subordinates is Brainwriting.

Brainwriting is a mind-liberating technique used to generate lots of novel ideas in a hurry. The technique works by effectively addressing six realities of creative thinking:

- People shy away from unconventional ideas if they think someone might criticize their ideas as silly, stupid, or unworkable. Anonymity liberates the mind.
- People are most creative when left alone to work at their own pace.
- Outside stimuli can trigger entirely new ways of thinking.
- The best way to come up with great new ideas is to generate lots of ideas—the more the better. *Every idea*—crazy, wild, sensible—should be viewed as equally valuable.
- Great ideas are rarely usable in their original form; like new wine, they need to mature.
- Creative thinking and critical thinking are contradictory brain processes. Do not mix them by evaluating the goodness or badness of ideas as you generate them. Get as many ideas on the table as you can *before* you evaluate any of them.

Here is how Brainwriting works. Each person receives a blank sheet of paper and writes the challenge across the top of the sheet. When looking for new ideas (e.g., how are we going to raise money for our organization?), you and your team members should preface your idea-generating need with:

In what ways might we . . . ? (e.g., In what ways might we raise money for our organization?)

If you are trying to identify what could go wrong before it does, preface your troubleshooting challenge with:

What things might we need to think about when . . . ? (e.g., What things might we need to think about when trying to implement our outreach campaign?)

The actual Brainwriting starts by having your team members, each working on their own, write down any and all thoughts that come to mind and are related to the *In what ways might we* challenge. Once an idea is on paper, it stays there as is—no editing is permitted, no matter how flawed it seems to be. If a participant thinks of a better way to say what she had in mind, she should add it to the list as a new, separate entry.

When a person's output of ideas begins to slow, she should not labor to squeeze more ideas out of her depleted head. Instead, she should say "switch!" aloud and trade sheets with someone.[2] Those who have traded now read through their newly acquired Brainwriting sheets. Doing so usually triggers new ideas, which are recorded beneath the sheet's other ideas.

The singular goal of Brainwriting—and every other idea-generating technique—is to generate as many ideas as possible. The presumed quality of an idea does not matter: seemingly *good, bad, ridiculous, sensible, and off-the-wall entries are equally valuable.*[3]

Participants should switch sheets with a new person each time their flow of ideas begins to ebb. After eight to ten minutes of Brainwriting, the sheets of recorded ideas are collected.

Brainwriting is an upbeat way to end a meeting because there is a real sense of collaborative accomplishment. Dozens of novel ideas are created in only a few minutes; moreover, every single one of those ideas is preserved permanently as a written record. With a bunch of new ideas on paper, you and your team can now evaluate—using your other brain hemisphere—which ideas have promise.

As suggested earlier, it is important to recognize that few ideas will be ready for showtime in their initially proposed form—most will need further refining or development. So do not dismiss promising but flawed ideas too quickly. Anytime you find yourself saying or thinking "Yeah, but . . ." about a tantalizing idea, try this: Brainwrite ways to make the idea better. For example:

- In what ways might we change the proposed animal-riding fundraiser to make it acceptable to animal rights activists?
- In what ways might we tweak the proposed event X to make it more fun?

This second round of Brainwriting (where you are looking for ways to overcome a perceived weakness) is followed by a second round of evaluation.

---

2. When to switch sheets is up to each individual; it is not a group decision, and not every member of the group needs to switch in unison. That said, if someone requests a switch, go ahead and switch sheets with the person, even if you have not yet exhausted your own storehouse of ideas.

3. *Evaluating* the goodness or badness of ideas comes later and is an entirely different mental process.

This back-and-forth method between Brainwriting and evaluative thinking is one of the main ways that trained problem solvers make novel ideas workable. The back-and-forth only works, however, if the two very different brain activities are kept separate. *Do one or do the other—do not try doing both at the same time.*

Getting People in a Meeting to Say What They Are Really Thinking

Domineering personalities have a chilling effect on the meek and mild. One way to counteract this problem is to equalize dominance in the group: separate out the dominant members and place them in freestanding teams of three to five, and do likewise with the meek and mild.[4] Once teams are formed and members are seated together, explain the mission and time constraints and specify the output that you are looking for (e.g., ideas, ranking of ideas, articulation of concerns).

The separate teams now work independently, with each team producing a written summary of its conclusions, recommendations, ideas, or concerns. Because summaries are group efforts, no individual is identified as being the originator of an idea.

Two other approaches that work well at getting people to say what they are *really* thinking are the Facilitator-Recorder Approach to Running Meetings (below) and the Improved Nominal Group Technique (described a bit later). Both approaches rely on an impartial facilitator creating an environment where participants feel comfortable sharing their thoughts. Every shared thought or idea, regardless of its perceived value, is written on a flip-chart sheet and treated as a contribution to the group as a whole. The strengths and weaknesses of entries are not discussed until the group has exhausted its outpouring of ideas, and every idea has been transcribed to a flip-chart sheet.

The Facilitator-Recorder Approach

The Facilitator-Recorder Approach increases participation in meetings by equalizing differences in power and authority within the group. It also works well at neutralizing hostility among group members.

---

4. The boss should join whichever team has the most aggressive members.

The facilitator's role is to create a meeting environment where group members feel free to share ideas without fear of ridicule or verbal assault. That is critical because timid participants will not share their thoughts openly unless every person is respectful of every other person's thoughts. It is the facilitator's job to ensure that happens by treating all ideas fairly, respectfully, and equitably. The role of the recorder is to keep track of ideas, turning spoken thoughts into written entries without editorializing. Good recorders summarize ideas quickly and legibly on the flip-chart sheet, using the speaker's own words, and they ask members to correct them if a transcription veers from what was actually stated. As for meeting participants, their role is to participate actively and respectfully and to correct the recorder when ideas are not summarized accurately.

In setting up the meeting space, participants are seated in a semicircle facing the recorder and a flip chart. Shared thoughts are thus directed to the flip chart and, by association, to the group as a whole. Once participants are seated, you—as the facilitator—explain everyone's role. When everyone is clear about their individual missions, suggest a way to proceed. Facilitators most commonly propose three separate phases of sharing: the first is an uninterrupted outpouring of ideas, the second is a clarification of confusing entries, and the third phase is a discussion of strengths and weaknesses of promising ideas. If participants want to proceed differently, that is fine because your role as the facilitator is to be the shepherd/cheerleader, not the decider.

Following that, you read aloud the first agenda item and explain where you would like attendees to focus their attention—exactly what you want from them. Participants *must* understand what you are after or their well-intentioned contributions will wander in every direction imaginable. The recorder notes the participants' responses on a flip-chart sheet; when one sheet fills, another is started. If many ideas are forthcoming, more than one recorder may be needed. Completed sheets of comments are then posted prominently on a wall, in sequential order, so that the meeting process is readily apparent to everyone, including late arrivals.

Displaying the collection of ideas on flip charts for everyone to see— without identifying who came up with the idea—changes the idea's ownership: it is no longer *one individual's* idea, it has become the *group's* idea. That makes all the difference in how members interact with one another when ideas are discussed.

Discussing items on the flip-chart sheets (typically the third phase of sharing) can get animated. The facilitator should set clear ground rules about what the discussion phase is and *what the discussion phase is not*:

- The discussion phase is *not* a debate or lobbying session.
- The discussion phase is *not* about deciding which ideas to keep and which ideas to toss. It *is* about efficiently exploring the merits and liabilities of each item on the flip-chart sheets.

As for protocol and rules:

- Any item on the sheet *may be* discussed, but an item *does not have to be* discussed.
- Participants should avoid saying what someone else has already said.
- Speeches and diatribes are not permitted, comments need to be short and to the point.

When someone strays from this protocol, which often happens when people are agitated, the facilitator quickly and politely reminds the wandering speaker to stay on track. A good way to do this is to ask, "Does the speaker have something new and specific to add?"

The discussion of pluses and minuses will reveal some items as promising and some items as obvious losers. Making final decisions on items is typically a separate exercise that may or may not include the whole group. The recorder can, with the group's approval, highlight items that command especially favorable or unfavorable discussion. When tasks are assigned or decisions are reached, highlighting can be used to eliminate uncertainty about what has been decided on, or who is going to do what by when. Volunteers and appointees are more likely to remember and carry out their duties if their responsibilities are prominently displayed.

For the Facilitator-Recorder Approach to work, all assembled members must believe they are being treated fairly and equitably. Toward that end, facilitators and recorders must not be defensive when someone suggests that ideas have not been advanced accurately or fairly. Offer thanks for the feedback and mean it.

The Improved Nominal Group Technique

The Improved Nominal Group Technique (INGT) also works well at drawing out thoughts and ideas from group members who hesitate to say what they really think. This is a common problem when members are of different status, rank, or power, or when the level of support for an idea depends on who suggests it. To neutralize this counterproductive dynamic, ideas and comments need to be anonymous. That is what INGT provides.

INGT resembles the Facilitator-Recorder Approach in many respects, but it requires more orchestration so it is wise to test the waters to see if it is worth trying. To do so, distribute a comment card to each meeting participant a few days before your next meeting with this question on it:

> I am searching for ways to make our meetings more inclusive and rewarding for everyone. Would you feel more comfortable, and would you be more willing to contribute whatever is on your mind, if your inputs were anonymous? (I am asking this of everyone, and I would like your honest, anonymous response).

Have people return their anonymous responses back to you in a neutral ballot box in time for tallying of results. Use this feedback to decide if INGT is worth a try.

Running an INGT meeting is not difficult, but it may seem weird to those who are unfamiliar with it. The technique works best when groups meet regularly, or when participants know each other well.

The key to INGT is anonymous inputting of ideas and anonymous evaluation of ideas. Differences in status or aggressiveness are irrelevant in INGT because everyone contributes ideas the same way, and submitted ideas are introduced to the group only after anonymity has been assured. Ideas are discussed and evaluated on merit alone.

Submitting anonymous index cards provides a forum for people to share ideas without worrying about how their ideas will be judged by others. This protective cloak of anonymity is a major strength of INGT. The discussion phase of INGT provides a forum for exploring the strengths and weaknesses of ideas without knowing whose idea is being discussed. Decoupling the merits of an idea from the generator of the idea is a major strength of INGT.

The INGT process begins when meeting participants receive a copy of the agenda ahead of time and are asked to record their thoughts about the agenda items on 3 x 5 cards.[5] This premeeting exercise jump-starts the actual meeting by getting participants to think about agenda items beforehand. The meeting therefore starts and ends at a higher level.

Meeting participants bring their cards to the meeting, receive new cards as they enter the room, and seat themselves in a semicircle facing the facilitator and a flip chart. Participants are then asked to submit one or more cards, facedown, for collection. Participants who completed a card before the meeting turn it in now; participants who did not complete any cards beforehand turn

---

5. Two digital alternatives are Mentimeter and Poll Everywhere.

in a blank card face-down. This process of everyone always submitting at least one card (face-down) ensures that inputs are anonymous.

Having collected this first batch of cards, you—as the INGT facilitator—now introduce an agenda item and ask members to spend a few minutes recording their thoughts about it on one or more cards. While participants are writing, you shuffle the cards you collected earlier and then transcribe (assisted by a recorder if necessary) ideas from the shuffled cards to a prominently displayed flip chart at the front of the room. The transcribed ideas will be the focus of group discussion, so you should be prepared to add ideas of your own if most of the collected cards are blank.

Once the ideas have all been transcribed from cards to the flip chart, you collect the newly completed cards, face-down. As with the first batch of cards, the collected cards are shuffled and the ideas on the cards are then transcribed to flip-chart sheets. Completed flip-chart sheets are hung on the wall for all to see.

Transcription of this second set of cards will take longer than the first set, so you may need additional recorders and sheets to keep pace with the input of ideas. While the ideas are being transcribed by recorders, you could run through announcements, updates, and other information that does not require much input from the group.

Once transcription and meeting preliminaries have been completed, you ask participants to review items on the flip-chart sheets for clarity. Any participant can propose a rephrasing of any item to make it more clear, but at this stage no other discussion of items is permitted. A proposal to rephrase an item requires approval from the group before the change can be made. You can manage this by asking if anyone objects to changing the item as proposed. If no one objects, the proposed change is made on the flip chart by lightly crossing out the original (so it is still visible) and replacing it with the newly phrased version. If anyone objects to the proposed change, there is no further discussion or argument; the original item is left unchanged, and the proposed change is added to the flip-chart sheet as a new item.

Once the transcribed items have been reviewed and clarified, you ask for another session of anonymous card writing where each member records new ideas that were triggered by items on the flip chart. After a couple of minutes of reflection and silent writing, you collect at least one face-down card from each person (individuals having nothing new to add submit a blank card), the collected cards are shuffled, and new items are transcribed to a new flip-chart sheet.

As with the Facilitator-Recorder Approach discussed earlier, discussing items on the flip-chart sheets (the next stage of INGT) can get out of control if the facilitator allows members to stray from INGT protocol. Set the following ground rules early—and enforce them:

- Keep comments short and to the point.
- No lobbying for or against an item.
- No speeches.
- Avoid repeating what has already been said.

When someone is out of line, you need to immediately but respectfully remind the errant speaker to stay on track. You can send this message with a gentle question: "Is there something new and specific you would like to add?"

Discussing the many ideas generated by card writing eats up more time than you would expect. If you find that the group will not be able to discuss every item adequately in the meeting time that remains, a time-out is needed to decide how to proceed. Should the present meeting be extended? Should there be a time limit on discussion of remaining items? Should another meeting be scheduled?

When time is running short, the temptation is to blitz through remaining items for the sake of completion. Do not do that.

The Difference between Offering Ideas, Evaluating Options, and Making Decisions

Getting meeting participants to say what they are *really* thinking can reveal unexpected sentiments that you may not want to hear. Be honest with yourself before claiming that you want to know people's inner thoughts. How will you react if people express contrary or unwelcome sentiments? Will you lash out and become argumentative or defensive, or will you be able to tamp down your inner emotions and listen respectfully and appreciatively—*and value*—the divergent views? Never pretend that you want to hear what people are really thinking if your ego can't handle what might be said.

Also never let team members imagine that they are part of the decision-making process if they are not. People tend to assume that, if they are part of generating or discussing ideas, they will also be part of decision making. But *offering/discussing* ideas and *making decisions* are entirely different undertakings—do not confuse the two. And don't assume that the difference is obvious to participants; often it is not. Nip that assumption in the bud or prepare yourself for hard feelings.

So decide and be up-front about it from the get-go: who will have the final say when decisions are made? The leadership? The group as a whole? A subgroup? An independent decision-making body? Make sure everyone knows the answer to this question from the start!

If you choose to be the sole decision maker but wish to know how group members feel, be absolutely clear and unapologetic that you alone will make the final decision but that you would appreciate their input through an advisory straw poll. Use secret, written ballots and count the ballots in private if you conduct the poll.

Secret balloting makes sense for two main reasons. First, individuals are likelier to vote their conscience when they are not worrying about how others will view their vote; voting by a show of hands does not necessarily reveal everyone's true preference. The second reason for secret voting is that it shields you (the decision maker) from needing to defend a decision that goes against the group's will. When a vote is open and public, everyone immediately knows the group's preference. If you ultimately decide to take a road that differs from the expressed preference of the group, prepare for major headaches. To minimize the fallout, you can explain and defend your decision, and you can remind everyone that you told them that the vote was advisory, not binding. Do not expect it to do much good, though: those who voted will take your decision as proof that what they think does not matter. Regaining their trust will not be easy.

Some Closing Thoughts

Work with any group of good people long enough, and some of them are sure to get on your nerves. Add to this team tinderbox other near certainties—personality differences, a firm belief that *your* way is the *right* way (with others in the group feeling the same about *their* way), and chronically worthless meetings—and it is only a matter of time before bad things happen.

Effective leaders keep those bad things from happening by changing the dynamic. They make meetings worth going to, and they keep people focused on the same desired outcome so that everyone pulls in the same direction. They get the most out of their team by recognizing that no single person—themselves included—has all the skills or personal traits needed to solve tough problems. Last, and most impressively, effective leaders exercise humility—they admit to themselves and others that *their* way might not always be the best way.

This chapter, and the one preceding it, are about connecting with people. The next chapter, "When Town Hall Becomes Battlefield," builds on those teachings to show how experienced leaders handle contentious meetings with grace.

6

When Town Hall Becomes Battlefield

How to Survive Contentious Public Meetings

Some decades ago, I was working as a ranger at Alaska's Glacier Bay National Park when then secretary of the interior James Watts—our boss—decided to visit. His reason for meeting with park rangers and staff was obvious: to tamp down the public outrage that park employees had been directing at him.

I felt almost sorry for Watts: more than half of the seated rangers, including several in uniform, were wearing Dump Watts buttons. We *hated* our boss—he was doing his utmost to destroy the park we loved. We couldn't wait to let him have it.

On the day we were to meet him, Secretary Watts was nowhere to be seen. His absence only stoked our resentment more—it felt like he was wasting our time. But suddenly, there he was among us, in jeans, an old flannel shirt, muddy boots, and a giant grin. "Sorry I'm late," he said. "A Humpback Whale was breaching off Gustavus Point!"

Secretary Watts would eventually do jail time for his misdeeds, but at that moment, he came across more like an excited kid in a candy store than like the three-piece-suited devil incarnate that we knew him to be. He gushed excitement as he recounted to everyone around him the amazing experience he had just had in the park. The effect on the assemblage of Watts-hating rangers was mind-blowing: the verbal venom we had planned to assault him with never materialized.

The secretary masterfully reset the meeting's tone, making the get-together a *discussion* rather than a battle. When still-angry rangers addressed him rudely, Watts maintained a calm, smiling, very human demeanor. In so doing, he disarmed the aggressive questioners and was able to keep the meeting a civilized exchange.

I learned lots from James Watts that day about diffusing people's anger—certainly a useful skill when tempers boil in a public meeting, which is something that, at some point in your career as an environmentalist, you'll almost certainly find yourself running. An even more useful skill, though, is knowing how to prepare for and run a public meeting so that emotions do not reach that boiling point. The first part of this chapter describes how to go about holding a public meeting that's civilized and productive. As you will see, it is easy—in principle, at least. But even well-planned meetings can go wrong and often do. The second part of the chapter describes what you can do about it.

Running Productive Public Meetings

Public meetings are held for a number of different reasons: to solicit feedback on a proposed action, to give people a chance to be heard, to answer questions, to address concerns. But whatever the meeting's purpose, one thing is entirely predictable: the people who show up for a public meeting do so because they care deeply about what is being discussed. Going into the meeting, you may not know if attendees are confused, concerned, frustrated, angry, or all of the above, but their lively comments and questions will make their feelings known. How you prepare for these emotionally charged interactions—the focus of this section—will help determine how the meeting goes for both you and them.

Meeting Preliminaries

An explosive meeting environment can develop anytime people assemble to talk about an issue about which they care about but disagree. You cannot do much to keep people from being upset—giving people a chance to vent might be the very reason you are having the meeting—but you *can* manage how the meeting proceeds. That begins with everyone having a clear understanding of the meeting's purpose.

Before any meeting takes place, attendees should know:

- the exact purpose of the meeting
- where and when the meeting will be held
- how long the meeting will last
- a little background on what will be covered (and why)
- the mechanics of how the meeting will be run, including how attendees will engage

- a contact person if there are questions (with email address and telephone number)
- where to go for additional information

The first order of business, of course, is to settle on the exact purpose of the meeting (see chapters 1 and 4 for help with this). The next decision is when and where to hold the meeting. Finalize those decisions at least a couple of weeks out so that interested parties have time to fit the meeting into their schedules.

Public meetings are typically held on a weekday evening. Unfortunately, that is when most other meetings also are held. To avoid competition for attendance when scheduling your meeting, first check with the town office, library, social clubs, and schools to see what is already been scheduled. School vacations, for example, are poor choices if you want parents at the meeting, just as hunting seasons are poor meeting times if you are seeking good attendance from hunters.

After settling on a meeting time and place and duration (longer than two hours is probably too long), the next order of business is getting the word out. To advertise the meeting broadly, place a sign outside your meeting location and contact radio stations about making a Public Service Announcement (see chapter 7). You will only be able to report the basics in these venues (e.g., Town Forest Meeting, Town Hall, Wed. eve, May 21, 7–9 pm) but more descriptive (and inviting) announcements can be made in posters and the local newspaper. Set a positive tone by being welcoming and friendly in the announcements to (e.g., Please join us for a community gathering to . . .).

Who knows about and attends the meeting—or doesn't—matters *a lot*, so do not rely on a single advertising strategy to get the word out. In this digital age, where most of us take electronic communication for granted, do not assume that everyone's computer savvy. Some are not. Do not overlook them!

Of course, the people who *most* need to know about the meeting are those who are likely to be most interested or concerned about the meeting's focus. Brainstorm who these parties may be—hunters, farmers, ATV riders, snowmobilers, loggers, and camp owners are sometimes overlooked—and find ways to reach them. Personally reaching out to key players, especially those who hold views different from your own, builds trust in your commitment to fairness.

In describing an upcoming public meeting, state the exact focus and intent of the meeting. For example, rather than advertising the meeting in general terms, such as "a meeting to talk about zoning," describe the meeting as "a question and answer information session about the proposed zoning change," or "a meeting to share opinions about options A, B, and C," or "a meeting to explain how we might guide future development so the town becomes the community we would like it to be." See appendix 9 for other nuts-and-bolts reminders.

Getting the Meeting Off to a Good Start

Dress in a way that is appropriate for the situation and the audience and that does not call attention to your being different from those attending. Doing so helps reduce the feeling of "us-versus-them." If you are from a government agency, for example, consider downplaying the affiliation to emphasize the fact that you are a human being, not a faceless government official. If you can, wear a plain shirt and simple nametag instead of the agency's logo-ridden hat, shirt, or nametag. If the meeting is for a bunch of loggers or hunters, dress more outdoorsy; if it is for bankers or high-level bureaucrats, dress more formally, perhaps wearing a jacket and tie.

Charles Johnson, a state naturalist who has hosted more contentious meetings than anyone I know, shared the following funny story about how perceptions affect how people receive you:

> When the Forest Legacy Program was just being instituted in the state, with much anxiety on the part of some landowners, I went on a statewide dog-and-pony show to explain how it worked. In Rutland, I met a hostile audience. One fellow in particular was ripping mad and started yelling at me, pointing and saying, "We don't need no damn bureaucrat in a coat and tie coming down here to tell us what to do!" I smiled, took off my coat and tie, and replied, "Now can we talk?" He paused as if at a loss for words, then he too smiled, then laughed with others in the room. The meeting went well from then on.

As the story suggests, humor can work wonders at lowering the boiling point—if it is not offensive, patronizing, degrading, or aimed at those in attendance. A little self-deprecation lightens the mood too.

It is important to project friendliness, so be welcoming. Nothing does this more effectively than a hello and warm smile. Chat with people as they enter. Shake hands, thank people for coming, and encourage them to fill out a nametag.

In starting the meeting, introduce yourself, even if you think everyone in attendance knows you, and briefly explain who you are, where you are from, and how you became involved. Use this brief autobiography as a personalized, conversational lead-in. Doing so sets the tone for the meeting. Thank people for taking time out of their busy lives to attend the meeting.

Offer a special thanks to committee members and other volunteers who have spent countless hours trying to make the community a better place. Remind the assembled body that working on these committees as volunteers is a thankless task, and that it is easy to criticize but much harder to come up with solutions. Acknowledging these realities makes audience members more sympathetic to your efforts.

In your introductory remarks, ask participants to include in their comments or criticisms a constructive recommendation for how to improve what has been proposed. If someone goes on a rant, you then can redirect him by asking if he has any recommendations for improvements. Being nicely challenged this way makes people realize *wow, this is really hard!* and softens their criticisms and outbursts.

Be clear that your role as chair is part cheerleader, part facilitator, part referee. One effective chair explains it in this light-hearted way: Chairing a public meeting is sort of like being a gym class teacher who is overseeing a tug of war with a rope having three ends. Getting people to pull together in a single direction without fighting one another is the challenge.

Remind people of the meeting's *purpose*—exactly what the meeting is about and what it is not about. As you offer this reminder, point to the written version of the purpose that you prominently displayed when you set up the room (appendix 9). A friendly reminder of the purpose of the meeting at the very start of the meeting gives you a leg to stand on when someone starts going off on a tangent. You usually can get the meeting back on track by gently referring back to the meeting's purpose, and then asking the speaker, in a friendly, neutral voice, if she has thoughts that pertain to that purpose.

If the participant refuses to return to the task at hand, acknowledge the participant's concern by recording its essence on a flip-chart sheet to show that the concern is taken seriously and not lost. Suggest that if there is sufficient interest in this or any other concern, additional meetings can be scheduled to address them. That assurance is often enough to get the meeting back on track. If it is not, you do have other options (discussed later).

Go over ground rules for the meeting (e.g., no clapping, no rudeness), pointing to the displayed rules as you go. Acknowledge that it is not easy to be civil or respectful when you are anxious, confused, alarmed, or otherwise upset, but ask people to please try. Last, explain the nuts and bolts of how the meeting will be conducted. The basics are explained below.

The Basics of a Public Meeting

Public meetings typically follow, at least loosely, parliamentary procedure, where a preset agenda defines how the meeting will be run. This includes the rules as to how audience members participate. Someone, usually a leader, chairs the meeting to maintain focus and order and enforce the rules. An overview of parliamentary procedure basics and rules of order can be found in appendix 10; jargon you are likely to encounter can be found in appendix 11. (Other types of meeting formats are described later in this chapter and in chapter 5.)

However the meeting is run, everyone *must* understand that they may not speak until their request (a raised hand) is "recognized" by the chair. This rule of recognition keeps people from interrupting or talking over someone else. When a number of people at the same time indicate a wish to speak, the chair identifies the order in which they will speak (e.g., Carl speaks first, followed by Jenny, then Molly . . .). People must not be allowed to speak out of turn.

An effective chair keeps things moving and does not let one person dominate; every person should have a chance to speak before there is any repeating. It is wise to decide ahead of time and to let attendees know how long an individual can have the floor and speak without interruption from others. Encourage people to keep their comments to the allotted time so that they are not interrupted when their allotted time runs out. To lessen the chance of needing to interrupt someone in mid-sentence, consider giving each speaker a one-minute warning.

Attending to meeting preliminaries, and establishing and following rules of order that everyone understands, sets the meeting in motion. How the meeting proceeds thereafter depends on the meeting's *purpose*—what you want to come out of it.

When you are seeking public input in a meeting that promises to be contentious, turn over the running of the meeting to a neutral, third-party facilitator. Doing so takes the spotlight off you and liberates you to really *listen* to what people say. Having a neutral facilitator run the meeting also makes it possible for you to express your views along with everyone else.

Whoever is facilitating the public meeting, that person must *never* put forth or hint at her personal opinion or deep-seated philosophy. Doing so destroys her credibility as being neutral, and it undermines the entire meeting process. The facilitator should have no stake in what is being covered.

A meeting that aims to keep people in the loop about humdrum goings-on will not attract many attendees, stimulate many reactions, or generate much emotion. No special provisions are needed to run this type of meeting; the chair can take charge and dominate what is said. That all changes if the purpose of the meeting is to explain or generate support for a controversial action, policy, or decision. Upset people need to have their say and let off steam—deny them this and you will have a revolution on your hands! Letting off steam is not enough, however: people also need to feel that *they have been heard and taken seriously.* Few things anger people more than feeling that a purported listening session is nothing more than an empty charade orchestrated to appease the crowd.

To send a strong message that audience comments *have* been heard and taken seriously, explain at the outset that a recorder or a scribe—not the facilitator or group leader—will record every contribution that an attendee makes.[1] The scribe legitimizes attendee comments in large print on flip-chart paper, using highly visible markers.[2] Effective scribes write clearly, process ideas quickly and accurately, remain neutral, and encourage audience attendees to correct any entry that misses the mark. When a flip-chart sheet is filled, it is taped to the wall in a prominent location and a new sheet is started. (See chapter 5 for other guidelines.)

It is the chair's (or facilitator's) job to engage meaningfully with the participants and to keep the meeting focused on the issue at hand. Reminding people of the meeting's purpose helps, but when people are upset about something, they will go off topic. A way to manage these peripheral comments respectfully is to record them on a separate sheet labeled "parking lot" so that the comments are not lost. Once recorded, you can redirect people back to the topic at hand.

Managing Yourself So You Don't Make Things Worse

When the meeting's purpose is to get public input, *your job is to listen,* so resist the urge to explain or defend a particular position. To show that you are paying close attention to what someone's saying, focus your attention solely on the person speaking. Small head nods show that you are following what is being said.

When the meeting's purpose is to announce or defend an unpopular action, policy, or decision, you can count on facing a large, concerned, anxious crowd.

---

1. Introduce the scribe, of course.

2. It is better *not* to record the name of the person who makes a comment. By not attributing comments to contributors, comments become the collective property of the group. That is desirable because it distances personalities and factions from comments.

How well the meeting ultimately goes depends, of course, on how well you manage the crowd. But it also depends on how well you manage yourself. Self-management needs to start the moment you consider holding the meeting.

Begin by taking stock of how you feel about the meeting. Are you looking forward to facing a room of alarmed, agitated, angry people? Of course not. Are you dreading the meeting? Probably. You must not dwell on the expected unpleasantness, however, or they will taint your attitude and how you interact with those who attend.

Instead, approach the meeting as an opportunity to accomplish something important, not as an ulcer-causing hell. Switching to this problem-solving mindset will lessen your sense of dread and make you less reactive when people say or do things that rub you the wrong way.

The attitude you bring into a meeting affects how you comport yourself. That matters because how *you* comport yourself affects how people in the meeting comport themselves. Upset people can and will say reactive things; there is nothing you can do to keep that from happening. You *can* keep yourself from entering into a defensive back-and-forth fray, however, by remembering that people are not reacting to *you* personally; they are reacting to an action, policy, or decision that troubles them. One friend offered this tip for keeping cool in tense moments: "Think of pointed comments as pebbles off a mountain. The meeting participants are the pebbles; you are the mountain. Pebbles that have merit will stick; those that are petty or disrespectful will just roll off."[3]

Avoid speaking sharply or showing frustration—people in the audience will respond in kind. When you feel your dander rising, smile. Treat smiling as your protective shield. Keep reminding yourself that *you are just the messenger.* Doing so makes it easier to stay cool, calm, and collected.

But staying cool, calm, and collected is easier said than done when someone is yelling at you or saying nasty things that are not true. How do you prepare for those personal attacks? There is only one way: practice your responses.

To prep yourself for difficult interactions, anticipate what surprised, confused, anxious, upset, angry people might do or say in the meeting. It is likely that some people will:

- raise their voices
- interrupt

---

3. Ethan Tapper, a consulting forester.

- not listen
- be rude and disrespectful
- challenge your authority
- be quick to take offense
- threaten with retaliatory action
- be unwilling to consider viewpoints other than their own
- go off on tangents that are not relevant
- hold distracting side conversations
- ignore stated rules on how the meeting will be run
- act on misinformation and faulty assumptions
- turn disagreements into personal attacks
- claim that the deck is stacked against them
- rant and rave
- storm out of the meeting

Do not be caught off-guard by these disruptions. Instead, prepare for them by practicing how you will respond to each and every one of them. Before any real public meeting, hold at least one mock practice meeting with role-playing colleagues who act out as angry, aggressive, confrontational members of the audience, hitting on all of the disruptions above. Practice your responses to their role-playing disruptions—and keep fine-tuning your responses—until you and your role-playing colleagues feel secure that you can handle all of the situations above calmly. The rehearsal will give you something to fall back on when unruly people give you a hard time.

How Things Go Wrong (and What You Can Do about Them)

Public meetings rarely go the way you want them to. To illustrate what can go wrong, let's replay a public meeting that was poorly managed.

The town of Gorham is trying to decide what to do with its newly acquired three-hundred-acre property.[4] Five people have volunteered to serve on the town forest subcommittee, their mission being to develop a plan for the property. The main interests from townspeople seem to be wildlife and mountain biking.

The subcommittee has hired an environmental consulting team to design a trail system and a naturalist to discern how the trail system would affect wildlife. They are holding a public meeting to talk about what they have come up with.

---

4. The town name, and some of the details, have been changed to preserve anonymity.

Here is what happened at the meeting (in italics). Each incident is followed by how the problem might have been averted.

Five hunters show up to the meeting hopping mad; no one had told them that the meeting was happening, and they learned about it by accident. The hunters accuse the subcommittee of leaving them out on purpose so they could railroad through an antihunting agenda.

The meeting leaders should have brainstormed in advance of the meeting constituencies that are likely to have a strong interest in the meeting and then devised ways to reach them. Telephoning a couple of hunters (the town clerk could help identify some) and asking the contacted hunters to spread the word would have given the subcommittee cover: they could have explained that hunters X and Y *had been called*, and the contacted hunters *had been asked* to spread the word to other hunters.

The trail supporters are mad because the naturalist hired to assess the trail's effect on wildlife is a well-known wilderness advocate. Trail supporters distrust the fairness of the naturalist's assessment because they believe she is strongly biased against trails. That such a biased individual was hired (instead of someone more neutral) leads them to believe that the town forest subcommittee is anti-trail, and that the whole meeting is just a sham.

To avoid any perception of conflict of interest when hiring consultants, the subcommittee could have run the names of possible consultants by representatives of the main stakeholder groups. (Making them part of the process would have made the subcommittee appear less autocratic.) Here is how they might have reached out to constituencies: "Hi, Jane/Jack/Jill/Jim, as you may know, the subcommittee will be hiring a naturalist to assess the trail's effect on wildlife. A couple of seemingly qualified people have been recommended to us: persons W and Z. We want to get the best person for the job, of course, so we are reaching out to see if there are any red flags that we should be aware of. Any thoughts?"

*An angry member of the audience challenges the chair with this question: Who gave **you** the right to decide what happens to the forest?*

This type of personal challenge, which happens all too often, puts the meeting chairperson on the defensive—a very bad place to be. To keep it from happening, the chair's opening remarks should have reminded people of the meeting's exact purpose—what it is and what it isn't—and reminded them that the trail system is only a concept, not a done deal. (Referring to it as a trail concept rather than as a trail system would have helped.)

As for the angry member not liking that an exclusive, small group (the subcommittee) was making all the decisions, the chair should have reminded people at the outset about the subcommittee's role, how it came about, and where its authority comes from. [5]

When a group has been charged to take the lead on an initiative, it assumes ownership of what it puts forward. It is possible to share the ownership, always a good idea, by presenting the preferred option alongside other options, giving each equal time. Early on in the process, long before the meeting is held, the subcommittee could have invited people to send in ideas for consideration. The subcommittee could have added its favored idea to the collection, ultimately promoting it as the one they felt had the most promise. If no one sent in ideas, the subcommittee could have generated a couple of other ideas to add to the one they favored. Having a suite of self-created ideas, they still honestly could have claimed to be promoting the one they felt held the greatest promise.

*We don't need a nature park; we **do** need a ball field! Why isn't that on the table?*

This question comes from the person assuming (mistakenly) that the acquired property could be used for any number of purposes—ball field, playground, dog park, nature trails, or whatever. In the case of the Gorham Town Forest, the property was purchased with funds that were earmarked for town forests; other uses of the property were not legally possible. If people had been reminded of this in the introductory remarks, the ball field idea would not have surfaced.

Many times, however, properties are acquired without preconditions on possible uses. When that is the situation, be sure that everyone knows from the outset *how* the subcommittee settled on the plan being considered. People must believe that the process was a fair, community-level decision.

This is the first we've heard of this! Why are we just hearing about it now?

This question can make your blood boil when you have gone out of your way to keep people in the loop. The chair could have lessened the chance of

---

5. Try to resist the urge to lash out at complainers who were conveniently absent when the committee was being formed.

this complaint being levied if her introductory remarks had explained how the subcommittee sought to keep people informed.

Sarah's ranting goes unchecked.

Trying to police people and their behaviors is tough if the rules are not clearly established beforehand. If everyone knew at the outset how long they would have to speak, the chair would have had established rules to back her up when she sought to stop the rant. An audience will support a chair who impartially enforces the rules.

It is best, of course, to avoid policing altogether. Clustering people in small groups as they sit down is a way to do that. When a large meeting is transformed into a collection of small meetings, it is very difficult for one person's ranting to affect the whole group.

Bill and his cronies have taken over the meeting. They are loud and overbearing, and they interrupt anyone who tries to speak. People who have other views are outraged that Bill and company have been allowed to dominate; some of them, totally frustrated, storm out of the meeting in a huff.

Breaking into smaller groups makes it harder for a single person or clique to dominate, and if they do dominate, only the small group is affected. It sometimes happens, however, that someone feels that his very important thoughts *must* be shared with the whole group, not just a small subset. When this happens, all you can do is let the person grandstand for a short while but then move on, holding the line.

Dominating personalities in any size of meeting can be neutralized, and participation from timid individuals can be promoted, by seeking written rather than spoken feedback. Briefly explain that, to maximize input from the group, and to be sure that every voice is heard, you want to give everyone a chance to share their thoughts on cards so you have a written record of the group's thinking. After passing out a pen and index card to everyone present, explain the exact feedback you are seeking. Make your request simple, direct, and specific. For example: "In the next three minutes, please write down as bullets your three biggest concerns about the proposed plan. Then for each concern, briefly explain why it troubles you. You can put your name on the card or not, that's your choice."

As people are writing their responses, fill out a card yourself to be sure that your views are represented. After time is up and it seems that most people have had time to record their thoughts, collect everyone's card, adding yours to the pile. Shuffle the cards to protect anonymity and then have a preselected, fair-minded scribe summarize feedback as bullets on flip-chart sheets that are posted prominently. (See chapter 5 for more on this and other techniques.)

As for what you do with the items on the flip-chart sheets once they are posted, that depends on the meeting's purpose. If the meeting's goal is to ferret out the full range of views, posting the flip-chart sheets may be sufficient. If your goal is to gauge support or resistance to an item, you may want to hold off reviewing written feedback until you have time to do it right (after the meeting). If your goal is to promote one favored item over others, plan beforehand how you will accomplish that in a way that will not seem like you are steamrolling your wishes over others. Whatever your purpose and strategy, however, be clear that a written summary of the feedback will be made available to all who are interested in reviewing it.

"Let's vote on it!" a trail supporter insists, even though that's not the purpose of the meeting. A vote is taken, and most people vote for building the trail system. (That result's not surprising given that most people who showed up for the meeting are trail supporters.) "It's decided, then!" the trail supporters proclaim.

People who do not want the trail are outraged. "There was no advance warning that a vote would be held!" they yell. "If we had known there would be one, many more people would have found a way to attend the meeting!" The town forest subcommittee tries to tone down their outrage by explaining that the vote is not binding, and that nothing has really been decided. Now it is the trail supporters who are outraged. "We voted on it!" they shout.

The meeting's purpose was *not* to hold a vote, but that was not made clear. If in her introductory remarks the chair had explained what the purpose of the meeting was and was not, the call for a vote could easily have been nixed. The chair could have pointed out that holding a vote would not be fair to those not present (who had no inkling that a vote was in the offing).

There are times, of course, when holding a nonbinding straw vote serves the meeting's purpose. Before taking that road, however, think through what will happen if the straw vote does not align with the action that you wish to take.

Taxes are too high already! I don't want my taxes going to buy a town forest that no one will use!

As it turns out, no taxpayer money was used to acquire the property. This complaint could have been averted if the chair, in opening remarks, had reminded people how the property was acquired.

A couple of aggressive, antagonistic hotheads are very disruptive.

Anger can bring out the worst in anyone, but some individuals have reputations as hotheads. The subcommittee should have identified likely hotheads before the meeting was scheduled. Once that identification took place, the subcommittee could have strategized ways to interact with the hotheads productively and respectfully. Connecting with them beforehand (explained later) would have been a good place to start.

"You're not letting us talk about what we want to talk about!"

Putting limits on what will happen at the meeting may disgruntle some individuals who believe that anything should be fair game. The chair could have contained the disgruntlement by being clear at the outset that the meeting (and its stated purpose) need not be the only meeting held on the issue. People could have been reminded that any number of other meetings (with different purposes) would be possible if there is sufficient interest, and if someone is willing to organize the meeting and make it happen.

Your request that participants save their tangential interests for a different meeting may be ignored by those who feel a need to have their say now. If you foresee that situation arising, structure the meeting around the Open Space Method (discussed later) so that multiple issues can be aired at once. The Open Space Method is a good escape hatch, in fact, when a meeting turns chaotic and you cannot get participants back on track. Be ready to transition into it quickly should the need arise.

The People Factor, Redux

I have never met a scientist or naturalist who grew up wanting to deal with agitated, opinionated, clueless citizens in a public meeting. Most scientists and naturalists I know, in fact, would sooner clean a barn stall with their toothbrush than run a public meeting. Some of them nevertheless still step forward and do what they least want to do.

Why do these gluttons for punishment do it? Why do they willingly subject themselves to unneeded aggravation? They do it because they understand that making an environmental difference—doing environmental good—revolves around people's attitudes and behaviors more than anything else.

What Makes People Mad

Of the many reasons why people act out in a public meeting like the one at Gorham, some arise from past events that have little or nothing to do with what the meeting is supposed to be about. Unbeknownst to you, people will have a pent-up anger walking in if they feel that:

- they have been left out, ignored, or not taken seriously
- something has been shoved down their throats
- their personal rights or values are under siege
- they will be on the losing end, no matter what

People who are not mad when they walk in the door can get mad in a hurry if they feel that you have been hostile, unfair, dishonest, defensive, argumentative, bossy, or uneven-handed. Wasting their time with a pointless meeting, or saying things that are not true, or not knowing what you are talking about will not win you points either.

Meeting participants become most agitated, however, when they feel that they are not being respected, listened to, or taken seriously. You can diffuse some anger by treating everyone with respect, including those who do not seem to deserve it. That is easier said than done when someone is unfairly giving you a rough time, but it is your best countermeasure. Practicing your interactions with role players who act in aggressive, unfair, hostile ways will prepare you for the real thing. And while it is hard not to take someone's smoldering anger personally, you need to try not to. Again, holding practice sessions with colleagues (described earlier) is your best bet. The following thought pattern can also help: *What I hear when I'm being yelled at is people caring—loudly—at me.* [6]

Handling Saboteurs

Most agitated people who disrupt meetings do so without intention; they are not scheming troublemakers. Saboteurs are the insidious exception. Working behind the scenes, saboteurs try to undo what you are doing or have done. Maddeningly, saboteurs will feign ignorance if you challenge them on their undermining behaviors. Even more maddeningly, they will hold off opposing something until it has worked its way through the lower ranks and seems poised for implementation. Then they will pounce.

Saboteurs quickly become known entities, however, and experienced colleagues can point them out to you. Once you know who they are, your natural inclination, of course, will be to stay as far away from them as you can.

---

6. From the television show *Parks and Recreation*.

Unfortunately, that is usually the wrong strategy. Saboteurs, when not met preemptively face-to-face, can create unmitigated hell for you and your efforts. The best strategy is to take the bull by the horns and meet with saboteurs prior to the scheduled meeting.

When you first meet with a suspected saboteur, be friendly. Break the ice by finding something positive to say about him or his accomplishments. Doing so sends a message of good judgment. She will think, "Anyone who is wise enough to see how great I am can't be all bad!" Recognizing that you are a decent human being may temper her inclination to sabotage you and your efforts.

Here are a couple of examples of how you might jump-start a first meeting with a suspected saboteur:

> "Hi, Frank, it's nice to finally meet you. I'm new to these parts, but I've been hearing since I got here that you're the one I should talk with if I really want to understand what's going on up at Dry Creek. Rumor has it that you're also quite a bass fisherman, which is a disease I've been trying to cure myself of but haven't had much luck."

> "Frank, thanks for agreeing to meet with me. As you may know, I'm really interested in what might or might not happen at Dry Creek. I don't know where you stand on this, and I'm not completely sure where I stand on it either, which is why I wanted to hear what you're thinking. I've heard that you're a person of integrity who talks straight and says what he thinks, so I thought I'd go straight to the source rather than wade through the pile of propaganda, partial truths, and untruths that others might try to push."

Meeting with suspected saboteurs and being friendly may seem manipulative or disingenuous. It is neither *if* you are sincere in what you say. Every human being has good qualities, even someone who undermines you or holds views that you cannot stomach. Your mission is to find and acknowledge that person's good qualities so that you treat her with respect before, during, and after the meeting.

The unfortunate reality, however, is that blocking the efforts of saboteurs is neither easy nor a sure thing. Building a political wall of support would probably be your best weapon. [7] But that takes lots of time and effort. Your surest bet is to get comfortable with managing unpleasantness.

---

7. Hans Bleiker's Systematic Development of Informed Consent, for example.

Managing Unpleasantness

Despite your best efforts to control the tenor, public meetings can turn unpleasant in a hurry. Even nice people can turn nasty, and their unfiltered outbursts can trigger counter-outbursts that, in turn, trigger retaliatory outbursts. If not nipped in the bud, these back-and-forths can become personal. And even if you, as chair, spend time anticipating what could go wrong and take actions to prevent that from happening, people with an ax to grind—like saboteurs—can be counted on to act out in ways that are not nice. To avoid being caught off-guard, practice how you will respond to nasty, personal assaults.

Smile when you are threatened or challenged, and practice smiling in your mock meetings. Smiling is the last thing you want to do when someone is giving you a rough time, of course, but a calm demeanor sends a message to all that you will not be drawn into a spitting match. Addressing aggressors by their first name, as though they are friends, also disarms them.

Sit or stand physically close to people during the meeting; doing so makes you seem more human and less authoritarian. You will also feel less nervous if you are *with* people rather than apart from them. Do not hide behind a lectern; it distances you from the audience and depersonalizes you.

People who see things one way often demonize those who do not share their view. To open communication between people who view others as enemies, try arranging a shared outdoors adventure or work session where people get to know one another as fellow human beings. Suggestions for orchestrating such an outing can be found in chapter 4.

Experimenting with Unfamiliar Approaches

It is helpful to recognize that most people have an immediate, knee-jerk reaction against change, even if the change is for the good. It helps to give people a chance to transition into a more receptive mode by connecting with small stakeholder groups before a big public meeting. Meeting with key groups beforehand also works at lowering everyone's temperature.

One strength of parliamentary procedure is that its structure is at least vaguely familiar to most participants. That matters, because when people are agitated, worried, confused, or angry, they are in no mood to spend time being schooled in an unfamiliar, newfangled meeting format. They lack patience and want to get on with what is troubling them.

If you are hoping to get concerned people talking with one another to find common ground or come up with novel solutions, however, the World Café

Method or the Open Space Method (both are described below) might work better than parliamentary procedure. But these two alternative approaches will work *only if*:

- Participants are open to trying a different approach.
- Participants are willing to truly *listen to* and *consider* what others are saying.

If either condition strikes you as problematic, a loose version of parliamentary procedure is a safer approach.

The World Café Method emphasizes collaborative dialogue, the premise being that meaningful conversation—where people *really* listen to one another—can solve lots of problems. Seven design principles guide how World Café sessions are run. [8]

The World Café Method is a good choice if the meeting's purpose is to bring together different perspectives into a more effective whole. The method often generates new possibilities through cross-pollination of ideas.

Very briefly, here is how the World Café Method works. Clusters of four or five participants gather together to converse about a chosen issue; a table host for each cluster takes notes on what is said. After twenty minutes of conversation, the clusters disband, and people form new clusters of members; only the table hosts stay behind. Once a new cluster forms, the table host brings the new members up to speed on high points of the first conversation. Twenty minutes later this cluster reconfiguration is repeated, and once again, twenty minutes after that. What results from this cross-fertilization approach is a sharing of ideas and perspectives and (hopefully) a merging of minds.

The Open Space Method creates discussion clusters around *shared* interests or concerns. [9] Participants create and manage their own agendas rather than following a single agenda item dictated by the chair.

The Open Space Method is a good choice if the meeting purpose is to zero in on what people feel is most important about an issue, or if the goal of the meeting is to draw people together more closely. The method is also effective at diffusing tension when people want to have their say about different things.

---

8. More about the World Café Method can be found at http://www.theworldcafe.com/wp-content/uploads/2015/07/Cafe-To-Go-Revised.pdf.

9. More about the Open Space Method can be found at https://www.mind.org.uk/media/9684099/open-space-method.pdf.

Very briefly, here is how the Open Space Method works: Sitting in a circle facing one another, participants respond to a broad question posed by the organizer by suggesting subtopics they wish to discuss. Every subtopic suggestion is written on a Post-it note that is posted on a designated bulletin board (usually a wall) for all to see. Participants then review the various subtopic suggestions and assemble around whichever subtopic interests them most. The assembled group members then discuss the subtopic, and a scribe takes notes.

Depending on a person's interests, some participants may choose to spend the entire meeting time in a single subtopic session, while others may choose to move from one session to another. A scribe in each subtopic session records main points of discussion and presents them to the group as a whole at the very end of the meeting.

Some Closing Thoughts

Before meeting with people—be they fence-sitters, chosen members of your team, or the public at large—you (hopefully) first think through exactly which outcome would cause you to feel that the meeting was a success. With that desired destination identified, you then strategize ways to get there and, if possible, run the chosen strategies by trusted colleagues before moving ahead with them. Careful planning and preparation greatly increase the likelihood of a meeting achieving its desired end, but they certainly do not ensure it. Even the best-laid plans can be thrown asunder by a single person's outburst.

Outbursts are all too common in public meetings, and many of them are unfairly directed at the person running the meeting. Many outbursts could be prevented (the teachings of this chapter) but some outbursts are inevitable. Practicing how you will deal with them when they arise will keep your ulcers at bay.

This chapter, and the two preceding it, have centered on people skills because you have little chance of moving the environmental needle without them. The next section teaches how to use your skills to mobilize people to action, along with ways to get support for your cause more broadly.

part III

TOOLS FOR FINDING SUPPORT— FOR YOUR CAUSE AND FOR YOURSELF

So far, we've covered two sets of tools: one for making sure that what you do, and how you do it, yields the outcome you're ultimately after; and another for working effectively with folks of all stripes. This final section covers tools for mobilizing support for your cause: from outreach strategies that compel people to take action, to how you go about securing needed funding for a cause. Finally, we address an overlooked dimension of effective environmentalism: supporting *yourself* so you don't burn out or lose hope as you fight the good fight.

Getting the Word Out
How to Communicate Your Cause to the World

Preceding chapters teach ways to connect, build trust, and work with people who may or may not see things the way you do. This chapter shows ways to get the word out to current and future allies and motivate them to action. Doing so has never been easy, but the Internet has probably made it harder. Every day, whether we are aware of it or not, we are bombarded with—and are numbed by—hundreds of messages to give, buy, or act in a particular way. We ignore most of them, even when the case for acting is strong.

But some messages do get through to us and motivate us to take action. The following story did that for me.

HOW THE CHILDREN'S RAINFOREST CAME TO BE

The story of the Children's Rainforest (El Bosque Eterno de los Niños) begins in 1987, when Eha Kern and her young students in Fagervik, Sweden, were learning about tropical rainforests. They were fascinated by the amazing array of wildlife but concerned when every TV documentary they saw ended with horrid pictures of those same forests filled with the wildlife they had come to treasure being chopped and burned. They wanted to do something to help. An American botanist, Dr. Sharon Kinsman from Bates College in Maine, was spending time in Sweden after studying the cloud forest ecosystem in the Monteverde Cloud Forest Preserve. When Eha met Sharon, she invited her to come to her classroom to share information with the children about the Costa Rican forest. Sharon's photos sparked the children's desire to help protect the rainforest. They began to raise money by putting on plays, having bunny-hopping contests, giving pony rides, selling home-baked goodies. They set a goal to save twenty-five acres, but they made more money than they expected.

Their enthusiasm grew, and so did their fundraising ideas. A newspaper article was written about their efforts; then a television report was aired. As more kids heard about their plan, more schools began to contribute. That is how Barnens Regnskog (Children's Rain Forest in Swedish) was born. The Swedish government matched funds raised by the children. In the first year they raised over $100,000.

Sharon helped arrange for threatened forest around Monteverde to be purchased through the Monteverde Conservation League. She also founded Children's Rainforest USA to help kids in the United States protect the forest in Costa Rica. The idea swept the world. Students in the United Kingdom, Germany, Canada, Spain, and Japan also created organizations to help. Eventually, children in forty-four countries contributed.

By 2020 El Bosque Eterno de los Niños, commonly referred to as the BEN, had protected 57,000 acres and become the largest private reserve in Costa Rica.

The story of the Children's Rainforest and the inspiring action of the children (picked up by the press and spread widely) sparked worldwide action. It touched thousands of others—myself included—and motivated us to send money to conserve the Costa Rican rainforest.

As with the Starfish Flinger story that this book began with, I taped this story above my desk so I would never stop believing that one person *can* make a difference, even when the odds are lined up against you. But the Children's Rainforest story offers another reminder: that getting the word out to the right people is how you magnify your impact and likelihood of success.

Directing Your Energy Where It Needs to Go

At the start of this book, we went over the importance of figuring out what the *right* thing to do is before doing anything. And even though it's natural to want to jump immediately to action and get the word out for our cause, that same idea holds here. Knowing where—and *to whom*—to direct your energy requires knowing what you're directing your energy toward.

But with so many environmental problems out there, how do you choose which one to tackle? Most of us would have a tough time answering that question right away. The difficulty lies not in our satisfaction with the status quo—just the opposite, in fact. There are so many outrageous problems and wrongs and concerns out there that it is hard to decide which problem needs your attention most. But decide you must.

As much as you may want to fix everything at once, resist dabbling in multiple causes at the same time. To make meaningful headway, you need to focus all of your attention on one cause at a time. And then stick with it.

If you are unsure about which cause to tackle first, it's worth going over again the following exercise from chapter 1—the repeat-why technique. Begin by imagining that you have a magic wand that, when waved, changes a situation to your liking. What change would you seek? (Write your answer on the lines below, being as specific as you can).

1. What change would you seek?

Now carefully analyze what you have written above and respond to the following questions: *Why* do you care about this? *Why* is it important? *Why* does it matter to you? (Think hard, record your answers on the lines below.)

2. Why it matters:

Now carefully examine your response (no. 2 above) by responding to the same set of *why* questions as before (Why do you care about this? Why is it important? Why does it matter?). (Think hard; record your specific responses on the lines below.)

3. Why it matters:

Now examine your last response (no. 3 above) and, once again, ask and answer the same set of *why* questions as before. (Record your response on the lines below.) Note: if answering these questions is not pushing your mind into uncomfortable places, you are not thinking hard enough!

4. Why it matters:

Now consider your last response (no. 4 above) and again ask and answer the why questions from before. (Record your response on the lines below.) Hang in there, do not despair or give up: if the asking and answering of questions seems to be leading you into existential realms, that is okay. Digging deep and finding the root cause is what you want.

5. Why it matters:

Working through this repetitive but mind-bending exercise probably frustrated and confused you. It also may have distanced you from identifying the exact nature of the fire in your belly. At least, that is what you might think.

Before dismissing the effort as wasted time, however, let's take a look at a colleague's progression of thought as she worked through this repeat-why exercise. The colleague began by stating:

- I want big business to stop exploiting poor communities.

Notice that in her first effort to articulate what she seeks to achieve, she left out a key ingredient—the individual *people* she is hoping to mobilize into action. Who are these people? In what specific ways does she want them to act if she waves her magic wand? She would make much more headway if she thought in those terms.

She completed the repeat-why exercise nonetheless, coming up with these responses to the first set of *why* questions (no. 2 above):

- because they have no right to do so—it's wrong
- because people in poor communities should be the ones who profit from and make decisions about how their land and water is used
- because the rich are getting richer and the poor are getting poorer
- because targeting the less fortunate just makes social problems worse
- because exploiting the resources of easily exploited communities just gets us deeper into the problem of overconsumption—rather than conserving resources, we're able to proceed as though the resources are limitless
- because environmental restrictions in poor communities are weaker, so there's less control over air, land, and water pollution

Her responses to the second set of *why* questions (no. 3 above) were:

- because it bothers me that the rich "haves" exploit the poor "have nots"
- because it's their land and their resources, not some economic bully's
- because I don't think that's the way it should be
- because it allows people to live unsustainably—to ignore future resource realities because air and water pollution in poor communities affects people's health

Her responses to the third set of *why* questions (no. 4 above) were:

- because the rich seem to have no conscience—they don't seem to care that when exploited people lose their resources, they lose much more as well
- because people should have control over their own destiny
- because the way we live our lives shouldn't be driven by how much money we can make
- because I'm worried about my kids—they're the recipients of our selfishness
- because pollution and resource exploitation in less privileged communities is a main cause of global problems

Her response to the fourth set of *why* questions (no. 5 above) was:

- Because this is not how we should live. If we're so uncaring about the welfare of others, what hope is there for a peaceful world? You know, it really comes down to conflict and self-centeredness. How can we expect or even hope for the "have-nots" to worry about regional, national, or global environmental problems when they're ineffective at protecting their own local interests? What has happened to the American way— liberty and justice for all? What has happened to our sense of morality, what has happened to our soul? We're hypocrites—how is it okay for us to defend our own freedoms and rights while destroying those of others? Is it because we think we're better than they are? Is it because we don't really respect them as people? That we think that their well-being is less important than our own? Is it because the "haves" are too isolated from the less fortunate to see their pain and suffering? When our value systems go astray, we lose our moral compass; that affects everyone. It's not right that the selfishness, greed, and injustices of the powerful should be allowed to transform and destroy the well-being of others.

Notice that her simple, cerebral, sound-bite responses (the first three responses) shifted into a free-flowing, heartfelt stream of consciousness in the fourth. That is exactly what you want. When this happens (and it often happens before the fourth response), you know you are on the right track—that you are zeroing in on the root cause of your outrage or passion.

In the repeat-why example above, it turned out that this colleague's initial blaming of big business was a bit off the mark. Her real outrage was with something else—how American culture (in her estimation) has degenerated to the point that Americans no longer respect or live by the American Dream.

For this person, using the magic wand to recalibrate the American psyche would accomplish much more than eliminating big business. What she *really* wants is for those from less privileged communities to be treated with equal respect and fairness. That is the magic wand that she would really want to wave.

The heartfelt outrage exposed by the repeat-why exercise greatly clarified what burns within this colleague. Getting to the heart of her internal fire allows her to better understand *how* she would like things to be different. With this understanding identified—how she would like things to be different *if* she is able to pull it off—she can effectively figure out strategies to get people from where they are to where she would like them to be.

But *which* people? Is everyone out there equally positioned to move a cause forward? Certainly not. So, don't worry (yet) about motivating *everyone*.

Targeting Your Message

Some people are more important to a campaign than are others, so tailor your message and delivery to those specific audiences. Which interest groups have the authority, respect, or star power to advance or derail your efforts? Target these groups first. Now is not the time to worry about trying to reach everyone else—everyone else can wait.[1]

To identify which people to target first, answer this question: *If you could influence only twelve people, who would those twelve people be?*

---

1. If, for example, you are concerned about land use along streams, focus your efforts on landowners and land-use planners. Don't spend precious time and energy trying to get your message out to the world at large—unless the audiences you most wish to target are completely unwilling to consider your point of view. In that case, you might need to take the long, slow road of building a groundswell of public opinion to force laggards into action.

These are the people (or type of people) you should focus on reaching first. But *how* do you reach these people effectively? By understanding where they are coming from—what they value—and tailoring your message accordingly.

Marketing Your Cause

The *way* you first present your cause to a target audience is critical, it opens the door for future engagement by making people receptive to your mission. A good elevator talk does that.

An elevator talk, also called a farmer's overview or sales pitch, is a key first step to engaging fence-sitters, political heavyweights, funding organizations, and anyone else you would like to win over to your cause.[2] A good elevator talk is also an important, but too often overlooked, part of effective consulting and research.

To mobilize others to action—or, at minimum, to make them aware of what you are up to and why—you must be able to articulate your undertaking clearly and compellingly in just a few sentences. An elevator talk accomplishes this by summarizing what you are doing, with enough context and background to make the explanation interesting and meaningful. A good elevator talk articulates your cause compellingly and explains—succinctly and convincingly—*why* your cause is so important.

To develop an effective elevator talk, start by just blabbing aloud to yourself about what you are doing and why it is important. Imagine that you are trying to sell what you are doing to the twelve people whom you most wish to influence (it usually helps to pretend that you are one of them). What could you say to convince those important twelve that the undertaking is meaningful and important? What could you say that might get them to buy what you are selling?

Your first few efforts to promote your cause to this imagined audience will not be very polished or effective. That is why, at first, you should practice on yourself rather than on someone else. But practice does make perfect, so experiment with different approaches and arguments until you come up with a delivery that you think sounds convincing. If it is longer than a minute, try to pare it down. Short and sweet is good; long and detailed is not.

---

2. Personally, I prefer calling the elevator talk a *farmer's overview* because farmers tend to be unusually clear-headed, perceptive, and practical-minded. They are also unafraid to call you out when you are not making sense.

Once you have an elevator talk that *you* like, try it out on a practice audience of friends or colleagues to see what they think. To make their reactions most useful, tell them which audience type they are standing in for, and ask them to evaluate your pitch accordingly.

Once you have a version that your practice audiences like, get it on paper so you have a record of it for future reference.[3] Never assume, however, that an elevator talk that works for one group will work for another. When an elevator talk fails to move listeners, it is usually because the talk did not jibe with the listeners' interests and concerns.

There is lots at stake when you give an elevator talk. You *might* get a second chance to win over those who are not moved the first time, but the odds of success go way down. First impressions stick.

Some Outreach Strategies

An elevator talk only works, of course, if there is an audience to hear it. The paragraphs below review some outreach strategies.

Talks, Presentations, and Broadcasts

Community and special interest groups (e.g., student groups, sportsman's clubs, Rotary Clubs) are always looking for guest speakers for their get-togethers. If you have an interesting presentation or talk that is not preachy, you will be welcomed with open arms. It is a very effective way to reach specific groups or publics.

Local television stations also actively look for interesting stories to include in their evening news programs. They are most enthusiastic about covering stories or presentations that provide photo opportunities.

Living Room Meetings

These are small, relaxed gatherings where people are invited to learn about an issue of interest. Held in someone's home (often a volunteer's), these gatherings allow a speaker to give a quick overview of the situation and then

---

3. Read it over occasionally, making adjustments if warranted, to remind yourself of what you are doing and why. The reminder keeps you on track and helps you hang in there when you are discouraged about how slowly change is happening.

lead the discussion that follows. To make it friendlier, the host usually provides tea and coffee.

Special Outreach Events

Events that are well planned, such as how-to workshops, work projects, and outings with celebrities, can work wonders at introducing new blood to your cause. Remember to tailor the special event to the group that you are trying to reach, however, and remember that preaching to the choir attracts few new recruits.

Many special outreach events that appear successful in the short term prove unsuccessful in the long term. To be successful (i.e., to mobilize others into action), a special outreach event must not end when everyone goes home. Specific, planned, action-oriented follow-up is essential. Motivation inspired by a special event fades quickly when it is not enflamed by action.

Opinion Letters

Letters to the editor (of a newspaper or magazine) and letters to elected officials are the most common types of opinion letters. Both can be effective at swaying opinion *if* the presented opinion strikes the right nerve in the targeted audience.

To write an effective opinion letter:

- Identify yourself, your affiliation, and your position. State your opinion clearly, rationally, and succinctly.
- Let your passion show, but moderate your rants and ravings. Be respectful, even when you are angry.
- Keep a lid on personal assaults on others.[4] Letters of opinion that are thoughtful and respectful are more likely to sway the uncommitted.
- Keep your letter of opinion short and to the point; do not exceed the number of words allowed (the editorial page usually provides submission guidelines and restrictions). Be aware that editors often edit opinion letters to make them shorter and more interesting, sometimes to the detriment of the intended message. Make your points clearly and succinctly to minimize editing.

---

4. Sometimes, newspapers and magazines choose to print especially outrageous letters for their entertainment value. Having such letters appear in print does not help your cause, however.

- Check your facts. Nothing undermines an argument faster than a fact that is not true.
- Double-space your letter, printing on one side of the paper only. Have someone literate proofread your letter for typos and misspellings before submitting it.

When you send a letter to an elected official, the audience you are targeting is obvious.[5] A little homework will provide plenty of insight about who the person is and how the person thinks. That insight is harder to come by when you send a letter to the editor because the audience is diverse. Also, whereas a letter to an elected official seeks to move a single, well-known individual to action, a letter to the editor seeks to move many people, most or all of whom are strangers to you. Study letters to the editor in the newspaper or magazine you're targeting to gain a feel for what the editor deems publishable.

Memos

Memos, usually sent electronically, are quick, efficient notes used to reach a desired audience. The guidelines for writing them are similar to those for letters of opinion and press releases (discussed later). Memos can be used to market ideas and rally troops, as well as to share information and keep people in the loop. Whatever your memo's purpose, keep it short, direct, clear, efficient, and easy to read. Also be sure that the memo's take-home message is abundantly and immediately clear, and that recipients of your memo know what—if any—action you would like them to take (e.g., ideas needed, decision needed, action needed). If your sole reason for sending a memo is to pass along information, say so up-front with an FYI (For Your Information).

To craft an effective memo, begin by asking yourself the following questions:

- Who is your audience? Is a memo the best way to reach that audience?
- What is the memo's intended purpose? Why are you bothering to write it?
- What specific action/response do you want your memo to elicit?
- What *needs* to be included? (Anything that is not needed is superfluous.)

---

5. Some legislative aides report that handwritten letters carry more weight than computer-generated letters because they have greater legitimacy (handwritten letters cannot be mass produced).

Use your answers to guide what you say and how you say it. See appendix 12 for examples of what an effective memo looks like.

Memos can be chatty or businesslike, depending on who is writing and receiving them. That said, memos of any type typically include:

- the date the memo was sent
- the recipient's name
- the sender's name, with a descriptive title or position if the recipient does not know the sender (when a memo is sent as a hard copy, the sender typically pens his/her initials next to the printed name)
- contact information so that recipients can find you easily
- a complete list of who is receiving the memo
- a subject heading identified by the preface *Subject*: or *Re*:. The subject heading is useful because it immediately tells the recipient what the memo is about. Strive to make it descriptive rather than bare bones. For example, "Subject: Effect of holding time on dissolved oxygen in water samples" is much better than "Subject: Water samples" because recipients do not need to read the entire memo to know what it is really about.

Here are some other ways to make your memos (and emails) better:

- Keep them short and direct—don't beat around the bush.
- Keep sentences short and simple.
- Use bullets or number main points to add emphasis.
- Be conversational in tone. Write as though you are conversing with the recipient.
- Be careful what you put on paper. Written words always seem to wind up where they shouldn't.
- When you write a memo in anger, sit on the memo overnight before sending it. Reread your angry memo (when your head is a little cooler) to see if you want to send the memo in its raw form. Probably you won't.
- Be specific about who needs to do what, and by when. For example, "Ellen: please measure pHs within two hours of collection; Nate: please acidify samples within eight hours of collection" is much better than "Water samples should be processed immediately." Fuzzy, generalized requests are ineffective because they don't specify who is expected to do what, or when. In the end, either no one takes responsibility or someone begrudgingly steps forward and resents the others for not doing so.

Press Releases

Press releases, also known as news releases, are short news announcements that are sent to the media (newspapers, magazines, radio stations) for dissemination. Like memos, they should be direct, clear, easy to read, and the main message or bottom line should be front and center. For example:

FOR IMMEDIATE RELEASE

Hospital Expert Announces Run for State Senate

Frank E. Dante, a lecturer at the University of Texas and chairman of the Texas Hospital Data Council, announced today he will seek the Democratic nomination for a State Senate seat from Ipswitch County.

Dante, who has spent 25 years writing about government as a reporter and editor, has never sought political office before. He said he hopes to focus on three major issues—the management of growth, health care, and education.

Dante will resign his post as chairman of the Data Council effective this fall. He will chair the August hearings of the council in order to provide continuity in the surveillance of hospital budgets in the state.

Dante came to Texas in 1987 to serve as managing editor of the *Ipswitch News Miner*. He left the *News Miner* in 2000 to write a book, *Environmental Justice*, that chronicled the political underworld.

Dante, 63, is married to Judith Dante, principal for JD Environmental Consultants, and has two children, James and Maureen. He holds a degree in political science from Rutgers University.

—end-

Contact: Jeffrey Hughes (Jeffrey.Hughes @XXX.org; 802-656-xxxx [w])

Date of Release: June 1, 20XX

To be publishable, a news release must be newsworthy. It must present something new or different—and it must do so accurately, truthfully, and in a way that is interesting to the intended audience. Examples of newsworthy announcements include new initiatives, new land acquisitions, new research findings, newly acquired grants or gifts, or new collaborations.

Since news releases are usually issued to advance a group's cause or profile, it is easy to go overboard in self-promotion and issue news releases when there really is nothing worth reporting. Exercise a little restraint—obvious self-promotion lowers your standing with the press—but don't be overly restrained, either. A press release does not need to change the world to be published; it only needs to interest the readership. Remember that news organizations have one mission and one mission only: to find news that they can report. A good news release makes their job that much easier.

To appear knowledgeable about what you are doing, use the media's own terminology:

- *Embargo until* (this is written at the top of the news release). This indicates that the news release must not be reported before a stated date. To publicize a special award that someone will receive on June 15, for example, you would write *Embargo until June 16* at the top of your news release to indicate that the news should not be printed before the event takes place.
- *For immediate release until* (this is written at the top of the news release). This indicates that timing is not a factor, your release can be reported any time.
- *Contact person.* This is the person to contact if there are questions. In addition to your name, include your email address and your home and work telephone numbers.
- *Date of Release.* This is the date when you issue the news release.
- *-end-* Write this at the end of a news release to signal the end of the release. "###" is another way to indicate the end.

It is important to send a news release to the right person—news releases that are sent to a place rather than to a specific person usually go nowhere. So do your homework. If all else fails and you cannot figure out the exact person who should receive your release, send it to the newspaper's city desk.

Writing effective news releases is a skill that does not come easily to everyone. If it proves difficult for you, don't despair; future releases will be easier and better.

Public Service Announcements

One overlooked opportunity for getting the word out is the Public Service Announcement or Public Service Advertising (PSA). It is a federal law that radio and television stations must broadcast messages that serve the public interest. A PSA is aired free of charge so it is a highly desirable way to spread your gospel if you can package your message in a way that fits the Federal Communication Commission's (FCC) definition of a PSA:

> any announcement for which no charge is made and which promotes programs, activities, or services of federal, state or local governments . . . or the programs, activities or services of nonprofit organizations (e.g., United Fund,

Red Cross blood donations, etc.) and other announcements regarded as servicing community interests, excluding time signals, routine weather announcements and (station) promotional announcements.

Managers of television and radio stations ultimately decide which PSA submissions will be aired on a given day, so give them what they want. Study a station's PSA broadcasts to gain insight into what the station finds acceptable.

To initiate your courtship of a station, make a quick, friendly phone call, asking whether they would prefer to receive your PSA by mail, telephone, or email. While you have them on the phone, ask how much lead time they would like, and if they prefer single-sentence announcements or PSAs that are more engaging.

To assess whether a PSA should be aired, station managers consider three factors:

- Does the submission fall within the FCC's definition of a PSA? If it does not, the station will let you know and ask if you would like to pay to have it broadcast.
- Is the submission relevant to the station's listening or viewing audience?
- Does the technical quality of the PSA submission meet the station's standards for broadcasting?

Petitions

People like to help, but few like to lead. Signing a petition is a nonthreatening way for people to feel, without putting themselves out much, that they are helping. A signed petition might not accomplish much in its own right but getting people to sign the petition is a way to build a list of contacts, telephone numbers, and email addresses for future use. When trying to push a legislator to action on an issue, casually mentioning the massive number of like-minded souls you have on your contact list is often enough to motivate the legislator to see things your way. An expansive list gives you credibility.

The Internet

Electronic communication (e.g., email, websites, blogs, chat rooms, social media) is a mainstay of getting the word out because large numbers of people from all over the world can be contacted instantaneously, at little or no expense, through a single sender's efforts. That is the good news. The bad news is that everyone else out there also wants to exploit the same communication advantages. So somehow you need to convince recipients that *your message* is worth reading. Fee-based services such as PRNewswire.com can do that. If you opt instead to spread the message yourself, try to send your electronic messages through friends or acquaintances of those you wish to reach. Personalized electronic messages from known senders are much likelier to be read and spread.

Joining Forces with Another Organization

If you are a small organization, or if your cause tracks the cause of another, better-established organization, consider pooling resources and joining forces. There are several possible advantages to doing so:

- The other organization probably has connections that you don't have.
- The other organization probably has skill sets or personnel that you don't.
- Joining forces makes your cause more noticeable and formidable; outsiders are therefore more likely to take it seriously. This matters because people with power, money, and influence are more willing to throw their support behind a cause that seems to have a chance of winning. A lone voice in the wilderness does not look much like a winner.

Joining forces with a like-minded organization can jump-start a campaign.[6] It can also affect how you are seen by friends, foes, and fence-sitters. If you are seeking to establish yourself as a bona fide, freestanding organization, or if you are seeking to raise your organization's profile or identity so it is clearly distinguishable from other organizations, joining forces with another group might make your organization *less* visible, not more. Also be aware that apportioning control will become an issue: Who is in charge of what? Who gets the credit? A mutually beneficial relationship can turn ugly if one side steals a disproportionate piece of the limelight.

Letting People Know That They Matter

It is hard to make much headway on your own or in a small group; that is why recruiting people to a cause and showing them how to do good is so

---

6. Small groups tend to be much more daring than large organizations; they also are much easier to manage.

important. But doing good accomplishes more than helping a cause or campaign, doing good gives people purpose and helps them feel good about themselves. Being recognized for their contributions makes clear that they are valued and respected—that they matter. Every human craves that recognition.

The good that comes from doing good can sour quickly, however, if the person's effort goes unrecognized or someone else unfairly gets credit for what she did. To counter any chance of that happening, credit others more than you need to and publicly acknowledge what others have done. Effective leaders operate on the principle that you cannot thank someone (or express appreciation) too many times.

When people feel valued and respected, they take ownership for what they are doing and invest more fully of themselves. That, of course, is what you want in your staff and volunteers, so support them by showing that you trust and value them. Do not micromanage—give staff and volunteers a piece of the leadership action—share the limelight, the glory, and the challenges. Praise their initiative and leadership efforts.

If you are the micromanaging type, letting a bunch of rookies run the show is a tough pill to swallow—especially when the cause you are fighting for is the *one thing* you care about most. Understandably, your inclination is to maintain control so that nothing gets screwed up.

Leaders may differ in how they share the leadership without giving up control of a campaign, but they all seem to share a few common traits:

- They make each team member feel important and valued.
- They communicate more than they think they need to.
- They cede whatever level of authority and responsibility a team member is able and willing to assume.
- They celebrate the accomplishments and contributions of others.

Work on the traits above by believing that you already have them, then regularly prove to yourself, through your actions, that you in fact do. Do this for a couple of years, and you will be able to write your own book on effective leadership.

Handling Propaganda and Spin

In trying to win over others to your cause, does the end justify the means? Propaganda and spin sway public opinion because they attack the subconscious where people are most vulnerable. Whether or not you play the game yourself, expect those on the other side to do so.

There are more ways than ever to spread propaganda (and professionals use all of them), but the raw elements of effective propaganda have not changed much—speak half-truths; make people fearful; use loaded words (e.g., patriot) even if they are not relevant; label the opposition in problematic ways (e.g., tax and spend liberal); and repeat distortions again, and again, and again. As political operatives would say, stay on message.

How to counter untruths? First, do not let your opposition's propaganda campaign gain a head of steam. You can gain the upper hand in public relations before a battle even begins by meeting with your opposition in a respectful, friendly manner and discussing the ground rules for how you will interact. Be forthright—state your hopes that the upcoming battle of ideas will be honorable and above-board, and that you will not resort to propagandizing unless your opposition does. Offer your hand to shake on it—"Is it a deal?"

If the opposition agrees to an above-board campaign (eschewing propaganda and sleazy tricks), publicize the agreement. If the opposition does not wish to partner in the publicity, all the better for your side; you will get credit for taking the lead.

With a *no propaganda* agreement firmly planted in the public's consciousness, you now have a stick to hold over your opposition's head. You can hold them publicly accountable if they break their promise, putting them on the defensive while you take the high ground. (Of course, they can do the same to you if you break the *no propaganda* pledge!)

If the opposition does *not* agree to a *no propaganda* campaign, that is even better. Publicize their unwillingness to agree to an honest exchange of ideas. Their unwillingness to behave honorably will taint their credibility and put them on the defensive—a place that is to your advantage.

Some Closing Thoughts

Spreading your message and getting the word out are how you build support for or against an action *if* those receiving the message take action or pass it on. So set higher goals for your outreach efforts than "raising awareness." Make "people taking action" your outreach target.

Changing the environmental status quo often takes time, however, and if you are anything like me, you want *results* and you want them quickly. Patience is not my strong suit—I want to get stuff done.

Early in my career, a number of prominent activists tried to convince me that meaningful change takes time and patience—that I needed to take the long view to be effective. Given my nature, that is not what I wanted to hear so I pretty much ignored that counsel. Pride, arrogance, and insufficient humility probably also factored into my stubbornness.

Eventually, however, their results—and my *lack* of results—got me listening to what they said. Their wisdom, in a nutshell, is this:

- Effective advocacy is all about personal connections and relationships.
- Meaningful change takes time, often *lots* of time (e.g., it took women 150 years to earn the right to vote).
- Trying and failing is how you get better.
- Timing and momentum matter; force-fitting does not work.

If your natural inclination is to run before you walk, try to dial back your approach a bit and proceed as though you are building a brick chimney: lay the bottom foundation of bricks first. Building a foundation is especially important when it comes to raising funds to support your organization or causes. The next chapter teaches ways to do that.

8

Fundraising, Proposal Writing, and More
How to Find Money for Your Cause

Since money paves the way to getting things done, it is not surprising that many organizations hire staff, recruit volunteers, or form boards to help fundraise. Ultimately, however, someone has to take the lead in finding where the money is and how to get it. That you are reading this chapter suggests that you are that someone.

This chapter alone will not make you a fundraising superstar—no chapter or book can do that. This chapter *will* get you over the hump, however, by changing how you think about asking others for money. Once you internalize the basic truth that fundraising is about doing good for others—not begging for money—your fundraising skills and success will jump by leaps and bounds.

In small environmental organizations, raising money is everyone's job. Passion for a shared mission is critical, of course, but money is critical too because it is the fuel that powers change. Without that fuel, there's little power; with little power, there is little movement; with little movement, there is little change. Fundraising may not be what you thought you had signed up for, but it sure helps move the conservation needle.

Fledgling fundraisers tend to assume that there's not much money out there. They are mistaken: *There is plenty of money out there*; you just need to go after it. Hone your skills, and it will start coming your way.

Asking Individuals for Help Is Not Begging!

The main sources of money are private individuals, philanthropic organizations (foundations), businesses, and government agencies. Since private individuals give more than all the others combined, that is where we will begin.

Asking someone to support your cause through a monetary gift has the greatest potential to yield a big return. But it is also the approach that fledgling fundraisers find most intimidating and distasteful. It shouldn't be.

If the prospect of asking someone for money makes you cringe, consider how uneasy you would feel if you did not ask for money when you *should* have asked. For example, imagine how you would feel if you let your favorite natural area be paved over when—with a little effort—you and others could have raised the money to buy the place and preserve its specialness forever. Do not live a life of regret knowing that you might have made a difference if you had only stepped forward and asked for help!

Equating fundraising with begging or favor-asking is probably why you're hesitant to ask someone for money. That reaction is completely misguided: raising money for a worthy cause is *not* about begging for money. It's not even about asking for favors. Instead, raising money for a worthy cause is about giving people a chance to do something good. People *like* to do good; it makes them feel good about themselves. If they choose not to give, so be it—at least you gave them the chance. And remember, no one will think less of you if you ask for money to support a selfless, worthy cause. Most people, in fact, will respect you for doing what others never get around to doing—putting themselves out there to make the world a better place.

There are several reasons why people may give money to an environmental cause. Doing good is usually the strongest motivation, but some other common motivations for giving are:

- It is a family tradition.
- It is good for business.
- It is a way to repay a past favor.
- It is an ego boost.
- It is a way to gain entry into a social set.
- It is a way to memorialize someone.[1]

Keep these possible motivations in mind when looking for clues as to why a prospective donor—or prospect, as we might call them—would be willing to give. Knowing what a prospective donor values in terms of benefit greatly strengthens your fundraising chances, so do your homework—learn everything you can about the person and what makes them tick. If a person does not see how they will benefit in some way from making a gift, they won't give—it is as simple as that. Your job as fundraiser, therefore, is not to try to

---

1. Adapted from Russ Alan Prince and Karen Maru File, *The Seven Faces of Philanthropy: A New Approach to Cultivating Major Donors* (San Francisco: Jossey Bass, [1994] 2001).

extort money from the unwilling; it is to help people understand how giving to your cause benefits them.

The Ins and Outs of Successful Fundraising

Changing your mindset about asking for money is the first essential part of becoming a successful fundraiser. Once you accept the reality that raising funds for a worthy cause benefits the donor as well as the receiver, fundraising becomes infinitely less daunting. It also becomes more productive.

The sections below explain how you go about the different parts of successful fundraising, from finding possible donors to developing relationships with prospects to presenting your cause to "making the ask," and managing the aftermath when the answer to your ask is yes or no.

How to Find Possible Donors

If your organization has been around for a while, it probably has received gifts in the past. Find out who has given and approach those donors first. Solicit their help in identifying other prospective donors.

As you are pursuing these leads, use other contacts and connections—friends, acquaintances, staff, friends and acquaintances of staff, volunteers—to expand your list of possible prospects and new connections. If you feel that you are not making much headway, find organizations with similar missions and get copies of their annual reports. Review them carefully—you never know what you will find within. If other organizations have newsletters, scour them for staff, contributors, and friends who share your interests or perspectives. Contact these people and get to know them. Attend parties, gatherings, events, conferences, and go to places where like-minded people congregate.

Finding prospective donors is about networking and keeping your eyes and ears open. Local and regional community foundations are fabulous resources in this regard because their mission is to connect funding groups with nonprofits who share their interests.

Getting the word out about what you are doing usually attracts at least a few donors. If your organization does not have a newsletter describing what you are doing, create one and distribute it widely. Get in the news, connect with a celebrity, get in front of a camera, have something to say. Become known. Favorable publicity through a newspaper or magazine story gives you credibility and makes donors much more likely to give. Chapter 7 details other ways to get the word out.

Fundraising as Development

Raising money for your cause necessitates that you eventually make the ask. We'll get to some tips about how to do so effectively in a moment, but it's important to recognize first that fundraising shouldn't be seen as a one-off thing. Instead, fundraising for a cause should be approached as a long-term venture. The time will come—sooner than you would like—when you will be looking for money again.

Fundraising is frequently referred to as "development" because that is how successful fundraisers go about their business. In fact, developing and sustaining relationships is what successful fundraising is all about. As professionals like to say, a fundraiser's job is "friend-raising."

Individuals are more inclined to make charitable contributions to people they like and trust, so cultivating relationships is a centerpiece of effective fundraising. If you have identified a prospective donor but have never met the person, try to find a mutual friend to accompany you on an introductory get-acquainted meeting. The mutual friend breaks the ice by introducing you, your affiliation, and your cause. For example, the mutual friend might say, "Mary, this is Jeff Hughes from Conservation International, and he is working to try to save mountain gorillas. He and I both thought you would be interested in learning more about what is going on." It is then up to you to quickly and convincingly introduce your cause, letting your passion and commitment shine through. Presenting your case in the form of a personalized story is the most effective way to do this (see chapter 4 for tips on how to do this well).

After a few minutes of storytelling, it is time to let the prospect take the lead in conversation. As advised below, listen attentively and search for clues about the prospect's interests, inclinations, and motivations. Be an active participant in the conversation; work to develop a fruitful relationship with the person. Don't be pushy, don't dominate the conversation, and don't ask for money. Ask open-ended questions to uncover the donor's interests.

If the conversation seems to be going nowhere, or if the prospect seems disinterested, present the challenges facing the mountain gorillas and ask for advice. For example, "I have been trying to meet with a few conservation leaders like you for ideas about how we should go about tackling this problem. Here is how things stand . . . one conservationist thinks we should . . . another feels strongly that we should. . . . What do you think?"

Asking a prospective donor for insights, feedback, and guidance can create a dynamic dialogue, so listen carefully to what is being said and not said. Take notes after the visit so you do not lose any of the ideas or insights you might gain by the response. Also, after the meeting (before you forget what transpired), draft a plan of action for your next meeting with the person. Ideally, you want to create a dynamic where the person begins to take ownership for your cause.

When you meet the person next time, acknowledge the prospect's valuable ideas, and how you have used them to create a very rough plan of action. Introduce just enough of your draft plan to engage the prospect and then be quiet, letting the prospect run with it and take ownership of it. Remain an active participant, but—again—let the prospect have the floor. As you did in your introductory meeting, make notes after the visit to capture insights, ideas, and inclinations that you can work into a revised action plan.[2]

Hopefully, the prospective donor will begin to internalize your jointly developed action plan as a personal call to action. Actually putting the plan *into action* then becomes the obvious next step. That is the time to make the ask—when you know the donor wants to give. Do not expect this to happen on the first or second visit!

Finally, remember that when meeting with a prospective donor, how you comport yourself matters. Here are a few pointers:

- First impressions are made only once. Be personable, friendly, and presentable. Dress nicely. Details matter.
- Relax, be casual, be human, and be yourself. People give to human beings, not to faceless, lifeless machines.
- Have on hand relevant, engaging pictures and reading materials. Leave them with the prospective donor to keep your cause front and center in her consciousness.
- Present a small gift as a way to say hello, just as you would when going to someone's house for dinner.
- Send a friendly note as a follow-up to your visit.
- Do not put all your eggs in one basket. Be prepared to introduce other angles or initiatives if the cause that you are pushing falls on uninterested ears.

---

2. Many fundraisers use Donor Management Systems (DMS) to keep track of donor information and insights. DMS is a powerful tool that makes it easy for a new person to take over if the original fundraiser moves on. Like any information management tool, however, it only works well if it is kept current.

Getting Donors to Care for Your Cause

People are likelier to give if they are interested in what you are advocating for, and if they can see that it benefits them in some way. They also need to believe that giving to your cause will actually make a difference. For that to happen, prospective donors need to trust that you will put their gift to good use. You earn that trust by explaining how their gift will be used.

Generalized pleas from wild-eyed crusaders (e.g., we need to save the tropical rainforest!) do not work so well because there is nothing tangible for donors to get their arms around. Unless the donor has witnessed rainforest destruction and its effects firsthand, a plea to save the tropical rainforest does not really *mean* anything—it is just a vague abstraction.

To be moved to invest in a cause, prospective donors need to *feel* and *internalize* the exact cause that you are fighting for, and they need to care about the cause. If they don't care much, or cannot *feel* the problem, or cannot see how their hard-earned money will be part of the solution, they probably will not give. So be clear and specific about what your cause is really about—what you are fighting for and why—how it aligns with the person's interests, and how a gift would be used to make a difference.

People are more moved by their hearts than by their heads, so the most powerful commitments to a cause are emotional or value-laden, not rational. That is why imagery—photographs and videos—is the fundraiser's best friend. Pictures move people in ways that words cannot.

To illustrate how you might present your cause, let's say that you are seeking to raise money to save the tropical rainforest. As noted earlier, saving the tropical rainforest is a vague, uncompelling abstraction that does not grab people— you need to make the cause real and meaningful so that people *feel* it. What about the loss of tropical rainforest grabs you? Why do you care? Is it the injustice of native peoples being driven from their land and culture? Is it loss of a charismatic species that you hold dear? Is it concern over the effect of rainforest loss on global warming? Is it all of those things? Is it something else?

Identifying what you most care about helps you zero in on steps or strategies that you can employ to attack the problem—if you come up with the money. Tell prospective donors what those steps or strategies are—convince them that their monetary gift really will make a huge difference.

It is easiest to raise money from people who share your heartfelt passion or outrage because they are probably moved by the same storylines and pictures as you; when you speak from the heart, you touch them. The number of like-minded people for any cause is always limited, however, and finding them is not easy, so effective fundraising is about broadening the pool of potential donors. You do this by tapping into *other people's* passions rather than just your own.

To illustrate, let's say that *your* drive to save the tropical rainforest is spurred by outrage over the injustice of native peoples being driven off their land. If you speak passionately of this social injustice to similarly outraged souls, they will be immediately receptive. The same social injustice pitch to people who do not already feel your outrage, however, will fall on deaf ears. Trying to convince someone to care about *your* passion (if the person is not already so inclined) is a losing proposition. So always present your cause in terms that resonate with the *prospect's* passions. If a prospect loves jaguars, for example, concern for jaguars, not social injustice, should guide your pitch and time together. In the end, if you are able to save the tropical rainforest, does it matter that your reasons for wanting to save it differ from the donor's?

Of course, you may not know much about a prospect's passions when you first meet, so you need to test the waters. In a first meeting with someone to raise money for the tropical rainforest, for example, toss out reasons that you and others feel a need to save it. After fertilizing possible avenues of discussion, encourage the prospective donor to take the lead by asking them what *they* find most troubling about losing tropical rainforest. Be attentive and engaged, *but let the donor do most of the talking*; you will learn much more that way. Look for clues as to the person's interests; those interests are what might motivate the person to give.

Making the Ask

The *right time* to make the ask is when it seems like the obvious thing to do. If the conversation is not headed in the right direction, or if the time just does not feel right, it is probably not the right time to ask.

Before making any ask, try to ascertain how much the donor might be able to give (a little sleuthing can usually provide a ballpark estimate of assets), then ask for a little more. Do not ask for $50 if the person can give $50,000!

Be realistic about the cost of achieving your desired result—do not claim that you can do something for less than what is reasonable. People with money know how much it costs to get things done. They distrust bargain basement claims.

As for actually making the ask, try always to do it face-to-face. Less direct asks—by telephone, mail, Internet—may be simpler and less stressful for you, but they are too easily turned down.

Make your ask a direct, upbeat proposition rather than a plea for survival. People like giving to winners, not to sinking ships, so avoid desperate pleas such as *our organization will fold without your help!* (even if that is just what will happen).

Here are some examples of possible asks:

- A gift of $200 will allow one inner city child to attend Conservation Camp for a week. Is that something you can make happen?
- We are looking to endow the Conservation Leadership Graduate Program. For every $400,000 going into the endowment, we will be able to guarantee that every year—*forever*—one new conservation leader will lead the charge to undo environmental wrongs. Can we count on you to sponsor one future conservation leader?
- A gift of $5,000 will enable us to restore a hundred feet of riparian habitat along the most damaged reach of Trout Brook. We are hoping that this is an investment that you would like to make. Is it?

IMPORTANT! Once you make the ask, seal your lips until the donor responds; do not break the silence! This can be uncomfortable, but it is *essential*. Let the prospective donor stew on your request for as long as he or she wants. Anything you say at this point will undermine your fundraising request.

When the Answer Is No

Offering someone a chance to do good does not mean, of course, that the person will immediately hand over her wallet. No matter how worthy your cause and sales pitch, some people will *not* give—at least not right away.

When a prospective donor says no to your request, do not leave in a huff or with your tail between your legs. "No" is not a personal rejection of you; "no" simply means that the person is not going to support your cause at this time.

The way you respond to a "no" speaks volumes about you and your cause, and it can affect whether the person contributes in the future. Recognize that the person has given you her time, so thank her for considering your request. Then ask if she might be willing to share her thoughts about the cause with you. This keeps the conversation going and may provide insights into how you can convey your message more effectively to other prospective donors. The transition also gives you a little more time to develop your relationship with the person.

Failure is part of fundraising, but failure goes hand in hand with success. If you asked ten people for money and five said no, for example, you *could* interpret that as failing five times, or you could interpret that as *winning* five times. Salespeople would jump up and down with joy if even a tenth of the people out there said yes to what they were selling!

Approach your fundraising effort in terms of number of asks rather than in terms of number of failures or successes. Put fifteen pennies in one of your pockets and transfer one penny to the other pocket each time you ask a potential donor for money. When you have transferred all fifteen pennies to your other pocket, you have met your fundraising goal. Along the way, you have probably also raised some money.

Last, remind yourself that *if you do not ask, you will not receive. The main reason people do not give is this: no one asked.*

After the Gift

Fundraising does not end when the donor's money arrives; it just moves into a different stage. For starters, be sure to keep donors apprised of how their gift is being used, and how it is making a giant difference. Videos, pictures, site visits, and interactions with those who have benefited from the gift are all effective ways of convincing donors that their money is being put to good use.

Professional fundraisers stress the importance of maintaining a close connection to donors if there is *any* chance that you may seek future gifts from the same donor. Ken Burnett, author of *The Zen of Fundraising*, offers the following (somewhat massaged) advice:

- Send a warm, personal, appreciative, handwritten thank-you note for the gift—right away.
- Assure the donor that the gift will be used in an important way. Explain the sort of thing you might do with the gift so that the donor feels the gift is going to good use.
- After a few months, update the donor on how the gift is being used.
- Offer first-class customer service to each donor—go the extra mile. If a donor calls with a question or concern, get back to the person *right away.* Be sure to treat every question and concern with the utmost respect.
- Be sure that anyone in your organization who might possibly interact with the donor knows who the person is and how he or she likes to be addressed.
- Looking to the future, how soon can you approach the donor for another gift? One request per year is the standard.

Other Ways to Raise Funds from Private Individuals

In addition to a direct ask (discussed above), there are two other common approaches to raising money from private individuals: sell something or stage a special event like a Casino Night. Rarely does either approach raise much money—they are likelier to be friend-raisers than lucrative fundraisers—but selling stuff or staging an event are easier on more hesitant or inexperienced fundraisers who may liken direct asks to begging.

Selling something can take the form of services or products, with bake sales, raffles, and car washes leading the pack. But there are endless other opportunities for generating funds if you use your imagination.

To jump-start your imagination about possibilities, take stock of the special or unusual skills, talents, and interests of your staff, volunteers, and friends. What are they? Calligraphy? Beekeeping? Fly-tying? Massage? Whitewater kayaking? Drawing? Palm reading? Cooking? Gardening? Genealogy? Windsurfing? Mushrooms? Wild edibles? Rock climbing? Bird watching? Parachuting? Spelunking? Gold panning? Taxidermy? Bagpipes? Orienteering? Housecleaning? Painting? Yard work? Carpentry? Plumbing? Electricity? Investing? Public speaking? Computers? Songwriting? Singing? Beer making? Weaving? Blacksmithing? Glassblowing? Salsa dancing?

Looking over the interests, talents, and skills that you have identified, is there anything here that you could sell? For example, could you get Mary to donate a few pieces of pottery, Eric to teach Chinese cooking, Frances to lead a mushroom hunting walk, or Julia to teach salsa dancing?

With a little brainstorming, you will probably be able to identify quite a few different services and products that your group could sell at little or no cost to the organization. That is a start, but give thought as to which ones would garner outside interest. How many people are likely to knock down your door to learn glassblowing, for example, or pan for gold, explore caves, or buy handmade horseshoes? Gauging interest is important to protect supporters from offering their products or services only to have no one show interest. You can protect against this demoralizing possibility by presenting a collection of services and products through a "Yankee Swap."[3]

Yankee Swaps, auctions, concerts, special dinners, and outings with celebrities are examples of special events that can be held to raise money from private individuals. Even when such events don't raise much, they build

---

3. Google *yankee swap* or *white elephant* for numerous examples of how such an event is orchestrated.

camaraderie and can be fun, effective, interactive ways to friend-raise and introduce your cause to those outside your immediate group. The possibilities for a special event are limited only by your imagination and by the outlay of cash and risk needed to implement the event. If your cash reserves are low or nonexistent and your special event is built around individuals who charge a fee for their services, try to negotiate an arrangement where they are paid an agreed-upon percentage of the take rather than a flat fee.

A word of caution: virtually every special event has up-front costs—from facility rental to constable hiring (required by many towns and cities). These can eat into profits significantly, leaving you with lots of PR and good will but little extra cash.

Finally, recognize that holding a successful special event takes much more advance planning and staff time than you would initially expect. For a large event, start planning a year in advance; you may need that much time to advertise properly and recruit and train volunteers. For smaller events, a few months may be adequate.

Convincing Businesses to Support Your Cause

Owners of small, local businesses are likely to be personally invested in their community's well-being. They are also more likely to know you and to feel that they have a responsibility to help. As a result, local business people are usually receptive to personal appeals if they see the cause as doing something good.

All businesses are interested in their financial bottom line, of course, and opportunities that might attract future consumers are considered good investments if the price is right. Your challenge as a fundraiser is to convince business people that their business will profit from making a gift by getting favorable publicity at little cost. Be aware, however, that local businesses are constantly barraged with requests for money, so they are subject to donor fatigue. Do not wear out your welcome by knocking on the same door too often.

Most businesses will consider donating an item from their stock to an auction or yard sale. The wholesale cost of the item is much lower than the advertised price, so the business appears generous and supportive for relatively little in outlay. The favorable publicity that comes from a donation is well worth the business's small expense.

As you would with direct requests to individuals, work behind the scenes to gauge how much each business is likely to give. Then ask for a little bit more.

Since competition is a reality of the business world, you can sometimes pry a new or larger gift from an unenthusiastic business by casually letting the business know that a competitor has already made a gift and will be recognized for it. Not wanting to be left behind, the unenthusiastic business will usually surrender and make at least a small contribution.

When approaching a business, know who has the authority to make a gift; that person is the one you should approach. If it is unclear who that person may be, or if it appears that any one of several different people might have that authority, zero in on the person who is most likely to be personally interested in the cause that you are advancing. Behind-the-scenes sleuthing can help you figure out who that might be.

Remember that businesses are staffed by human beings, not by money-grubbing automatons. While it is true that businesses are more likely than private individuals to give to a cause whose main selling point is that it will burnish their image, raising money from businesses usually comes down to the human factor and personal connections. Passionate, engaging individuals who have good people skills will always raise far more money than those who are socially awkward or just doing their job. Those who know the prospective donor personally will do even better.

As with private donors, your job as a fundraiser does not end when a business makes a gift. At minimum, follow-up each gift with a prompt, personal thank-you note that briefly explains how the business will be recognized for its contribution. Take every opportunity to thank the business publicly. Good public relations is worth a lot—it gives businesses something for their money.

To summarize, probably no one grows up dreaming of becoming a fundraiser, but that does not mean that it cannot be a job you learn to love. Raising funds for a worthy cause is more than filling a suitcase with money; it is a charitable service that you provide for people who want to do good but do not know how. Looking over "Some Fundraising Reminders" (appendix 13) will help keep you on track.

Funding from Foundations and Government Agencies

The main way to obtain money from foundations and government agencies is through a grant. To receive a grant, you need to convince those holding the purse strings that your idea meshes closely with what they value or want. Your proposal is therefore a sales pitch—a course of action that you are proposing to address a problem, challenge, or question that the funding organization cares about.

Virtually all proposals ultimately take the form of a written document that is submitted to the funding organization. Experienced grant seekers go above and beyond writing proposals, however: they work to establish personal relationships with people in funding organizations. As with fundraising from private individuals, there is plenty of truth to the saying that money follows relationships.

On occasion, a funding organization will decide to channel its funding into a very specific problem or question that it deems critical (e.g., the effect of road building on the spread of kudzu in Alabama). To encourage proposal submissions, the organization will release an RFP (**R**equest **F**or **P**roposals) or NOFO (**N**otice **O**f **F**unding **O**pportunity) that spells out what the funding organization is looking for. Here is what an RFP or NOFO might look like:

REQUEST FOR PROPOSALS

To Assess Whether Forest Access Roads Are Spreading Kudzu in Alabama
(Deadline for receipt of proposals is March 15, 20XX)

To meet a heightened demand for forest products, forests in Alabama are being harvested and planted at unprecedented rates. The increased activity has been a boon to rural economies, but the increased road building that accompanies harvesting and planting may expedite the spread of invasive weeds. Of particular concern is kudzu, a high-climbing, rapidly spreading, invasive vine from Asia that has become a serious management problem in the southeast United States.

To better understand the relationship between road building and kudzu spread in Alabama, the Department of Conservation seeks proposals that answer one or more of the following questions:

- To what extent do Alabama's forest access roads serve as vectors for kudzu spread?
- Are some forest types at greater risk of invasion by kudzu than others?
- As new access roads are cut through forests, what "best management practices" can be implemented to prevent spread of kudzu?

A total of $260,000 is available for the 20XX–20YY period. It is anticipated that several awards will be made, each ranging from $40,000 to $60,000, but awards up to $100,000 will be considered if thoroughly justified. Awarded funds may be spread over a one-, two-, or three-year period. Those wishing to submit a proposal are encouraged to review further details about this RFP at http://www.xxx/xx/xxx/. Questions should be addressed to Jill Doe at xxx-xxx-xxxx.

Responding to an RFP or NOFO like the above fictitious example is the easiest way to target a likely funding source because the funding organization tells you what it wants. Reviewing current and upcoming RFPs and NOFOs is therefore a good place to start your search for possible funding. Three no-subscription-required websites list current and upcoming RFPs and NOFOs:

1. www.fdncenter.org (The Foundation Center)
2. www.guidestar.org (Guidestar)
3. www.grants.gov (government grants)

Another website that is worth looking into is www.grantadvisor.com. Unlike the three above, this site charges a subscription fee of several hundred dollars a year. The good news is that, as a goodwill gesture, Grantadvisor donates a subscription to two public libraries in each state. Contact a reference librarian at a city or university library to find the nearest public library with a subscription that you can access at no charge.

Of the more than seventy thousand foundations, corporate donation programs, and government programs that give money to charitable causes each year, only governmental programs can be counted on to advertise all of their funding priorities through RFPs. If you cannot find an appropriate RFP for your cause or interest, you will therefore need to sleuth out organizations that might be interested in funding your project. The four websites above have search engines to help you identify promising prospects; they are a good place to start.[4] Also try these (lower-tech) approaches:

- Seek help from professionals who are familiar with your type of project.
- Search newsletters and annual reports of organizations similar to yours to see who is funding them.
- Seek advice from colleagues from organizations similar to yours. Ask about their funding successes—how did they do it?
- Check out local foundations and corporations—they may be receptive to your proposal even if it is somewhat outside their main area of interest.
- Identify and approach nonprofit organizations that are likely to be interested in what you are proposing. These organizations may not be able to offer financial support, but they may be willing to join forces with you or suggest possible funding avenues.

---

4. All four websites are helpful, but www.fdncenter.org and grantadvisor.com (if you can access them) are absolute gold mines. Be sure to browse through them so you know what you could be missing.

After identifying possible sources of funding, check the website of each to get a better handle on its funding history and its current and upcoming priorities. If the priorities are unclear, call the organization's contact person, introduce yourself, and briefly pitch the idea you wish to propose (see "Research Overview," chapter 2). To have any chance of your proposal being funded, it must be a good fit with the organization's interests. If it is not, look elsewhere for money.

The Art of Grantsmanship

Grantsmanship, like talking someone into joining a cause, is about selling an idea convincingly and compellingly. If you sell the idea sufficiently well, your grant is funded.

Writing a grant proposal is more straightforward than other fundraising approaches because the components of a proposal, and how you present them, are set by the funding organization.

What a Proposal Looks Like

A proposal is a sales pitch that is built around a compelling, clearly stated question or challenge. The organization of elements in a proposal can vary from one proposal to the next and be labeled differently, but the main ingredients vary little. In one form or another, every winning proposal includes the following elements:

- A **Title Page** that includes a descriptive title of the proposed project (no more than thirteen words), the principal investigator's (PI's) name, institutional affiliation, address, telephone, fax number, and email address.
- An **Executive Summary/Abstract** that provides a short (less than a page) but intriguing encapsulation of what your proposal is about, why it is important, and how you propose to pull it off.
- A **Project Overview** that explains the problem or need or challenge in greater detail and how you propose to address it.
- **Justification** for why your proposed undertaking is incredibly important and why *you* are the best one to do it (sometimes this is folded into the Project Description/Overview).
- Explicitly stated **Goals and Objectives** that articulate exactly what you hope to accomplish. Collectively, the stated goals/objectives should

convince the funding organization that your proposal gives them everything that they are looking for.

- **Methods/Procedures** that describe, step-by-step, exactly how you propose to meet your goals and objectives.
- **Work Schedule/Timetable** that provides an overview of when the various parts of the proposed project will be undertaken and completed (sometimes this is folded into the Goals and Objectives section).
- **Qualifications** of the main players who will be working on the project.
- **Itemized Budget** that spells out anticipated expenses (e.g., salaries, benefits, travel, supplies, copying, mailing, shipping, phone, equipment).
- **Budget Explanation/Justification** that briefly explains why each expense is needed (sometimes this is folded into the Itemized Budget section).

These other proposal elements are also sometimes included:

- **Expected Results** forecast what you will learn or achieve.
- **Project Evaluation** explains how you will assess the effectiveness of your effort.
- **Anticipated Difficulties/Troubleshooting** assesses what could go wrong, with a description of how you propose to neutralize their impacts.
- **Deliverables** describes the tangible products that a funding organization can expect to come out of the funded project.
- **Public Outreach/Getting the Word Out** describes how relevant information from the project will be communicated to those who can use it.

Examples of what these proposal elements look like can be found in appendix 14.

Last, a brief (less than a page) cover letter that introduces you and your proposal is included with your submission. When appropriate, the cover letter includes a reminder of past discussions that you have had with the funding organization about your proposed idea.

IMPORTANT! Even as the list above identifies common winning proposal elements, you should always attempt to give funding organizations *what they want* in your proposal. If a funding organization specifies how it wants proposals packaged, follow their guidelines *exactly*. If no precise proposal format is specified, check www.fdncenter.org for different format options.

How to Write a Proposal

When it comes to grantsmanship (writing proposals), the more you know about grant makers (those who give money) and how they think, the better. The following three websites, created to help grant makers share information and ideas, are worth scanning periodically:

1. www.ega.org (Environmental Grantmakers Association)
2. www.nng.org (National Network of Grantmakers)
3. www.cof.org (Council on Foundations)

These sites are not efficient places to look for funding opportunities, but browsing through them will give you an inside look at what grant makers are thinking about.

Many books and guides have been written on proposal writing; a few of the best are listed in the Recommended Reading section. All of them say about the same thing, however: proposal writing is about selling ideas and solving problems. If you are a good, credible salesperson, you will be an effective grant writer if you are crystal clear about the problem that you are proposing to solve.

Reviewers cannot evaluate the likely effectiveness of the strategies you propose, or whether your idea is even worth pursuing, if the problem or question that you propose to tackle is unclear. So make it clear, right off. As a move in that direction, try writing—in a single sentence—the problem that your proposal seeks to solve. To illustrate, here are some examples of problems around which a proposal might be framed:

- Landowners are selling off their land to developers because their yearly income from the land does not cover their taxes.
- We do not know if road building is responsible for the rapid spread of kudzu in Alabama.
- The town's landfill cannot accommodate the town's stream of waste.
- Is nest parasitism contributing to an ecologically meaningful decline in some songbird species?
- In the arid West, free-roaming livestock concentrate in riparian zones for food and water but, in so doing, they cause major water quality problems.

Each of the above is a problem in need of a solution. If, for example, you had an idea for how to solve the first problem (i.e., how to keep landowners from needing to sell their land), you would first locate a funding organization that is interested in solving that problem. You would then learn what you can about the organization, including how and when they entertain proposals. After making contact with the organization and floating some ideas past them and getting feedback, you would start crafting your proposal.

In writing your proposal, you would start off by quickly but compellingly presenting the problem. In so doing, you would briefly but convincingly build a case that solving the problem is critically important. With that as your foundation, you would then explain—in detail—the suite of specific steps that you propose taking to solve the problem. Along the way, you would convince the funding organization that you and your proposal are the perfect fit—that no one out there could possibly implement your proposed plan as effectively as you would. That is all there is to proposal writing.

To put yourself in the right frame of mind as you sit down to write, think of yourself as a salesperson who is selling an unknown product to a bored, tired, skeptical buyer. The problem you are proposing to solve through selling your bill of goods must appear very important, your way of solving it must be believable, and your proposal as a whole must be convincing, engaging, and readable in one short sitting. Accomplish those things and you are two-thirds of the way there!

How Your Proposal Is Evaluated

A crucial part of your approach is figuring out who might review and evaluate your proposal. Who are they likely to be? What are their backgrounds? What are their expectations? What will they want to know? What criteria will they use in evaluating your proposal? What will excite or intrigue them?

Funding organizations commonly spell out the factors that they weigh most carefully when they evaluate proposals. As a rule, however, the evaluative criteria below are the ones that most commonly factor into decisions about which proposals are funded and which are not:

- Does your proposal match the organization's interests?
- Does your proposal address an important problem or question?
- Is it exciting?
- Is it innovative or unique?
- Is the proposed action realistic? Is there a thoughtful, convincing plan behind it?
- Is it likely to succeed?

- Is the proposed budget appropriate and realistic? (An unrealistically low budget is at least as damning as an inflated budget.)
- Do you have the skills to pull it off? In the final analysis, organizations award funds to *people* they believe in. A stellar proposal will not save you if the funding organization doubts your ability, dependability, or integrity. Your reputation and the impression you make on people within the foundation are how they evaluate your worthiness.

IMPORTANT! Always tailor your ideas so that they directly address the organization's priorities. If your funding need is broader than what is specified in an RFP (let's say that you are concerned about the effect of road building on the spread of three invasive plant species in the South—not just kudzu, and not just in Alabama), limit your proposal to what the funding organization is looking for (in this case, road building, kudzu, and Alabama). Do not clutter your proposal, for example, with tangential discussions about your wish to study other invasive species in Alabama, or your intention to study kudzu in Tennessee or Georgia. That may be what you ultimately are interested in and intend to do, but it is not what the funding organization is paying for. Stay focused on what *they* want; keep your other interests and pursuits to yourself.

The Personalized Touch

Once you have framed your ideas in a way that makes sense, and you have identified a likely target for your proposal, try to schedule a sit-down meeting with an officer from the funding organization to premarket your ideas and yourself.

Before making the request for a sit-down, however, flip back to earlier pages of this chapter and study two sections: "The Ins and Outs of Successful Fundraising," and "Convincing Businesses to Support Your Cause." Those sections are as relevant to having your proposals funded as they are to having people write you checks.

Having internalized those sections, learn what you can about the wishes and interests of the granting organization before you sit down with them. Use any avenues you can think of to get the inside scoop—Internet searches, contacts within the organization, annual reports, newsletters, and so forth.

Use the sit-down meeting to (subtly) sell your ideas and to gauge which parts of your imagined proposal will generate the most interest. Listen carefully and adjust your sales pitch and conversation accordingly. If the meeting goes well, the funder will start seeing your ideas and priorities as being the same as her own. When that happens, you are in business.

Revise, Revise, Revise!

When I am on a proposal roll, the words—and terrific ideas!—just flow from me like water, and I go to bed energized and very pleased with myself. If I sit on the draft a couple days before picking it up again, however, my hitherto terrifically expressed ideas never look as great as I thought they were. "Huh?" I invariably find myself wondering, "why did I think that made sense?" and "Thank heavens I didn't send *that* out!"

Always sit on a draft proposal (overnight at minimum) before reviewing its suitability for submission. Also, *always* have colleagues critique drafts of your proposals and then revise, revise, revise! Last, *always* have a literate colleague proof the final draft before submission. Typos and other oversights send a message of carelessness that undermines the sense of professionalism and excellence that your proposal should be projecting.

Some Closing Thoughts

Asking people for money is not about begging; it is about showing people how they can do good. Doing good makes people feel good about themselves, but they need to believe that their gift *will* do good. That is why selling your product compellingly is essential.

Raising money through grant writing is also about selling your product convincingly (appendix 15 offers some reminders of how to do that). Practice *does* make perfect or, if not perfect, a lot better. Some people enjoy writing proposals, and I am one of them. To me, dreaming up and presenting great ideas is incredibly stimulating.[5] If my proposal is funded, hooray! But if it is not funded, that is okay too. The effort resulted in getting concepts onto paper that I can work over, improve, and use to seek funding at another place or time. Getting constructive feedback from the organization that turned me down increases my chances next time.

---

5. Great to me, at least!

9

You Are Your Most Valuable Resource

How to Save the World without Going Nuts or Burning Out

One person *can* make a difference if you have commitment, focus, and some practical know-how to keep you on track and out of trouble. The first eight chapters of this tool kit book teach skills that will make you more effective as an individual or member of a team. None of those tools, techniques, or tips matter or do any good, however, if your personal well-being is not where it needs to be. This last chapter, an important one, suggests ways to protect yourself from the frustration, discouragement, stress, and burnout that are always nipping at your heels.

The story of my friend Paul is an illustrative example of burnout. Paul was the environmentalist every one of us *should* be—a tireless crusader for whales, recycling, tropical rainforest, biodiversity, environmental justice, and every other environmental cause out there. If it was important, Paul was in the thick of it.

Paul and I didn't know one another before Fish and Wildlife tasked us with documenting salmon runs on tributaries of Alaska's Yukon River. The two of us shared a backwoods cabin that lacked electricity and running water, so I saw firsthand how Paul lived, slept, and breathed environmentalism: from shunning shampoo because it polluted waterways and spurning multinational products that did not pay workers a fair wage to insisting that we recycle our empty bean cans—even though we were in the middle of nowhere and had no place to recycle them.

Paul's singular life purpose, to right the world's environmental wrongs, spotlighted my self-centered, guilt-ridden tendencies. Despite Paul's disapproval, I continued to shampoo my hair to get rid of the grease, and I bought cheap coffee rather than the expensive, free-trade stuff. And when Paul wasn't around, I even buried smelly sardine cans rather than save them in hopes that we would someday find a way to recycle them.

Paul's extreme commitment to environmental correctness may have been virtuous but it didn't make him likable. When we parted ways at summer's end, I was glad to escape his overbearing judgment. I knew we would not stay in touch.

A few summers later, I was walking down a busy Seattle street when a passerby yelled, "Hey, Jeff!" Jeff *is* my name, but I didn't know a soul in Seattle—so I kept walking.

"Jeff, hold up!" the guy yelled again. I turned to see a grinning guy in a three-piece suit running toward me.

"It's me, Paul!" he said.

Paul? I wondered. I didn't know any Pauls, but I hid my cluelessness so I wouldn't hurt his feelings.

After a minute or so of mutual backslapping and handshaking, the guy calling himself Paul stepped back and with an even bigger grin asked, "You don't know who I am, do you?"

I admitted that I didn't.

"I was your cabin mate on the Yukon!"

"You are *that* Paul?" I blurted out disbelievingly. "What happened?"

"The frustrations and failures got to me. I just burned out," he answered. "It's not that I stopped caring about the environment; it's that I just couldn't take it anymore. I needed to do something for *me*."

His admission stunned me. If *Paul*—the ultimate environmental crusader—couldn't hang in there, how could *anyone*?

When I asked what the new, clean-shaven, three-piece suit Paul was doing now, his answer floored me. "I trade stocks," he said. He responded to my stupefied reaction with a laugh. "I know what you're thinking, but you know what's great about my move to the dark side? I have a *life*!"

We hung out for a while and, to my enormous surprise, I actually enjoyed being around him. As we parted ways, I said I hoped we would stay in touch, and I meant it.

A few years later I got a call from Paul asking if I would serve on his board. When I reminded him that I knew nothing about stocks, he laughed. "No, not that!" he said. "I'm no longer a stockbroker. I'm back to saving the world."

I asked what had changed, he laughed again. "I learned some things."

This concluding chapter is about those things and others that, if taken seriously, will keep you from going nuts or burning out. Here is a short list:

- Do not take on too many causes at once. Focus on the one (or possibly two) that you care about most.

- Do more of what lifts you up and less of what drags you down.
- Give yourself *real* breaks.
- Keep meetings short and infrequent, and do not hold them unless you know exactly what you want for outcomes. Follow preset agendas and start and end on time.
- Nurture an upbeat attitude. Surround yourself with optimistic and fun-loving people.
- When you find yourself thinking that you *must do* X or you *need to do* Y, know this: you probably don't. The world will not go to hell if you step off the treadmill.

We will address this last one first because it is the force behind most of the others.

Don't Treat Assumptions as Truths

A great deal of unnecessary angst comes from people acting on hidden or faulty assumptions. It is easy to believe, for example, that you *have to* do item W or that you *need to* do item X or that you *should* do item Y or that you *must* do item Z. But do you really? Are those musts necessarily true?

In actuality, there are few things that you truly *have to do* or should do. Most such beliefs are self-created *assumptions*. People who internalize lots of *have to's*, *need to's*, *shoulds*, and *musts*, however, have talked themselves into believing that everything will fall apart if they are not in the thick of it. That assumption, which they treat as a truth, is constantly reinforced by their *yeah, but!* reflex—*Yeah, but* if I don't do item X, there will be disastrous consequences!

The *yeah, but!* reflex is triggered by two assumptions:

1. that the action is critical (there is no way around it)
2. that you are the one and only person who can pull it off

Rarely is either assumption accurate or absolute.

It is hard to know how much faith you should place in your *yeah, but!* beliefs if you don't know the hidden or faulty assumptions behind them. To help reveal what you are *assuming* to be undeniably true, try examining your musts through the eyes of people unlike you: a hardscrabble farmer, a Wall Street executive, a factory worker, a foreigner—in short, a person of different age or gender or socio-economic status. If those other folks likewise agree that you—and only you—*must* do it, that is one thing. But if people from other walks of life do not see you as the sole savior, it is time for a reality check because hidden assumptions are at play.

In truth, the world will not collapse if you jettison some of your shoulds and musts. *Your* world, however, *will* collapse—in the form of ulcers and burnout—if you shoulder too many faulty should and must assumptions. So whenever you are thinking that you *have to, need to, should,* or *must* do something, try this: imagine it is a couple of months from now, and you are looking back on what you did or didn't do. Would it *really* make a difference one way or the other? When seen from a distance, you will find that most of today's *must do's!* are not as absolute as you make them out to be.

Here is another way to counteract the stress and burnout that comes from worrying about all the things that (you feel) need to be done. To get off the treadmill and give yourself a *real* break, start by making individual lists of everything you think you must do, should do, or want to do.[1] Getting all of your perceived tasks and responsibilities on paper reveals the giant cloud of background worries in your head. That alone can be psychologically uplifting and stress-relieving because it elucidates what you think needs to be done. You are able to see it in black and white rather than just imagine and worry about it.

Once you have your tasks codified on paper, create a timeline for each "must" task on your list (ignore your *should* and *want to* lists). Specify the *needed* completion date for each *must* task, and estimate the amount of time it will take you to complete it. Subtract that estimated time from the completion deadline to show when you should start working on it. Record that day on your calendar and assign it a start time.

For example, let's say that a particular funding opportunity that you wish to apply for has a submission deadline of October 25. If you estimate that you will need ten days to complete the proposal once you get going, subtract those ten days from October 25 to show when you need to start working on the proposal—October 15. Record that start date in your date book and indicate a specific time when you will begin (e.g., 10:15 am).

Establishing a specific start date *and time* gives you license to truly let go— to put the proposal out of your mind until 10:15 am on October 15. Until then, the proposal is not in your consciousness, which gives you unfettered time to focus your attention on a different task or to recharge with a *real* break.

---

1. Remember to be discriminating about what you really *need* to do, and what you think you *should* do, and what you *want* to do.

People on the road to burnout do not approach distant deadlines that way. Their approach is: *I will get to it when I can.* That sounds like a relaxed, hands-off approach, but it is the opposite—it actually stands in the way of allowing yourself a real break. Sure, you might recognize the warning signs that you need a break, so you go ahead and take one. But would that "break" really rejuvenate you? Highly unlikely. The specter of the funding deadline would still hang over you, lurking in the shadows of your inner being. You would feel guilty about being a lazy bum when you *could* be using that time to work on the proposal and keep from falling even further behind.

Is There Really Too Much to Do?

Believing that there is too much to do is stressful and draining. But *believing* that there is too much to do does not make it true. Here is how I learned that lesson:

I was working eighty hours a week but did not have enough time to get everything done. It was mighty stressful. And then I got married. I wanted to spend time with my wife, of course, so I stopped working evenings. I made up for the lost time by working later into the night after my wife went to bed.

And then my son was born. I wanted to spend time with him, of course, but cutting back on hours of sleep wasn't possible. I had been running on caffeine fumes for a year and a half and was fried long before my son was even imagined.

And then my daughter was born. Beam me up, Scottie! Something had to give but I was too wiped out to imagine what that could be. Fortunately for me, the retirement of a colleague, Jessie, showed me the way.

Jessie was the hardest-working, most indispensable, and most chronically stressed worker I had ever seen—she always was everywhere doing every-thing. Fortunately, the boss recognized that no single hire could ever replace her so, when Jessie decided to retire, her position was turned into two positions.

As job descriptions were being crafted for the two positions, a staff member, Pat, filled in as the Jessie stand-in until two replacement Jessies could be hired. Pat shadowed Jessie for a couple of weeks to get a handle on all the things that needed to be done.

Two months into her interim assignment, just before job candidates for the two positions were invited for interviews, Pat (the stand-in for Jessie) resigned. Pat's reason for resigning shocked everyone—*she said she didn't have enough to do.*

How could that be? How could she not have enough to do when Jessie had been so overwhelmingly busy?

When asked, Pat explained that of the many things Jessie had been doing, almost none of them really *needed* to be done. Pat theorized that over time, Jessie became more focused on *doing* and lost sight of the *why* behind it. The doing became the end, not the means to a thoughtfully targeted end. Jessie had not been able to see that because she was too busy and stressed to step back and assess whether her musts were, in fact, *true* musts. She was working harder, not smarter.

After two months without a Jessie replacement, the wheels *had not* fallen off the bus, and we were no worse off than when Jessie had been working full tilt. In fact, I was *better off* because I applied the Jessie lesson to my own life by no longer doing some things that I had thought were essential but weren't. As a result, my blood pressure went down, and my effectiveness went up.

When It Seems That There Is Not Enough Time

Leonard Bernstein, the famous conductor, had this to say about not having enough time: "To achieve great things, two things are needed: a plan and not quite enough time." For procrastinators like me, that is completely true: when my back is against the wall to get something done and I have no wiggle room to slack off, a concentrated burst of imaginative energy hits me. My foggy, unproductive brain miraculously kicks into high gear.

Not everyone, of course, responds that way to having too much to do in too little time. If you are a last-minute type like me, however, try painting yourself into a time-crunched corner with the scheduling trick described earlier. Estimate the time needed to complete the looming task *if you work hard*, then subtract that time from your completion deadline to establish a nonnegotiable *start time*. Record this *start time* (day and hour) on your calendar and put the task out of your mind until that *exact* start time. When the start time arrives—no sooner and no later—drop whatever else you are doing and focus solely on the scheduled task. If something else comes up, too bad, it will have to wait.[2] Establishing firm deadlines without wiggle room forces you to stay focused when something comes up—which it always does.

It is tougher to manage the *there's not enough time!* perception when there is no firm deadline by which a task must be completed. When you face this

---

2. Unless it is a true emergency, of course.

situation, kickstart your brain by committing to an inviolable completion time. Decide how much time you will allocate to the task, erring on the minimalist side, then decide on an exact *start time* as described in the preceding paragraph. Add the allocated work time to the specified start time to show when you *will* have the task completed—no matter what. Record the start and completion times for the task in your calendar and stay on schedule—*come hell or high water.*

Setting firm start and completion times—and sticking to them no matter what!—helps you accomplish more in less time. It also keeps you sane by giving your mind a break from that constant gnawing, background worry that time is ticking away and you might not be able to get everything done. Knowing that you have reserved specific time blocks for working on and completing tasks makes it easier to give yourself guilt-free, worry-free breaks. Make those breaks happen: you need them to stay sane and productive.

Placing bounds on how much time you will spend working on something has another advantage: it shifts the mindset from *there's not enough time to do it right* to *there's not enough time to do it wrong.* Two simple behavioral changes will help:

1. Set aside the hours when you are most clear-headed for substantive work; stay away from emails, social media, and cell phones during those hours.
2. Delegate more and micromanage less.

Stop Judging Yourself

If you are a Type A personality, you probably enflame your neuroses without knowing it. Are you setting high standards for yourself? Good. Are you setting standards beyond the reach of mere mortals? Bad.

All anyone of us can do is the best we can do. Consider a runner who completes a marathon in four hours when healthy. Is it fair to expect a similar result if they run with a head cold or sprained ankle? Would you expect a four-hour marathon run if they are sleep deprived or severely depressed? Would you think less of them if they ran injured, gave it everything they had, but barely broke five hours? Would you criticize their slow time or would you applaud their superhuman effort?

Judge your own performance with the same critical and appreciative eye as you would judge the performance of someone who puts in an equal level of effort. Work on your shortcomings, of course, but also give yourself credit for what you do well. Pat yourself on the back when you give it your best, even if the results fall a little short of perfection.

If that is hard for you—if you are always beating up on yourself when, at the same time, you are congratulating others for giving it *their* best—you need to level the playing ground with a humility check: do you really think you are so much better than everyone else that you should be judged by different and higher standards?[3]

Making Good Things Better and Unpleasant Things Less Bad

Reducing tasks and situations that drag you down will make you less miserable. Increasing tasks and situations that lift you up will make you more joyful. Doing both will make everything seem better.

If you find yourself whining about how rough you have it—the *too much of this and not enough of that* syndrome—do something about it. Find ways to do *less* of the stuff that drags you down and *more* of the stuff that lifts you up.

Begin by identifying and writing down the everyday tasks, situations, and activities that wear on you (e.g., answering emails, going to meetings). If you need help imagining what they are, see appendix 16 for possibilities.

Now take each of your identified burdens and strategize specific ways to minimize its impact on you. For example, if *dealing with computer problems* drags you down, imagine ways to minimize its impact on you—for example, get a backup computer to use when one goes awry; set a limit for the amount of time you will mess with a problem before seeking help; find someone on staff who will take care of computer problems for you; limit your computer work to tasks with few technological wrinkles. You then can work the more promising strategies into your daily life to lessen the annoyance of dealing with computer problems.

Follow the same approach with everyday tasks, situations, and activities that *boost* your joyfulness. If you need help imagining what such things may be, see appendix 17 for some possibilities.

For example, if you identify *getting aerobic exercise* as an activity that lifts you up, strategize ways to make it happen more often—for example, schedule exercise time into your daily and weekly calendars; find someone who is committed to exercise with you on a regular basis; pay money to join a health club

---

3. Seems a little arrogant, doesn't it?

so you will feel obliged to use your membership regularly to get your money's worth. Work the most promising possibilities into your daily life to make your days more fulfilling.

Choosing the Right Staff and Volunteers

Volunteers are the backbone of many environmental campaigns, especially in organizations that have few if any paid staff.[4] Volunteers can help relieve your stress and keep you sane because, after all, they are free. Well, that is actually far from being true: volunteers are *not* free. Managing them takes time and effort, and attentiveness to their expectations, which are:

- to be appreciated
- to be recognized for their efforts
- to do something important
- to meet interesting people
- to have fun
- to be part of a team
- to be shown what to do and how to do it
- to be kept in the loop about what is going on
- to be listened to
- to be adequately supervised
- to have someone to turn to if they have questions
- to have maximum flexibility about when they work and when they don't
- to know why the boring task that they are being asked to do (e.g., stuff envelopes) is important to the cause

If you are not able to meet most of those expectations, think long and hard before you welcome in volunteers.

Without guidance, support, cheerleading, and enough clearly defined tasks, volunteerism does not work. Disgruntled volunteers will poison your organization, discredit your cause, and drain you of time and energy.

Also recognize that *every* volunteer—disgruntled or not—will carry the banner of your organization and represent you. So scout out potential recruits

---

4. For more on the nuts and bolts of implementing a successful volunteer program, see https://www.volunteermatch.org/.

carefully before inviting them in. Know this: *once a volunteer is on your team, you are stuck with the person. She* will decide when to leave, not you.

When choosing volunteers (or board members or staff), look beyond pedigree, experience, and training. Skills and experience are revealed in applications, transcripts, and resumes, but personality traits might be even more important. Is the applicant dependable? Honest? Moody? High maintenance? Does the person have a sense of humor? An attitude? An upbeat personality? These personality traits, or lack of them, matter.

Of course, written recommendations may offer some insight into an applicant's personality traits, but don't count on them revealing traits that are problematic; most recommenders avoid saying anything that could raise a red flag. People who have read lots of recommendations know this, however, so they look for what is *not* said as well as what is said.

To gain greater insight into an applicant's personality—before it is too late—ask those who know an applicant well to react to contrasting personality traits. Here are some examples of questions that can reveal much:

- Does she always get stuff done on time—no matter what—or do things sometimes come up that get in the way?
- Is she cheerful and upbeat (or) is she sometimes a little on the moody side?
- Would she be a good person to represent you at a board meeting (or) would someone else probably be better?
- Would she be a good person to answer sensitive phone calls (or) would someone else probably be better?

Hypothetical questions can reveal important things about an applicant too. For example:

- If you were shipwrecked on a deserted island, why would *Elizabeth* (the applicant) be a good person to be shipwrecked with? Why would you be glad to be with her rather than someone else?
- Over time *anyone* would get on your nerves, of course, and that includes Elizabeth. What things about her would wear on you?

Appendix 18 provides a more expansive bunch of questions to ask references; it also suggests how to orchestrate the question asking. Before using it for keeps, practice running through the questions with colleagues. A good question-asking session is a relaxed conversation that takes only ten or fifteen minutes.

Some Final Closing Thoughts

Staying healthy, upbeat, and recharged is a never-ending challenge for people trying to move the environmental needle—there always seems to be too much to do, in too little time, with too few resources. And making headway always seems to take longer than forever, and it can feel like you are losing more ground than you are gaining. The discouragements and frustrations can sour even the most optimistic campaigner. Unless . . .

Unless you reflect on how much has been accomplished by a handful of committed people like you. *One person can make a difference if the person stays healthy, happy, and connected to supportive people who matter.*

It is insidiously easy to become isolated when you are superbusy, but you need to keep friends and family in your life to stay sane and happy. Keep their supportive spirit alive by scheduling a telephone call to a different friend and family member each week. Try blocking out a specific time each week for the call—put it on your calendar—to ensure that these calls do not fall by the wayside. Friends will be surprised and delighted to hear from you, and touching base with them will help put things in perspective when unpleasant interactions with people have been gnawing away at your inner peace.

It is hard not to take it personally when someone forcefully challenges, criticizes, or argues against your strongly held environmental beliefs or actions. For most of us, our immediate, knee-jerk reaction is to get mad, defensive, argumentative, or all three. We react that way because we interpret the opposing view as a personal attack on us, not as a difference of opinion that is grounded in a different set of experiences and beliefs.

It is worth remembering that two wonderful people can have diametrically opposed views and can argue and trash one another's notions heatedly, but still love and respect one another and enjoy doing something together afterward.[5] For that to happen, however, one of you must refuse to personalize the difference in opinion. Since the other person probably will not do it, that leaves it up to you.

I find it helpful to think of conflicting opinions as a stimulating battle of the minds, not as an opportunity to destroy the other guy. I also try to remember that people—no matter their beliefs or inclinations—*will* lash out and say things they shouldn't when they are upset or feel threatened. Some of those reactionary things will come across as personal. Whether you

---

5. Think of contrary family members!

internalize them as personal assaults on *you*, however, will affect your overall sense of well-being.

In the end, so much of your well-being—and your effectiveness as an environmental leader—is defined by your attitude. Your attitude affects how others interact with you, and it affects how you feel about yourself. And it is one part of the equation that you have complete control over.

So stand tall, smile a lot, and look people in the eye when you talk with them. And stay away from naysayers, misanthropes, and cynics—surround yourself with kind, upbeat, can-do, fun-loving people. Tell yourself that you are a good, kind, respectful person, then prove to yourself—every day—that you are. Last, believe that you will do great things. Believe it because it's true.

appendix 1
Telling Stories with Your Graphs

Graphs are efficient, effective ways to tell stories about the place or thing about which you have collected data. Aim to make every graph a clear, complete, straightforward, understandable, stand-alone storybook of information.[1] To illustrate, let's say that you have collected data on the abundance of nonnative plants and animals in both suburban and rural settings to see if suburban sprawl really is linked to higher numbers of nonnative pests. A few (of many) ways that you might present your data are shown in figures A-1.1 to A-1.6:

Figure A-1.1a compares sampling plots within the suburban landscape and how they differ from one another; Figure A-1.1b does likewise for the rural landscape. But is that the story you want to tell? Would anyone care whether

(a)

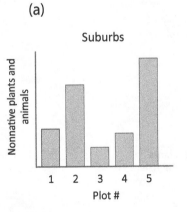

(b)

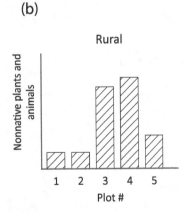

FIGURE A-1.1.

---

1. Do not forget to label all axes, specify units, and include a clear, descriptive caption for each!

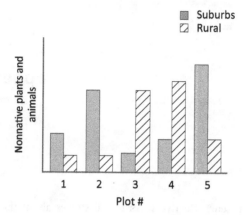

FIGURE A-1.2.

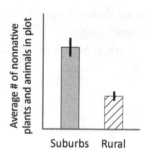

FIGURE A-1.3.

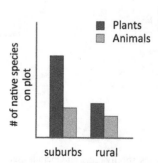

FIGURE A-1.4.

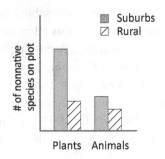

FIGURE A-1.5.

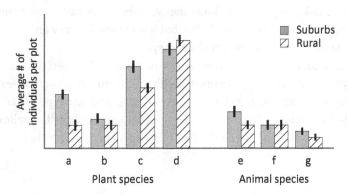

FIGURE A-1.6.

one arbitrarily numbered plot is different from another arbitrarily numbered plot? Of course not.

In principle, figure A-1.2 is a slight improvement because it compares suburban and rural plots side-by-side. The story is still meaningless, however, because the five plot-by-plot comparisons are arbitrary—if plots had been assigned different numbers, the side-by-side comparisons would be entirely different (and equally meaningless).

Figure A-1.3, in contrast to figures A-1.1 and A-1.2, actually tells a meaningful story. By summarizing results from each landscape type, side-by-side, the story is clear: on average, there are almost twice as many nonnative organisms on suburban plots as on rural plots.[2]

---

2. The vertical line at the top of each column indicates variability in the data that yielded the average for that landscape. A short line (as over the rural landscape) means that all of the plots from that landscape had similar numbers of nonnative organisms. A tall line (as over the suburban landscape) means that the plots from that landscape had vastly different numbers of nonnative organisms, some very high, some very low, and some in-between. The importance of measuring and reporting variability is explained more thoroughly in chapter 3.

Figures A-1.4 and A-1.5 both separate out suburban and rural landscapes, as well as plants and animals, but they focus attention on different comparisons. As a result, they tell different stories. According to figure A-1.4, there are many more nonnative plant species than nonnative animal species, and this holds true on both suburban and rural sites. The main story of figure A-1.5, in contrast, is that there are many more nonnative species on suburban sites than on rural sites, and that this holds true for both plants and animals. Given the question you wish to answer, figure A-1.5 therefore tells a far more interesting and useful story.

Figure A-1.6 tells a similar story to figure A-1.5, but with greater specificity. Like figure A-1.5, figure A-1.6 shows that suburban sites have more nonnative plants and animals than do rural sites, but it also tells the story on a species by species basis—a much more revealing story.

As the graphs above illustrate, *how* you present data determines which story you emphasize. Experiment with different graphing styles and versions—for example, try changing axes, units, and the type of data you present—to reveal the full range of stories that you might tell. Applications such as Microsoft Excel offer a number of approaches to play with.

appendix 2
Suggestions for Conducting an Effective Inventory

Conducting an inventory takes time, energy, and, oftentimes, lots of money, so pare down your questions (and your inventory) to the bare essentials. When considering which questions to tackle, focus on important questions that need answers *right away*. Don't waste time collecting data unless you know—in advance—*exactly* how you will use them.

Some inventory questions that *might* be worth your while trying to answer:

- Are there any rare, endangered, or threatened species on the property?
- Is the property special in some way? If so, in what way?
- How much would the property sell for?
- Does it have development potential?
- What is the property's best use?
- What is the current and future value of the property's timber?
- Are there valuable mineral resources on the property?
- Are there hazards or problematic issues on the property that we should be aware of?
- Are there any biological hotspots? If so, where are they?
- Which game species are using the property?
- What is the quality of habitat for species X, Y, and Z? (i.e., the species that you care about most)
- How many different plant species are there?
- Which species nest or den on the property?
- Where on the property are problematic populations of nonnative, invasive species?
- How difficult would it be to restore the site to its precolonial condition?
- Are there places on the property that could be managed to appreciably increase the number of individuals of species X, Y, and Z? (i.e., the desired species)

- Are there vernal pools on the property? If so, where are they?
- What natural communities are found on the property? Where are they located?
- Are there problematic pests or diseases on the property? If so, where are they?
- Is the property worthy of special protection?
- Does the property serve as a wildlife corridor for any valued species?
- Might management of the property affect water quality?
- Who is using the property? For what purpose? When? How often?

appendix 3
Statistical Jargon That You Are Likely to Encounter

alpha (α):   The probability level (usually 0.05) that is used as a benchmark for deciding whether data are sufficiently compelling to reject the **null hypothesis** (see definition below). The 0.05 value (or 0.01, or 0.10, or any other alpha level that you choose) refers to the probability that the null hypothesis will be rejected when it should not be. For example, if your null hypothesis were *honeysuckles are no more abundant along roads than they are in the interior forest,* and if you set α = 0.05, you would be saying: I can live with a 5 percent chance that I might mistakenly conclude that honeysuckles are more abundant along roads when, in fact, they really aren't. (If you were to choose α = 0.01 instead of α = 0.05, you would be setting the bar higher: you would be deciding that a 5 percent chance of making the wrong conclusion is too risky; you are only willing to take a 1 percent risk.)

analysis of variance (ANOVA):   A statistical technique used to compare things to determine how likely it is (based on probability) that they really are different.

confidence interval (CI):   The range of values (high and low) that circumscribes, with known probability, the true value of something that has been sampled. For example, if you were to sample mosquito abundance in Hidden Marsh (as a way to estimate how many mosquitoes there really are), you might report an average density (an estimate that is based on the data you collected) and a 95 percent confidence interval. The confidence interval would signify—according to your probabilistic calculations—that you're 95 percent sure that the *true* density of mosquitoes in Hidden Marsh falls between some range of values—for example, 0.3 and 2.7 mosquitoes per cubic meter of air.

correlation: A statistical measure of the strength of relationship between two different variables. Correlation should not be confused with *causation*.

For example, a strong correlation between dirty sneakers and good grades does not mean that dirty sneakers *cause* good grades, or that good grades *cause* sneakers to be dirty.

correlation coefficient: A calculated value, between −1.0 and +1.0, that indicates the strength and type of relationship between two variables of interest. A positive value indicates a positive relationship, such as the relationship between human height and shoe size (as a person's height increases, his or her shoe size also usually increases). A negative value indicates a negative relationship, such as the relationship between latitude and air temperature (as distance from the equator gets larger, the air temperature gets lower). The closer the correlation coefficient is to +1.0 or to −1.0, the stronger the relationship; a correlation coefficient of zero would indicate that there is no relationship whatsoever between the two variables.

data set: the collection of measurements or observations.

degrees of freedom (DF, df, d.f.):   The number used in statistical calculations that accounts for number of samples measured (i.e., **sample size**). The larger the sample size, the more degrees of freedom.

dependent variable: The thing you measure to determine if the independent variable has any effect. If, for example, you wanted to assess how different concentrations of a chemical affect algal growth in a river, the dependent variable would be algal growth and the independent variable would be concentrations of the chemical (see also **regression**).

H_1:   The alternative hypothesis—what you predict is true.

H_0:   The null hypothesis (see **null hypothesis**).

independent variable: See **dependent variable** and **regression**.

mean: Another word for average.

n: See **sample size**.

null hypothesis: The opposite of what you predict is going on (i.e., the opposite of the alternative hypothesis). For example, if you hypothesize (believe) that the number of nesting bobolinks in Illinois is lower now than it was ten years ago, your null hypothesis would be *the number of nesting bobolinks in Illinois is at least as high as it was ten years ago*. (Your alternative hypothesis would be *the number of nesting bobolinks in Illinois is lower than it was ten years ago*.)

observation: The term used to refer to one element in the data set.

P value (P):   A value calculated from your data set that establishes the likelihood of your null hypothesis being true. If the calculated P value is lower than the alpha value that you set as a benchmark, then the null hypothesis is rejected (and your alternative hypothesis is supported).

If α is set at 0.05, for example, and if the P value (calculated from your data) is lower than 0.05, then scientists would reject the null hypothesis (which is the same thing conceptually as saying that they are 95 percent sure that their alternative hypothesis is correct).

random sampling: Where every site or individual within a study area has an exactly equal chance of being sampled. To answer comparative and process-type questions you *must* sample randomly. (And remember: random sampling is *not* the same as sampling all parts of a study area equally!)

regression: A way to describe the relationship between two or more variables, where the value of one (the dependent variable) is determined by the value of the other (the independent variable). The strength of the relationship is expressed mathematically by the r^2 value (see below).

r^2: A statistical calculation that indicates the strength of a relationship between two things. The possible values of r^2 range from zero to 1.0—the higher the r^2, the stronger the relationship.

sample: Something that is measured or observed (the collection of samples constitutes your data set).

sample size (n): The number of observations or measurements you have for a thing of interest. For example, if you measured the phosphorus level of five different streams, your sample size would be five.

sampling: The act of collecting data.

significant: The term used to indicate that the null hypothesis is rejected (which is as close as you can get to saying that your hypothesis is true). For example, if the alpha level is set at 0.05 (i.e., $\alpha = 0.05$), and if the calculated P value (from your data) is less than 0.05, then the results would be significant. Based on a pre-established, α-value benchmark, this is the same as saying that the data did not support the null hypothesis.

Note: in science, the terms *significant* and *significance* are not used casually—they have specific, statistical meanings that are grounded in probability. Avoid using these terms until you fully grasp their statistical meaning.

standard deviation (s, SD): Like variance, standard deviation is a measure of how similar or different individual measurements or observations are to each other. Said another way, it is how close the individual data points are to the mean—the greater the spread, the larger the standard deviation. (In mathematical terms, the standard deviation is the square root of the **variance** (see below).

standard error of the mean (SE): A measure of data variability that is similar to standard deviation except that sample size is factored into the calculation.

statistic: A value that describes a sample (e.g., the mean, the standard error, the confidence interval).

stratified random sampling: A data collecting approach to sampling where the study area is divided into zones of interest or distinction, with random sampling taking place within each zone. For example, if you wished to ensure that high, low, and medium elevations on a mountain were all sampled adequately, you could stratify your mountainside study area into three separate zones (high, medium, and low elevation) and then sample randomly within each of the three zones.

variance: A calculated value that describes how similar individual observations (data points) are to the mean. The higher the number, the more the data points vary from the average value and from one another.

Some symbols that you may encounter if you interact much with scientists or their reports:

Σ: The sum of everything listed.

α **(alpha)**: See **alpha**.

±: plus or minus: This symbol indicates the spread away from a mean value. For example, 8±3 means the average value is 8, with a range from 5 to 11.

*: indicates a *significant* result (usually that the P value, calculated from your data, is less than 0.05). (See **significant** above.)

**: indicates a *highly significant* result (usually that the P value is less than 0.01) a more compelling finding than *.

***: indicates a *very highly significant* result (usually that the P value is less than 0.001) an even more compelling finding than **.

- Clearly identify the exact question(s) you need answered before you start worrying about which techniques to use. The question dictates which data you need to collect and how you need to go about collecting it.
- Recognize that no "standard" method or technique is universally applicable. Whether it is appropriate for *your* use depends solely on the question you seek to answer.
- With almost no exceptions, you will learn more by collecting lots of data on a few things than you will by collecting just a few data on lots of things.
- Discuss your data collecting plan with a statistician before filling data sheets with numbers.
- Store data in a secure, accessible location that is known to all.
- Store all maps, file names, contacts, and detailed descriptions of data collecting methods and analyses *with* the data.
- When setting up a monitoring program, find a committed, responsible individual who will watch over the program into the future. Monitoring efforts that lack such a person break down or are abandoned.
- If there is any chance that you or someone else might someday wish to revisit or collect data at the same exact spots, permanently mark the locations before walking away from them. Record GPS coordinates, of course, but also install nondegradable, permanent physical markers such as lengths of PVC pipe driven into the ground, or aluminum tags secured to trees with aluminum wire or nails. (Never hammer iron or steel nails into trees; they are hazardous to loggers and sawyers when trees are cut.) Iron reinforcement bar (re-bar) is sometimes used to mark locations, but it is difficult to cut, heavy to transport, and tough on the shins when tripped over. Also, relocating re-bar stakes with a metal detector does not work as well as you might hope. Be advised that most

plastic flagging (surveyor's ribbon) breaks down after only a couple of years in the field, even sooner if it is subjected to direct sunlight. Nylon and fiberglass marking materials generally last longer.

- Take lots of pictures. To keep track of where each photo is taken (and to provide a sense of scale), write the photo's location in bold print on a sheet of paper and include it in the photo.
- Do not cram too much information on a data sheet. It breeds confusion. Set aside a column or leave wide, blank margins on the bottom and sides of data sheets where you can write notes, explanations, qualifications, uncertainties, changes in data collection protocol, problems, or anything else that is relevant to interpreting data on the sheet. If, for example, you decide midway through your data collecting effort to adopt a coding system to save time, explain the coding scheme in the margins of your data sheet.
- To avoid mistakes, do not copy over data sheets to make them neater—fix the originals instead.
- If you will be collecting lots of data on paper, use 8.5 x 11" sheets of paper—smaller sheets are easy to lose or misplace and they are tougher to run through a copier.
- Attach brightly colored flagging to your clipboard, backpack, and other field gear so they are easily located when they are dropped or left behind.

When you need financial or political help to conserve a property, the most effective way to engage people and get them onboard is to let the property do the talking for you. Every place has an interesting story to tell; you only need to find it. Your ability to figure out a place's story and tell it (chapter 4) is how you make a seemingly unspecial place come alive to others and become worthy of protection. The teachings below show some of the approaches and clues that landscape detectives use to demystify a place and accentuate its value.

Looking Beyond the Site's Boundaries

Establishing context—how a place fits into the bigger regional whole—is fundamental to understanding the place's story and its values. In fact, the value of a property—be it as a wildlife corridor, a biodiversity hotspot, or a refuge—often depends more on the surrounding acreage than on the property itself. For example, an island of undeveloped land that is surrounded by square miles of city such as Central Park in New York City has very different values from an identical property that is surrounded by thousands of acres of undeveloped land. If you were trying to provide a connection to other protected parcels for wide-ranging mammals—if that was the value you were assessing—a Central Park-type parcel would prove worthless. If you were assessing its value as a place for people to experience nature, however, or if you were assessing its worth as a stopover place for migrating birds, an island parcel like Central Park would be judged immeasurably valuable. As realtors would say, it is all about location, location, location. A site's surroundings define its location.

Landscape context is also critical when dealing with nonnative invasive species on a site. Trying to clear a place of invasives is labor-intensive, so survey surrounding properties for invasives before committing to an eradication effort on your site. Many problematic species such as barberry, buckthorn, and bush honeysuckle produce seeded fruits that birds eat and spread in their droppings. If surrounding properties are infested with these invasives, one-time efforts to remove them from *your* site have virtually no chance of long-term success. Birds will see to that.

A parcel of land can distinguish or separate itself from its surroundings in many ways, and you can identify some of them before ever stepping foot on a place. Studying aerial photos is a good way to start.[1] Where is the place? Is it an inholding in a larger, similar landscape, or is it an isolated island of greenery surrounded by agricultural fields, housing developments, or industrial parks? Is it in a high- or low-value district? Record your observations so that you can refer to them later.

Topographic maps also reveal a parcel's relationship to its surroundings by showing roads, power lines, quarries, nearness to urban areas, wetlands, rivers, steep landscapes, and other landforms that may affect whichever characteristics or values you are assessing.

You can gauge the market value of a property by checking real estate listings for comparable properties. Zillow.com is especially useful because it shows the selling history of parcels, including those that are not currently on the market. Comparing the expected selling price of your parcel of interest against comparable properties elsewhere tells you much about a site's desirability for development.

USDA County Soil Surveys provide landscape analyses of almost every acre of land in the United States.[2] The first few pages of every survey summarize physical features of the region—the county's climate, geology, and topography. Thereafter, the survey shows maps of the county's soils and describes their specific characteristics and uses. You need not know much about soils to make use of the survey, just find your parcel on the survey's map and look up (in the survey) what the lettered abbreviations (e.g., LyD, BeC) in and around your parcel stand for. Each labeled soil type (called a "soil series") details depth to bedrock, drainage, fertility, stoniness, steepness of slope, crop productivity, likely tree and wildlife species, and the site's most appropriate management use.

---

1. Two free online sources of aerial photographs are Google Earth and Bing Maps.
2. These publications are free (https://websoilsurvey.sc.egov.usda.gov/App/HomePage.htm).

Landscape detectives heavily rely on County Soil Surveys. Surveys are so useful, in fact, that some environmental consultants have been known to assess a parcel without ever visiting the place—relying solely on what they glean from the soil survey.

Seeing the Forest for the Trees

When you first step foot on a place, you immediately notice things of all sorts, and those landscape "pieces" shape your impression of the place. Without thinking about it, you naturally focus on landscape pieces that dominate or are striking, noticeable, or interesting (e.g., hilliness, temperature, sameness of tree size). As you become more familiar with a place, however, your landscape viewing becomes more reductionist, and you focus more on individual pieces and less on the landscape as a whole. At some point, interesting discoveries such as a fox den may become more important to you than a less exciting landscape feature like site hilliness.

When trying to figure out a place's story, you *do* want to seek out and tell reductionist discoveries like the fox den, of course, but you also need to factor in the big picture background in which the small-scale discoveries find themselves. The best time to capture and record the big picture of a place is during your first visit because, as time goes by and you become increasingly familiar with the site, big picture things become forgotten background noise. If you have not taken measures to capture and remind yourself of the bigger picture, you can stop seeing the forest for the trees. Then you miss a critical part of the place's story.

To capture the big picture of a place before it retreats from sight, I always take these precautionary measures on my first visit to a site:

- I take lots of photographs; and
- I pretend that I am describing the place in a letter to a close friend who lives across the country. I spend five to seven minutes writing first impressions and whatever else comes to mind about the place.

Searching Out Clues and Indicators

Everyone naturally focuses on what they find interesting, of course— geologists, for example, examine a site's landforms and rocks in great detail but are likely to pay less attention to the site's birds, just as birders scan the landscape for birds but probably pay less attention to the rocks. The landscape elements that do not immediately attract your attention can reveal much of a place's story, however.

One effective way to expand your radar so you do not miss revealing landscape clues and indicators is to conceptually break a site into its contributing parts or "layers"—the site's terrain, its rocks and soil; its trees, shrubs, and ground cover; its wildlife; and its human artifacts—and then search for clues and indicators in each layer, one at a time.

Some Terrain, Rock, and Soil Clues

A site's terrain—its slopes, hills, and valleys—results from geologic forces and soil development that have been massaged by wind, water, and human activity. To get a handle on the basic geology underlying a place—and the role it plays in configuring the place—start with the geologic overview in the introductory section of your county's soil survey. For more detailed insights in the United States and Canada, check out the *Roadside Guide to Geology* series.[3] The geology departments of regional colleges and universities can also provide useful assistance, as can the maps and documents librarian at your state or provincial university.

The rocks and attendant forces that create a site's topography and terrain also help create the site's soil.[4] All things being equal (which they often are not), if you dig a hole in an older forest, the soil will change color, texture, and composition as you dig downward. At the ground surface you will find recognizable leaves and twigs; immediately below you will find partially broken-down leaves and twigs underlain by dark, decomposed, unrecognizable organics. Those unrecognizable organic fragments, usually within a few inches of the surface, grade into and mix with fine mineral particles until, at greater depth, the organics disappear and the soil is just mineral sand or clay. If you dig deep enough, you eventually will run into solid, impenetrable rock. That is what you *expect* to find when you dig a hole in the forest.

Expectations are useful because they give you things to look for when you are sleuthing a site. Deviations from the expected—or adherence to them—provide clues and insights that can help you unravel a place's story. Here are some clues to watch for:

- The ground is pretty flat and smooth. If the site is forested and the land surface lacks dips and mounds, the site was probably smoothed out by

---

3. You can find the series at https://mountain-press.com/collections/roadside-geology.
4. Passage of time, and a place's climate and living things, also play important roles.

plowing or pasturing sometime in the past. (Unmanaged forested land is naturally bumpy from pits and mounds created by past uprooting of trees.) Site flatness also may mean that the place was under a beaver pond or other quiet body of water for a number of years. When silt particles in water settle to the bottom, they fill in depressions, and the fine, dark silt sediment—often four to six inches deep—becomes the topmost layer of soil. Look for this.

- Rocks have rounded edges. Rounded rocks got that way by tumbling in water over an extended period, just as broken glass on the beach loses its sharp edges after continued pounding by ocean waves. Rounded rocks in a place therefore tell you that they came from a place that was once an ocean shore or streambed with lots of current or wave action. If your place is in a northerly glaciated region with no hint of a stream or seashore nearby, the rounded rocks had to come from a distant place, plucked up by the glacier and dumped on your site.
- Loose rocks are different types. As a rule, the underlying bedrock on a site tends to be of one single type. Since loose rocks are nothing more than small chunks of bedrock, seeing different types of loose rocks on a site tells you that they did not originate onsite; they came from different places and were somehow transported to the site, most likely by humans or glacier.
- The surface soil is pretty much rock-free. All else being equal, every site *should* have loose rocks because every site has underlying bedrock. Sites that lack surface rocks are places where, sometime in the past, wind or water deposited enormous volumes of silt or sand or clay particles over the underlying rocks.
- The onsite rock is limestone or another calcium-rich rock.[5] This tells you that your site was once under a warm, shallow sea (think coral reefs and where you find them). After millions of years of calcium-rich coral and seashells settling to the bottom and ultimately becoming rock, movement of underlying tectonic plates transported the limestone-rich rock to its present location your site. Identifying areas with calcium-rich rock is important because it helps you identify places that are likely to be biologically rich. Rare plants are often found growing on, or at the base of, calcium-rich cliffs; streams running through calcium-rich rock have more life than identical streams that do not.

---

5. You can learn this from geologic maps or from the County Soil Survey.

- The soil is dominated by sand or clay, or by fine-grained silt. These textures suggest that at some time in the past water deposited sediment on the site.[6] When water moves quickly, only heavy particles (pebbles and large-grained sands) are left behind; as the water slows, smaller, less heavy particles (finer-grained sands) fall out and sink to the bottom. Eventually, if the water becomes completely still, the finest particles (clays and silts) settle to the bottom. (You can observe this process in real time by following a stream from its gushing headwaters in the mountains, where the bottom is rocky, to its imperceptible flow in the flat lowlands, where the bottom is mucky. Watch also for differences in sediment type in channels and eddies.)
- The soil is soggy, and surface water has a multicolored, oil-like sheen. This sheen *might* be a pollutant but, more probably, it comes from naturally occurring metals in the saturated soil rusting (oxidizing) when they seep out of the saturated, oxygen-deficient soil. To tell if the sheen is oil or oxidized metal, poke the sheeny film with your finger. If it breaks apart into pieces, you are witnessing naturally occurring metals emerging from a permanently saturated place. If the sheen does not break into distinct units, the sheen is an oil-based pollutant.
- You come across blackened wood. Blackish chunks of wood might indicate a past fire, but rotting wood can also be blackish. To differentiate charred wood (and past fire) from wood that is just decomposing, rub a black chunk on paper. If the chunk leaves a bold, charcoal-like mark, it came from a fire on the site. Rotting wood does not leave a bold mark.
- You dig a hole, and the mineral soil has grayish and rusty splotches. This tells you that the site's water table fluctuates up and down, and that the soil is sometimes saturated with water, causing iron and other naturally occurring metals in the soil to rust.
- The soil has an unexpectedly thick organic layer. This hints at a number of possible goings-on. A soil's organic layer develops when fallen leaf litter and other organic material break down slowly or incompletely. Chronically low temperature, low moisture, low oxygen, few soil nutrients, or high acidity (or some combination) are the likely culprits. Consider each when seeking to understand why a site of interest has an unexpectedly thick organic layer.

---

6. Wind is also a possibility, but water is more likely.

- You dig a hole and encounter a distinct layer of bleached sand or ash about six to ten inches down. This usually signifies that the soil is acidic and has not been plowed for a very long time, if ever.
- You dig a hole, and the top six to twelve inches of soil (measure it) lacks noticeable layering—it all looks the same—but the soil color changes noticeably as you go deeper. This homogeneity in surface soil appearance indicates that a farmer plowed the soil sometime in the past and, in so doing, mixed the top horizons of soil. You know, therefore, that crops were once planted on the site. (The depth of the plow layer [soil scientists refer to it as the "Ap horizon"] suggests how recently the site may have been plowed. Plowing to a depth of eight or more inches may not be a problem for tractors—which became common farm implements in the 1920s—but plowing to that depth was nigh impossible before that time, when a horse, ox, or family member was pulling the plow.)
- The soil of your forested site has no organic layer of soil, or the organic layer is unexpectedly thin. One possibility is that the site is a young forest that has not produced enough years of abundant leaf litter to make much of an organic layer. Another possibility is that fallen leaves and other organics were eaten by animals or decomposers before they accumulated. This is common in the moist tropics, but night crawlers (large, nonnative worms) do the same thing in some northerly places. (Look for holes in the ground that are surrounded by worm castings.)
- The fine (hair-like) roots in soil concentrate in a particular place. "Fine roots" (the thread-like roots that take up most of a plant's water and nutrients) proliferate where resources are most available, so you can surmise the nutrient or water status of a site by where fine roots are most concentrated. But fine roots also cluster near the surface of soils that are flooded for extended periods. If you dig a hole and find gray and rusty soil mottling, saturated soil is behind a buildup of fine roots near the soil surface.

Some Plant Clues and Indicators

Plants (once you are able to identify them) can tell you lots about a place, but their relevance is very region-specific. Local experts can tell you which species to look for.[7] In speculating on why a tree is where it is or isn't, however,

---

7. Alumni of the Field Naturalist Graduate Program (https://fnepalumni.com/) and staff of The Nature Conservancy can usually help you with this.

think beyond the site as it currently exists. The current growing environment only tells you that the tree is *tolerating* the place now—it does *not* tell you that the place is necessarily better than places that lack the tree. Trees are most sensitive to shortcomings in the growing environment during their first year of life; anything short of a near perfect growing environment means that a seedling will not survive its first year. To understand why a mature tree is in a place, you therefore need to understand the site's growing conditions in that first year; those growing conditions reveal much about the site's past.

Knowing the life history requirements of tree seeds and seedlings helps you narrow down what the growing site was like at time zero. In North America, two free publications from the US Forest Service, *Silvics of North America* and *Seeds of Woody Plants in the United States* are fabulous resources.[8] For example:

- A cluster of paper birch on a site tells you that the birch seeds established in a large clearing that received full sunlight and that, almost certainly, had exposed mineral soil rather than a thick layer of leaves at the surface. Knowing the site's growing environment at time zero strongly hints at what probably created those conditions—fire or extensive logging.
- Finding hemlock, in contrast, tells you a completely different story about what the place was like when the seed germinated and grew into a seedling. Hemlock seeds and seedlings need steady, relatively cool temperatures to survive, so they establish under the shade of existing trees.[9] A site hit by large-scale fire or logging would not create that growing environment.
- You find one or more ancient-looking apple trees in the forest. In the past, when people relied less on buying food from stores, they planted apple trees near their houses. Apple trees need full sunlight to produce a good crop, so you know that the land was open (probably pasture) when the apple trees were planted. If you aged the apple trees by counting their growth rings, you could tell when the apples were planted; if you aged the co-occurring trees and added ten or fifteen years to their age, you could get a rough idea of when the landowner stopped caring for the apples and let the field develop into forest.

---

8. *Silvics of North America* is available at https://www.srs.fs.usda.gov/pubs/misc/ag_654/table_of_contents.htm; and *Seeds of Woody Plants in the United States* is at https://www.fs.usda.gov/treesearch/pubs/32626.

9. Paper birch and hemlock are just two examples of species that can tell you much about conditions of a site at time zero.

- Trees have similar diameters.[10] An "even-aged forest" is brought on by a site's growing conditions suddenly improving, so that a pulse of new trees comes in. Letting cropland or pasture revert back to forest (i.e., no longer plowing or grazing the site) accomplishes this, as does a severe disturbance that wipes out established vegetation (e.g., fire, logging, hurricane).
- Dead trees or snags cluster in a place. If running water is nearby, even a trickle, the area with snags was probably once a beaver pond. Look for old beaver chewings along the forest edge, remnants of a beaver dam downstream, silty soil with few rocks, and a smooth ground surface.
- The base of some trees is blackened. Rub paper on the blackened wood: if the rubbing leaves a dark charcoal mark, the place was burned. If the rubbing does *not* leave a charcoal mark, bacteria and fungi caused the black, not fire.
- Most trees growing along the shore of a water body are conifers (pine, spruce, fir, hemlock, or cedar) but most inland trees are broadleaf, not conifer. It *may* be, of course, that the waterfront sites favor conifers over leafy, deciduous trees. It also may be that beavers removed the tastier aspen, birch, and other deciduous stems and left behind the less tasty conifers. Look for beaver chewings near the water's edge.
- Tree roots are exposed. Trees send roots *into* soil, not on top of it, so some past event(s) must have removed the topsoil that covered the roots. Erosion seems the likeliest explanation, but what *prompted* the erosion? Look for clues that would suggest foot traffic, mountain bikes, horses, ATVs, overgrazing, or logging.
- A tree has stilted roots (see fig. A-5.1). The tree grew from a seed that germinated on, and sent its roots into, a rotting stump. When the stump's wood rotted away, the roots in the rotting stump were exposed.
- A farm field has a large tree in it. If the rest of the field is plowed and planted in crops, the isolated tree is probably growing over a ledge or a large boulder near the soil surface where the farmer could not plow. (The tree also might mark where the farmer piled rocks to make plowing the cropland easier.) Isolated trees in a farm field might also have been left to provide shade on hot days for livestock.

---

10. Neither diameter nor height of a tree indicates its age in years, but trees of the same species that have similar diameters and heights probably established at about the same time and, therefore, are about the same age.

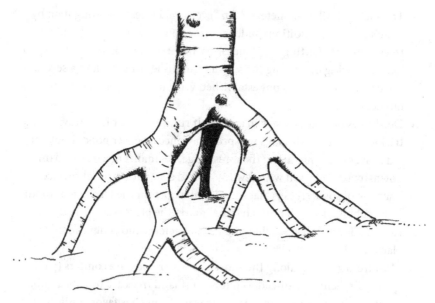

FIGURE A-5.1. Exposed, stilt-like tree roots indicate that the tree began life growing on and into a rotting stump. Roots that had grown through the stump were exposed when the stump's wood rotted away.

- Some trees have large lower limbs. These trees grew up in an open, unshaded place (probably a pasture).
- Buckthorn, or another nonnative shrub, completely dominates streamside vegetation. Beavers probably cut and removed native trees and shrubs but left the invasive nonnatives because they tasted bad. The opportunistic nonnatives exploited the high-light environment that was created by beavers removing the native competitors. (Unfortunately, the monoculture of nonnatives can persist long after beavers leave the site because the established nonnatives shade out native species that might otherwise establish.)

Before moving on to other clues and indicators, two misconceptions about trees are worth noting. The first is that "selectively harvesting trees" is good and "clearcutting" is bad.[11] There are cases where this is true, of course, but there are other cases where it is not. Some species, like birch and aspen, *only*

---

11. Trained foresters bristle when they hear people advocating "selective harvest" because too often "selective harvest" winds up being the same thing as "high grading"—cutting out the good trees and leaving the lousy ones behind. That practice dooms the future forest.

establish and form stands in large forest openings that receive full sunlight. Removing a tree here and there ("selective harvest") does not provide that growing environment, complete removal of overstory trees ("clearcutting") does. A large forest opening (created by clearcutting) also promotes the abundant, diverse understory growth that numerous animals require for food and cover. "Clearcutting," therefore, when practiced by a knowledgeable forester, is sometimes an effective conservation practice. "Selective harvest" may not be.

A second common misconception is about a tree's monetary worth. A single tree *might be* worth a lot of money, of course, but usually it is worth far less than imagined. A large beech, birch, or aspen tree in New England, for example, may yield no more than fifteen dollars total (if that) *once it is delivered to the mill*. Of that fifteen dollars, probably only five dollars would go to the landowner; the rest would go to pay the logger, the trucker, and the forester.[12]

Changing market forces affect a tree's value, of course, but the money you might get for a cut tree depends on species, diameter, straightness of a sixteen-foot section of its trunk, wood soundness, and number of large branches. The money you might get for a harvested tree also depends on how far the tree has to be dragged through the woods before it is loaded onto a log truck, and how many miles it has to be trucked to a mill that is willing to buy the type of logs that you are delivering. Also recognize that a logger needs to fill at least a couple of log trucks with sixteen-foot logs to make a logging job worth his while. Getting logging equipment onsite costs time and money, so if a woodlot cannot generate several loads of logs, you the owner of the trees may need to *pay* the logger to take your trees![13]

Human Artifacts

You can deduce much about a place and its story by paying attention to these human-created clues:

- *Cemetery.* As any grave digger knows, the soil should be deep, easily dug, well-drained, with few rocks, and the water table should be more than six feet down.

---

12. For those who have not orchestrated a timber sale, I strongly advise working with a forester.

13. Google *extension forester, consulting forester,* or *Forest Service* to find someone who can help you understand the value of trees on a parcel.

- *Silo.* A silo indicates that, when the silo was installed, the place was mainly a dairy or cattle farm. (Silos are built to store silage food for cows and cattle, not so much for other livestock.)
- *Wire fence.* Wire fences, barbed or otherwise, are strung for livestock containment. Check to see to which side of the post or tree the wire is attached; the attachment side is the livestock side. (Pushing wire against a post will not detach the staple, but pushing wire away from the post might.)
- *Stone wall.* Older stone walls and fences were built for functional reasons, rarely for aesthetics.[14] A stone wall may have been built to mark a property boundary or to contain livestock, but it also may be nothing more than a linear place where rocks from a plowed field were dumped. You can deduce the main reason someone built a wall by inspecting the size of rocks in the wall. If the rocks are all large, the wall was probably built to fence livestock (probably cows) in or out. If the wall has smaller rocks also, the wall was a dumping place for unwanted rocks taken from a crop field to make plowing easier. Since it is easier to carry rocks downhill than uphill, the rocks in a wall probably came from an upslope or adjacent location. As for which location was plowed, look for the place with an even ground surface (as noted earlier, plowing smooths out the ground surface).
- If you find a stone wall that runs along the slope's contour, compare the distance to ground on the uphill and downhill sides of the wall. If the distance from the top of the wall to the ground on the downhill side of the wall is noticeably greater than on the uphill side, that tells you that the upslope land was severely eroded, almost certainly by plowing or severe overgrazing. (When the eroding soil from the upslope hit the stone wall, it settled, raising the ground level.)
- *Rock pile.* Moving rocks out of a field to facilitate plowing is hard work. If the rocks removed from a crop field could be used to fence livestock in or out, farmers may have gone to the extra trouble of building a wall with the removed rocks. If livestock containment was less important, however, or if the location for a livestock fence was distant, dumping rocks in piles was quicker, easier, and made more sense. (As with rock walls, the size of rocks in a pile suggests why they were placed there.)

---

14. Mansions and wealthy estates are possible exceptions.

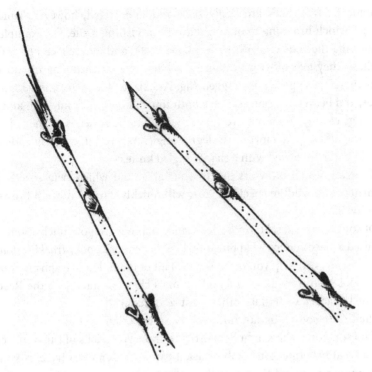

FIGURE A-5.2. The twig with a torn, ragged tip (on left) was browsed by a member of the deer family (e.g., deer, elk, moose). These mammals lack upper front teeth, so they remove twigs by pulling or tearing rather than by biting twigs off cleanly. The twig with a sharply cut tip (on right) was browsed by a rabbit or rodent. These mammals have upper and lower front teeth, so they bite twigs off cleanly, often at a forty-five-degree angle.

- *Painted blaze on a tree or post.* Blazes have meaning and purpose, but the color and designs vary regionally. In New England, red paint is used to mark property boundaries, and blue paint is used to mark trees for cutting. Different conventions are sometimes used elsewhere, however.[15]

Some Wildlife Clues

Many wildlife clues are subtle or short-lived and are keyed to weather, season, or time of day. As a result, they can be tougher to see and interpret than clues from other layers.

---

15. Local foresters and surveyors can tell you the meaning of blaze colors and designs in your area.

Some wildlife clues are easily seen and interpreted, however. You can deduce which browsing mammals have been visiting a site, for example, by examining the ends of browsed twigs. Deer, elk, and moose lack upper front teeth, so they tear off twigs rather than bite them off cleanly; remnant twig ends therefore appear a bit ragged (fig. A-5.2). Rabbits, hares, mice, porcupines, and beaver, in contrast, have both top and bottom front teeth and bite off twigs cleanly. They remove twigs by angling their heads to the side and snipping off twigs at a forty-five-degree angle. As a result, cut twig ends look like they were removed with a sharp, angled knife.

Knowing which browsers live in your area, and which twig species and diameter each wildlife species favors, will quickly narrow down a browser's identity.

Of course, tracks, scat, trails, dens, and rubbings tell you much about who has used a place and for what purpose. Paul Rezendez's book, *Tracking and the Art of Seeing*, will help you make sense of all of them. Photographs in Rezendez's book also show how different animals chew on nuts. (See the Recommended Reading section for other great resources.)

The best resource by far, however, is an experienced hunter or trapper. To find someone who might be willing to show you tricks of the trade, contact a local fish and game club or ask a game warden for advice. If you do get a chance to spend time outside with an experienced hunter or trapper, *watch how she walks.* Here is what you will see: *she spends very little time looking at her feet.* You will see many more animals, and many more of their (and other) clues, if you learn to walk *with your eyes up* rather than down.[16]

If your site has a stream or pond nearby, check it for snails, clams, and mussels. These animals need lots of calcium for their shells, so an abundance of shelled animals in a place indicates that plenty of calcium is present. That is worth knowing, because calcium-rich sites are productive and biologically rich.

---

16. Scanning the landscape while walking is easier said than done. One's natural inclination is to scout out the ground ahead to avoid tripping. To develop the hunter's "heads up not down" skill, practice first on a flat, uncluttered lawn or parking lot. Start your walk by glancing at the few feet of ground in front of you and then lifting your head and scanning the horizon as you take several slow steps forward. Then take another quick glance downward to see what lies in your path for the next few steps, memorize it, and then lift your head and take another few steps forward. Practice until you are able to walk twenty steps without looking down. You are now ready for more challenging terrain.

Some Legacy and Land-Use History Clues

You can learn a great deal about a place's past by studying old aerial photographs and by connecting with members of a local historical society. The United States Censuses of Agriculture, compiled at ten-year intervals from 1840 to 1930, and at five-year intervals thereafter, can tell you lots about a place also.

A surprising amount of information can be gleaned from town office records, including information that you might assume is nobody's business. Here is just a sampling of what is public information:

- the names and addresses of current and past owners of the parcel
- when the property was purchased, from whom, and for how much
- how much it is worth today (and how the assessed value has changed over time)
- the property boundaries and acreage
- easements, rights-of-way
- property taxes, and whether the landowner paid on time

Again, all of this is public information so do not hesitate to (nicely) seek the clerk's help. Real estate speculators do it all the time.

To go back further into the historical record, query the special collections librarian at your state university for possible information sources. While you are at it, ask if your place of interest is covered in a *Beer's Atlas*.

appendix 6
Some Ways to Make Meetings Better

- Don't hold a meeting when you can get away with not doing so.
- Be clear what the meeting is *not* about. For example: *Tonight, we will not be getting into the weeds about zoning, and we won't be rehashing last week's debate . . .*
- Keep meetings small when you want participants to engage actively; the larger the group, the less responsibility each individual will take for what happens.
- When you are aiming to get lots done in a hurry, schedule fifteen-minute meetings where everyone stands rather than sits.
- Review past minutes periodically to avoid rehashing what has already been decided.
- Stay humble—people resist being led by an arrogant jackass.
- Don't assume that *you* are the best person to run a meeting—oftentimes you are not.
- Motivate participants with honest and direct post-meeting memos. For example: *Jack—Good meeting today, thank you for your input. We made good progress generating ideas about xxxx; our next step (in our next meeting) is to decide what to do. Please do your best to help us move this along. Thanks!—Jeff. (next meeting is Tuesday, March 14, at 11am, same place)*
- Anticipate the physical needs of meeting participants—people cannot concentrate when they are hungry, thirsty, tired, or need a bathroom.
- Recap the main points of a meeting before adjourning; thank participants for their time and participation.
- Reserve a few minutes of quiet time for yourself after each meeting to review and record what went well and what didn't.

What an Effective Agenda Looks Like

When running the meeting, always cover items in the order listed on the agenda, placing the most pressing items first. And don't run over the time allocated for an item!

Meeting Agenda for the Clear Creek Conservation Commission
to be held January 13, 20xx, 6:30–8:00 pm, in Room 112 of the Sumner Town Hall, Sumner, Tennessee
Note: If you have questions or if you cannot attend, please contact [provide a name, telephone number, and email address] by January 5.

THE PURPOSE OF THIS MEETING IS TO [spell out the reason for meeting, and what you're hoping to achieve]

CALL TO ORDER: [identify the person who's chairing the meeting in parentheses]

ROUTINE BUSINESS (eight minutes)

1. Review the agenda
2. Approve the minutes from the last meeting
3. Informational announcements and updates (presented by the chairperson)
4. Status reports
   - from the chairperson
   - from other members of the group [identify who they are]
   - from committees [identify who they are]

UNFINISHED BUSINESS

1. Item under discussion when the last meeting adjourned [state clearly what this item is; also clearly state the meeting objective—what the

desired outcome is]. For example: We ended last meeting identifying the pros and cons of joining forces with the White River Conservancy. Let's wrap up that item in these next five minutes by identifying additional pros and cons. Please keep your comments short and to the point so we can get them into the minutes and move on (five minutes).

2. [Another] Item prompted by the last meeting (four minutes).

NEW BUSINESS

1. State clearly the most important or pressing item (what the item is); also clearly state the meeting objective (what the desired outcome is). For example: To reach a decision about whether we should hire a lawyer to fight the proposed development along the East Branch tributary (six minutes).
2. The second most important or pressing item (seven minutes).
3. The third most important or pressing item (five minutes).
4. Other business (five minutes).

SET NEXT MEETING TIME
ADJOURN AT 8:00pm

Minutes for the Clear Creek Conservation Commission Meeting
Held January 13, 2xxx (6:30–8:00 pm) in the Sumner Town Hall
Chair: Susan Fink
Attending: Rachel Bossee, Karen Cooney, Susan Fink, Dana Good, Jeffrey Hughes, James Jensen, Mary Moore, Frank Smith
The meeting was called to order by Susan Fink at 6:33 pm.
MINUTES of the Sept. 6, 2xxx Planning Meeting were approved as submitted.

ANNOUNCEMENTS AND UPDATES

- Farmer Jones has received a grant from the state to restore fifty meters of failing streambank just downstream of his dairy barn.
- The town of Sumner has scheduled an open town meeting to discuss its draft of the town plan. The meeting will be held in the Sumner Fire Station at 7–9 pm, March 2, 2xxx.

REPORTS

- Karen Cooney attended the Huntington River Watershed Association annual meeting. She reported that the Huntington River Association is willing to coordinate its fundraising efforts with the Clear Creek Conservation Commission. She will follow up on this by scheduling a meeting with them by mid-April 2xxx; she will announce the meeting time, place, and agenda at our next meeting.

UNFINISHED BUSINESS FROM LAST MEETING

1. Dana Good completed his discussion of concerns about the upcoming election for Bristol Selectboard and how the outcome of that election might affect the Lewis Creek Watershed. James Jensen and Mary Moore volunteered to work with Dana to make and install twenty campaign signs supporting Jerry Meyer by May 1, 2xxx.

NEW BUSINESS

1. Extending the sewer line to Pheasant Heights—Susan summarized the issues as:
   - Quality of drinking water in homes downslope of Pheasant Heights is sometimes compromised by failing septic systems in Pheasant Heights.
   - The cost of extending the sewer line to Pheasant Heights will be borne by Sumner residents who do not live in Pheasant Heights. Monthly water/sewage rates of Sumner residents will probably increase by about $3.00/month if the sewage line is extended.
   - Extending the sewage line to Pheasant Heights will pave the way for development and subdivision of Sandy Hill's farm. Sandy is retiring from farming and apparently wishes to cash in on her land.
2. Frank Smith asked Susan to clarify what she meant by "compromised" drinking water quality. Susan explained that, as she understands it, some residents downslope of Pheasant Heights complain that their water tastes funny the day after a heavy rainstorm. Susan was not aware of any water quality tests that had been performed on this well water.
3. Rachel Bossee suggested that the Clear Creek Conservation Commission needs to act quickly to understand how serious the water quality problem really is. She volunteered to contact all homeowners immediately downslope of Pheasant Heights and ask them if they would be willing to collect a drinking water sample after the next large rainstorm. Rachel asked James Jensen if he could arrange to have the samples analyzed for fecal coliform.

ADJOURNMENT
The meeting was adjourned at 7:56 pm.
Recorded by Jeffrey Hughes

appendix 9
Checklist of Reminders When Preparing for a Public Meeting

- Post directional signs at confusing places in the building if the location of the meeting room is not obvious. Also post directional signs for the bathrooms.
- Be sure the room is neat and clean and a suitable temperature, and that chairs and tables are arranged the way you want them. If you are meeting in an unnecessarily large space and you want people to sit near the front (always a good idea), block off chairs in the back with flagging to keep people from sitting there. You can open these rows incrementally if more people show up than anticipated.
- Check projection equipment and lights to make sure everything works. Have tape and flip charts handy, and markers that work. If there is a chance that someone might wish to take notes during the meeting, have paper and pens on hand.
- Create a friendly, personalized meeting space. Snacks help establish a friendly, welcoming environment.
- Wear a name tag; have supplies handy so attendees can do likewise.
- In a prominent place for all to see, display the meeting's purpose and ground rules (e.g., treat one another with respect, please; avoid personal assaults; limit your comments to the topic at hand). Prominently displayed ground rules give you something to refer back to if someone goes off the rails and needs to be reined back in.
- Ask attendees to keep their comments brief so that everyone has a chance to speak and be heard—three minutes per spoken contribution protects against a few individuals dominating the meeting. If you do ask people to observe a time limit, be sure to enforce the time rule evenly and consistently. Doing so sends a message that you are in control and not playing favorites.

Overview of Parliamentary Procedure and Rules of Order

Strict adherence to parliamentary procedure and rules of order is more involved, time-consuming, and stuffy than simply asking meeting participants, for example, "Does anyone have a problem with that? OK, let's move on then." It is tempting to forgo formal protocol in favor of a more casual approach, and very often a more relaxed approach makes sense. Other times, however, such as when the assembly is large or has several strong personalities, strict adherence to parliamentary procedure is needed to keep the meeting on track and under control.

Below is an overview of what parliamentary procedure looks like. Note that many formal meetings (e.g., a governing board) have additional procedural steps, such as establishing a quorum and approving the minutes from the last meeting.

At the appointed meeting start time, the chairperson calls the meeting to order and thanks people for coming. The chair then gives a very brief (less than one minute) overview of what the meeting is about and how the meeting will be conducted—who will do what and when. This quick review of the meeting agenda and process orients people, settles them down, and gets the meeting off the ground.

The chairperson now quickly dispenses with the next order of business—announcements, updates, and information exchange about noncontroversial items. A good chair keeps things moving—expediency sets a tone of efficiency and professionalism for the rest of the meeting. It also fast-forwards the meeting so that you can start dealing with meaty stuff while everyone is still fresh.

With routine business out of the way, the meeting turns to the main matter at hand. When someone other than the chairperson wishes to speak, that person raises his hand and asks to be *recognized* (given permission to speak) by the chairperson. If several hands go up at once, the chair assigns them an order in which they will get to speak.

Once recognized, the speaker *has the floor* for as long as she wishes to speak, or until a pre-allotted time for speaking has expired. When the first recognized speaker has had her say or used up her pre-allotted time, the next person in line is recognized.

A speaker who has the floor may not be interrupted by another participant unless she is *out of order*—ranting about something that has no relevance or behaving in a threatening manner. The chair may intercede if necessary to maintain order.

When someone wants to introduce a matter for consideration (a *question* in the parlance of parliamentary procedure), he introduces the question as a *motion*. A motion is a statement of what he wants the group to vote on and approve; it will not be considered, however, unless at least one other person agrees that it is important. She would express that support by saying *I second that motion*, or *seconded*. If no one seconds a motion, the motion is abandoned.

Once a motion is seconded, members have the opportunity to discuss and debate the question before voting for or against the motion. When the chair feels that the question has been discussed adequately, she will call for a vote or ask people if they are ready to vote. To ensure that every voting member knows exactly what he is voting on, the chair restates the motion. The exact wording of the voted motion is recorded so there is a permanent record of what was decided. The result is binding—the question cannot be recycled for another vote unless a majority of the members vote to do so.

Parliamentary procedure has lots of jargon. See appendix 11 for what you are most likely to hear or use.

To make a motion or **I move that . . .**: how you introduce and propose an
action that you would like to be voted on or implemented.

I second that motion or **seconded**: what someone says after a motion has
been made. If a motion is not seconded, the motion is jettisoned and the
group moves on. (Seconding a motion only means that you think the
motion warrants consideration.)

Do I hear a second? or **Is there a seconder for this motion?**: what the
chairperson says to see if someone wishes to second the motion.

I speak in favor of the motion . . .: how you preface your comments when
you support a motion (this makes it clear where you stand).

I speak in opposition to the motion . . .: how you preface your comments
when you oppose a motion.

I move to amend the motion by . . .: what you say to propose a change
in the stated motion so that it works better. A proposed amendment, if
seconded, is debated and then voted on; majority rules. If the amendment passes, the main motion is amended as proposed.

The chair recognizes Mr./Ms. X: what the chairperson says to tell someone that s/he may speak.

I rise to a point of information: what you say to interrupt the speaker to
point out an inaccuracy in what is being said.

I call for the orders of the day: how you interrupt the speaker if an
agenda item is being introduced out of order. The chair immediately
calls for a vote to determine the wishes of the group—to proceed as
is or to switch to whichever item the agenda says they should be focusing on.

I move to limit debate: what you say when you want to control how long
a motion is debated. For example: I move to limit debate on the motion
to thirty minutes (or) I move to limit the time of each speaker to five

minutes. A *second* is not required, and this subsidiary motion is not debatable, but a two-thirds majority is needed to approve it.

I move to close debate on the motion: what you say when you want to end discussion and vote.

I move to refer the motion to a committee: what you say if you think a committee, rather than the full group, should deal with a motion. This subsidiary motion, when seconded, is voted on; majority rules.

I move to table the motion: how you propose to postpone action on a motion. If this subsidiary motion is seconded and approved by majority vote, the main motion is removed from further discussion until another time.

If there is no further business, the meeting is adjourned: what the chairperson says to officially end the meeting. In very formal meetings, adjournment requires a motion, a second, and a majority in favor.

August 13, 20xx
   To: Frank Blowhard, President, Blowhard Industries
   cc: Jill Bluth, Shelburne Town Manager
   From: Jeffrey Hughes, Chair, Shelburne Conservation Commission
   RE: Questions about the accuracy of the wetland delineation of Frogland Marsh

Several town residents believe there may be inaccuracies in the recently completed (August 1, 20xx) wetland delineation of Frogland Marsh. Of particular concern is the extensive, northeast corner of the marsh that abuts Mildred Jones's property.

The hearing on August 30, 20xx (at 7:00 pm in the Shelburne Town Hall) will be an opportunity for concerned citizens to ask questions related to the siting of your proposed theme park near Frogland Brook. I expect several residents to attend this hearing and ask questions. To ensure that the hearing proceeds efficiently, please be sure that your wetland consultant is present to answer questions. Thank you.

I can be reached at 802-656-xxxx or Jeffrey.Hughes@xxx.org if you have any questions.

December 11, 20xx
To: Pam
From: Fred
Subject: Where we stand on our proposal to the Ebeneezer Foundation

Hi Pam,
Here's a quick update on the parts of the proposal I've been working on:

- I've summarized our activities these past six months and how they relate to our stated objectives (attached). As you'll see, it's only a draft, but I think it hits the main points. Please check it over for accuracy and completeness and get back to me with your comments by 4 pm tomorrow afternoon. I'll make revisions and send a final draft of that section to you by 10 pm tomorrow night.

- Sarah and I have been working on the budget. I'll send it to you in the next two hours. How are your parts coming along?
- Will I receive a draft of the study design tonight by 8 pm as we planned?
- How many letters of support have you received? Who has sent them? Who hasn't?

I guess that's all for now. Get back to me ASAP, please, to calm my nerves! Thanks, F.

appendix 13
Some Fundraising Reminders

- The biggest reason for people not giving is that they are not asked.
- Don't apologize when you ask for money. Fundraising is not about begging; it is about giving people an opportunity to do something good with their money.
- Emotion is a more powerful force than rationality when it comes to gift giving. Facts and reason may strengthen emotions, but they cannot replace them.
- People give to people, not to organizations. Successful fundraising is more about developing personal relationships than it is about asking for money.
- People give to those they like and trust.
- Do not act desperate, don't cry poor, and don't try to guilt-trip a prospective donor into giving.
- When asking for money, speak from your heart—it is honest, it is genuine, and it gets results.
- Timing of the ask is key. Wait until it seems the obvious thing to do.
- Be able to articulate your cause and needs convincingly, in only two or three sentences.
- Donors need to believe that your cause is important and has a chance of succeeding.
- People want to believe that their gift is doing something useful, and they want to know what that something is—what need is being fulfilled or what wrong is being made right.
- To get larger gifts, make the ask face-to-face.
- Remember that you are asking for an important cause, not for yourself.
- Once you make the ask, be quiet and stay quiet. Let the donor break the silence. This may be uncomfortable for you, but it is essential.
- When you make an ask, a response of no does not necessarily mean no way. No may mean that the time is not right for the donor, or it

may mean that the donor is uneasy about certain parts of what you are pitching.

- If you are not passionately committed to your cause, don't expect others to be. If your cause is important enough to ask others for money, you should make a meaningful gift yourself. (A meaningful gift from you, or from anyone, is more than a token—it reflects a level of caring commensurate with the donor's financial situation. Thus, a $10,000 gift from a billionaire is only a token; a $10 gift from a minimum wage worker is meaningful.)
- When contacting a prospective donor to request a meeting, let the person know the purpose of the meeting—that you would like to meet and talk about your campaign. You probably will not say outright, "I want to ask you for money," but the prospective donor should understand ahead of time that fundraising is part of your mission. This gives the donor some time to think about giving.
- When meeting with a prospective donor, pick a quiet, comfortable place without distractions. After a little warm-up social chatter, get to the point. Keep the meeting short—no more than thirty minutes.
- When meeting with prospective donors, listen carefully to what is said but also to what is *not* said. It can reveal lots about what you need to know to win their support.
- Stewardship of donors (after a gift) is absolutely key to development. Donors want to be kept in the loop, and they want to know that their gift really is making a difference.
- Let donors know that their gift is appreciated. Say thank you promptly, more than once, and in more than one way. Some fundraisers believe that you should thank a donor at least five times.

appendix 14
What the Main Elements of a Funding Proposal Look Like

Title Page (one example)

The New England Environmental Technical Assistance Program (NEETAP)
A Proposal to the Xxxx Foundation

Principal Investigator: Jeffrey Hughes
267 Jeffords Hall
University of Vermont
Burlington, VT 05405
Tel.: 802 656-xxxx
Fax: 802 656-xxxx
Email: jwhughes@xxx.xxx
15 January 20xx

Executive Summary/Abstract (two examples)

Example 1

We propose to establish an environmental problem-solving help center for grassroots organizations in need of technical assistance. This pro bono service, the New England Technical Assistance Program (NEETAP), will be staffed by teams of graduate fellows from the Environmental Leadership Program at the University of Vermont working under the direction of Dr. Xxxx, Dean of the Environmental Leadership Program . . .

Example 2

Riparian corridors are the streamside land-water interfaces that extend from headwater streams to lowland floodplains. They are receiving increased attention because of their (presumed) biological diversity. They also are thought to connect distant and different ecosystems and thus contribute to biological exchange and ecological integration at the landscape level. The goal of our research is to critically examine these presumed trends and to attempt to understand spatial and temporal dynamics of populations and communities of vascular plants along and across riparian corridors.

Twelve sections of riparian corridor, 200m in length each, will be examined along each of three New England stream orders: headwater streams, mid-order streams, and fifth- and sixth-order rivers. Patterns of species richness and related environmental variables will be compared, as will differences in richness associated with distance and elevation from the stream. Five transects of six permanent plots each (0.5m x 2.0m, divided into 0.5m x 0.5m subplots to permit sampling at different scales) also will be established within each corridor to evaluate year-to-year differences in recruitment, survivorship . . .

Project Overview (two examples)

Example 1

State and federal agencies mostly focus on region-wide environmental problems, but many environmental concerns are local and too small to warrant the attention of a government agency. As a result, local concerns generally stay local and ignored until a body of concerned citizens steps forward. Those who join grassroots efforts may be passionately committed to the cause, but they eventually learn that dedication and great intentions are not enough to effect change. The reason that well-intentioned efforts so often fail usually comes down to concerned citizens lacking the technical expertise and problem-solving skills they need to be effective. Our proposal to create a pro bono assistance program addresses these shortcomings . . .

Example 2

Riparian corridor refers to the narrow land-water interface that extends from headwaters (first-order streams) to lowland floodplains (larger-order streams; fig. 1). Riparian ecosystems are characterized by two essential characteristics: (1) laterally flowing water that rises and falls at least once within a growing season; and (2) a high degree of connectedness with other ecosystems (Smith 2019). Connectedness can occur from adjacent uplands and/or with upstream-downstream riparian systems through: energy fluxes (kinetic energy of wind and water); hydrologic fluxes . . .

Justification (one example)

The Northern Forest (NFLC) spans northern New York, New Hampshire, Maine, and Vermont. The main industry and source of revenue for this twenty-six million acres of rural expanse is forest products, especially from red spruce and balsam fir, which are used to produce paper and materials for building construction. Forest-related jobs account for a total annual payroll of over three billion dollars (Frank and Jones 2021), but most of the region is economically depressed.

The Northern Forest is an important recreational resource for the seventy million people who live within a day's drive, for it provides wilderness values and opportunities that are not found elsewhere in the Northeast. . . . The purpose of our proposed study is to evaluate how roads and roadsides alter the forest resource base of the Northern Forest over the short and long terms. This has profound implications for ecological and economic sustainability of the forest and for all Northern Forest stakeholders.

Explicitly Stated Goals and Objectives (two examples)

Example 1

The goal of the New England Environmental Technical Assistance Program (NEETAP) is to create a pro bono environmental think tank that can help grassroots organizations tackle environmental challenges for which they are ill-prepared. Graduate students in the Environmental Leadership Program will augment their academic training with real-world experience by serving as NEETAP consultants.

To reach this goal we will meet these objectives:

Objective 1: To have the NEETAP website online and operational no later than March 15, 20xx.

Objective 2: To inform at least twenty New England nonprofits of NEETAP services by April 2, 20xx.

Objective 3: To complete NEETAP training of twelve Environmental Leadership graduate students by March 5, 20xx . . .

Example 2

The purpose of our proposed study is to evaluate the effects of three different road types on the surrounding forest ecosystem.

Our first objective (Objective 1) is to quantify road coverage (acreage and percentage of Northern Forest Land in roads) in ten randomly selected Northern Forest blocks (five thousand acres each) by Sept. 1, 2100.

Our second objective (Objective 2) is to quantify the density of spruce and fir seedlings, saplings, and trees along roads and at increasing distances into the surrounding forest. We will complete this by November 18, 2100 . . .

Methods/Procedures

See chapter 3.

Work Schedule/Timetable

See Goals and Objectives examples above. Another approach is to present the work schedule as a timeline:

1 May	1 June	1 July	1 August	1 September

Objective 1	_____
Objective 2	_____
Objective 3	_____

Qualifications

Briefly make a case for why you and your organization are qualified to complete this project successfully. Include resumes of all key participants.

Itemized Budget (two examples)

Example 1

BUDGET SHEET

Personnel

Salaries:	
Jeffrey Hughes (PI; 200 hrs @ $50/hr)	$10,000
Kim Watson (technician; 12 months @ $3,000/month)	$36,000
Total salaries	**$46,000**
Benefits ($46,000 x 0.36)	$16,560
Total personnel (salaries + benefits)	**$62,560**
Travel (6,000 miles @ $0.50/mile)	$3,000
Supplies	$1,200
Copying, mailing, and shipping	$600
Telephone	$960
TOTAL REQUESTED	**$68,320**

Example 2

BUDGET SHEET (another standard format)

	Funds requested		
A. *Personnel*	yr 1	yr 2	total
Principal investigator (PI)	$12,500	$8,000	$20,500
Other senior personnel	$6,250	$6,750	$13,000
Support staff—technician, clerical, etc.	$17,000	$17,500	$34,500
a. Total salaries and wages	$35,750	$32,250	$68,000
b. Fringe benefits (35%)	$12,513	$11,288	$23,801
Total	$38,263	$43,538	$91,801

B. *Equipment*	0	0	0
C. *Travel* (includes lodging and meals)	$11,620	$8,900	$20,520
D. *Materials and supplies*	$200	$200	$400
E. *Copying and publication*	$100	$600	$700
F. *Postage, telephone, computer, shipping*	$570	$620	$1,190
Totals (A+B+C+D+E+F)	$50,753	$53,858	$104,611
TOTAL REQUEST			**$104,611**

Before filling out the budget sheet, find out what the granting organization is willing to pay for and what it is not. Some organizations will not pay for large pieces of equipment, for example, and few will pay for food. Do not ask for what they won't give.

In finalizing your budget:

- Make the take-home financial picture clear and obvious. Place the budget justification page and budget sheet at the end of your proposal where they are easily found.
- Check with your business office to see if you need to include overhead. "Overhead" refers to the daily operational expenses (lights, heat, rent, and such) that need to be paid to keep your organization afloat.
- Check with your business office to see if you need to include fringe in personnel expenses. "Fringe" refers to the package of benefits (health coverage, insurance, and such) that an organization provides to employees. Fringe benefits are pricey, often 30–40 percent of an employee's salary and wages.
- Do not underbudget travel expenses. In 2022, a standard rate for budgeting is 50 cents/mile.
- Round off all expenses to the nearest dollar.
- Triple check your Budget Sheet so that numbers add up correctly.
- Do not inflate your budget, but do ask for what you need. An unrealistically low budget tells funding organizations that you don't know what you are getting into.

Budget Explanation/Justification (one example)

Personnel: The PI (Hughes) will oversee all aspects of the project. The largest time expenditures will be at the start of the project (locating appropriate field sites, setting up instrumentation, training the technician) and at the end of the project (analyzing data and writing up findings).

The project is personnel-intensive and requires the services of a full-time technician. The technician (Watson) will collect data, prep samples, and enter results into a spreadsheet. She also will be responsible for maintaining equipment.

Employee benefits are charged at 35 percent of salary.

Travel: Over the course of the study, we anticipate visiting our field sites fifty times. The average round-trip distance of each trip is 120 miles; 50 trips x 120 miles/trip = 6,000 miles. We request the standard reimbursement rate of $0.50 per mile.

Supplies: Needed supplies include data storage devices, two increment borers, reagents, insect and tick repellent, and Rite-in-the-Rain data sheets.

Copying, mailing, and shipping: The main expense will be shipping live specimens to Drs. X and Y for identification. The other expected expense is copying (data sheets and key research papers).

Telephone: We will need to telephone our research collaborators at least weekly. Our request ($960) is the ATS's annual service charge.

appendix 15
Some Grant-writing Reminders

- State the problem or question clearly and quickly, then explain how you propose to solve it. Remember that a proposal is just that—a proposed course of action to solve a specific problem.
- Be bold and specific rather than timid and general, even when you are fuzzy on details. Proposals that advance innovative, exciting, new ideas win; safe, generalized, humdrum proposals lose.
- Make your proposals lean and mean but full of muscle and substance. It is much easier to generate and sustain excitement for your project in a few pages than it is in twenty pages. Potential sponsors will ask for additional information if they need it.
- Write in short, simple, direct, uncomplicated sentences. A straightforward presentation suggests clear-headedness.
- Write in language that works for your audience. Avoid jargon unless you are sure the likely reviewers of your proposal use and understand the same jargon.
- Before submitting a proposal, always have at least one literate person proof it. People who know nothing about your ideas are the best reviewers.
- Make your proposals neat, clean, user-friendly, easy to read, and professional in appearance. Use twelve-point font, double-space everything, and leave wide margins. Print single-sided unless the proposal guidelines say otherwise.
- State your main points up-front while your readers are still paying attention.
- State your objectives explicitly, near the beginning of your proposal.
- Don't miss deadlines!
- Having officers of the funding organization know and like you gives you a giant leg up on the competition. As is true with other types of fundraising, development (of relationships) is essential to success.

- Think of your proposed action as being so important that nothing can stop you from finding a way to do it. That approach works much better than *give me the money so I can do the work*.
- Use the qualifications section of your proposal to sell yourself as well as your ideas.
- Don't abandon a rejected proposal if the idea is good. Repackage it and try again.
- Don't let rejection get you down. *No one* wins every grant he or she submits; you are a star if you win 30 percent of the time.
- Avoid the scattershot approach—generic proposals that you send everywhere don't work.
- Resist the temptation to play it safe and do what everyone else has done.
- It is okay to submit a proposal to different funding organizations to increase your chance of being funded. To have any chance of success, however, you need to treat each submission as a unique proposal that is tailored to the interests and style of the organization you are targeting. An effectively packaged proposal to USDA, for example, probably would not work well for a family foundation or vice versa, even if their priorities seem identical. Remember: a good salesperson adjusts the sales pitch to fit the buyer's interests.

appendix 16
Some Everyday Tasks, Situations, and Activities That Might Drag You Down

- answering emails
- dealing with phone mail messages
- making phone calls
- going to meetings
- working on the computer
- dealing with technology problems
- having too much responsibility
- being in a competitive environment
- trying to reach consensus
- being a peon
- being bossed around
- being micromanaged
- being caught up in routine, every day the same
- being stuck in mindless repetition
- having unstructured days
- spending too much time alone
- not spending enough time alone
- not having time to think
- having too much time to think
- not knowing what you are supposed to be doing
- not having enough to do
- having too much to do
- needing to juggle too much at the same time
- working all the time but never finishing
- ending the day with nothing to show for it
- spending the day milling around without a plan
- being overloaded with family responsibilities
- encountering conflict at home

- not getting enough sleep
- staying up too late
- getting up too early
- staying in bed too long
- spending all day inside
- not getting enough exercise
- not socializing enough
- having a life with all work and no play
- drinking too much caffeine
- experiencing low blood sugar
- turning on the TV or web-surfing when you are bored
- sitting in darkness

appendix 17
Some Everyday Tasks, Situations, and Activities That Might Lift You Up

- brainstorming
- thinking big
- launching new initiatives
- completing tasks
- organizing things
- having something tangible to show for your efforts
- teaching others
- troubleshooting
- networking
- having quiet time by yourself
- being able to work at your own pace
- implementing strategies
- being in charge
- schmoozing with big shots
- being challenged by others
- being in the spotlight
- engaging in competition
- winning
- collaborating
- taking a walk by yourself
- taking a walk with others
- engaging in gentle exercise
- taking part in aerobic exercise
- gardening
- listening to or playing music
- spending time with friends
- spending time outside
- staying in touch with people you care about

- enjoying the sunshine
- meeting new people
- eating chocolate
- drinking a bottle of beer
- drinking a glass of wine
- drinking a cup of coffee
- drinking a cup of tea

appendix 18
Querying References to Learn More about Candidates

Applications, resumes, and letters of recommendation showcase a person's qualifications and background, but they rarely reveal much about a person's character. If a person may be with you for a while though, you *do* want to know what you are getting yourself into if the person comes on board. The questionnaire (below) achieves that.

The questionnaire works by asking references to react quickly to a large number of opposing personality traits, with each question focusing on a particular character trait (e.g., is the candidate more of a team player or more of a solo operator?). When a reference hems and haws over a character trait question, move on quickly, because the reference's hesitancy is a response in itself—that the candidate's trait falls somewhere in the middle. So don't let references dwell on an unanswered question, deal with hesitancy by answering for the reference: "it sounds like the candidate is not really one way more than another" (then quickly move to the next question).

Keep the questions moving—*you want immediate gut reactions rather than measured responses*. Except for the last five (questions 38–42), no question should take more than a few seconds to answer.

Before using the questionnaire for keeps, practice on friends or colleagues. Call them on the phone and practice your delivery until you feel comfortable with it, and are able to get through all the questions in ten or fifteen minutes.

Some questions may not work for you or seem important, so discard those you do not like. Err on the side of *keeping* rather than rejecting questions, however, because the questionnaire works best when you ask lots of rapid-fire, seemingly innocent questions. References let down their guard and speak more openly when they are asked lots of questions.

A way to introduce yourself and the questionnaire follows.

Hello, _____,

This is Jeffrey Hughes, director of _____. Elizabeth has applied for a position with us, and you wrote a very supportive letter of recommendation for her—it's clear that you think highly of her. Do you have a few minutes now to tell me a little bit more about Elizabeth so I know her better as a person?

As a way to get to know her better, I'd like to run by you a long list of descriptors to see which personality traits fit Elizabeth, and which personality traits don't. As you'll see, the descriptors aren't necessarily good or bad, they just represent different ways of being.

Are you ready? I'll just zip through them; just let me know which ones describe Elizabeth. If you don't have a strong feeling one way or the other, that's fine.

So here they are. Does one personality trait come closer to describing her than the other?

1. talks nonstop/rarely speaks
2. easy going/more on the serious side
3. a team player/more of a solo operator
4. likes to talk things out/likes to work things out on her own
5. sometimes a little too confident in her abilities/she could use a little more self-confidence
6. a people person/more of an introvert
7. very conversational—you'd never run out of things to talk about/she's not much of a talker—keeping a conversation going with her can take some effort
8. a freethinker/more of a black-and-white thinker
9. likes to be in charge/likes someone else to make decisions
10. dependable/means well but doesn't always follow through or complete things on time
11. spunky/more subdued
12. what you see is what you get/sometimes it's hard to know what's really going on with her
13. a leader in the conventional sense/works more behind the scenes (more of a support person)
14. stays on task/can get sidetracked sometimes
15. seems to get along with everyone/sometimes rubs people the wrong way
16. goes with the flow/often critical of how things are going

17. fun-loving/takes self a little too seriously
18. seems young for her chronological age/seems old for her chronological age
19. always gives people the benefit of the doubt/more inclined to blame or find fault
20. headstrong/goes with the flow
21. cheerful and upbeat/can be a little moody
22. very organized/can be a little scatterbrained
23. low maintenance/high maintenance
24. dominates/takes a backseat
25. says what she's thinking or feeling/holds cards close to her chest (she could be burning inside, but you'd never know it)
26. immediately likable/she grows on you (you need to get to know her a bit)
27. likes supervision/prefers being left alone
28. opinionated/noncommittal
29. is too tough on herself/doesn't beat herself up over things
30. always meets deadlines and gets things done on time/she means well but obstacles sometimes get in the way
31. can be a little judgmental/doesn't seem to judge others
32. talks about others a lot/doesn't talk lots about others
33. her moods sometimes weigh on others/her moods are her own
34. quick to point out what's wrong or why something won't work/not quick to judge
35. always pulls more than her share of the load/sometimes missing in action
36. a good person to represent you at a board meeting/someone else would be better
37. a good person to answer sensitive phone calls/someone else would be better

And now a few hypotheticals:

38. If you were shipwrecked on a deserted island, would Elizabeth be a good person to be shipwrecked with? Why would you be glad it's her rather than someone else?
39. Why wouldn't she be your first choice?
40. Over time, anyone would get on your nerves, and that includes Elizabeth. What about her would wear on you?

41. How does Elizabeth deal with criticism?
42. How does Elizabeth deal with things not going her way?

That's it! Those are all my questions. I feel I know Elizabeth so much better now, thank you! Before I sign off, is there anything you'd like to add? Thank you again for supporting her application.

recommended reading

Chapter 1

Gregory, Robin, Lee Failing, Michael Harstone, Graham Long, Tim McDaniels, and Dan Ohlson. 2012. *Structured Decision Making: A Practical Guide to Environmental Management Choices*. Hoboken, NJ: Wiley-Blackwell.

Hughes, Jeffrey W. 2007. *Environmental Problem Solving: A How-To Guide*. Hanover, NH: University Press of New England.

Hull, R. Bruce, David P. Robertson, and Michael Mortimer. 2020. *Leadership for Sustainability: Strategies for Tackling Wicked Problems*. Washington, DC: Island Press.

Chapters 2 and 3

Feinsinger, Peter. 2001. *Designing Field Studies for Biodiversity Conservation*. Washington, DC: Island Press.

Olson, Randy. 2018. *Don't Be Such a Scientist: Talking Substance in an Age of Style*. 2nd ed. Washington, DC: Island Press.

Wheelan, Charles. 2014. *Naked Statistics: Stripping the Dread from Data*. New York: W. W. Norton.

Chapter 4

Ham, Sam H. 1992. *Environmental Interpretation: A Practical Guide for People with Big Ideas and Small Budgets*. Milwaukee, WI: North American Press.

Heath, Chip, and Dan Heath. 2007. *Made to Stick: Why Some Ideas Survive and Others Die*. New York: Random House.

North American Association for Environmental Education (NAEE). Guidelines for Excellence series. https://naaee.org/eepro/resources.

Tools for Engaging Landowners Effectively (TELE). https://www.engaginglandowners.org/.

Chapter 5

Margolin, Jaime. 2020. *Youth to Power: Your Voice and How to Use It*. New York: Hachette Go.

Patterson, Kerry, Joseph Grenny, Ron McMillan, and Al Switzler. 2021. *Crucial Conversations: Tools for Talking When Stakes Are High*. 3rd ed. New York: McGraw-Hill Education.

Chapter 6

Grant, Adam. 2021. *Think Again: The Power of Knowing What You Don't Know*. New York: Viking Press.

Washington State Department of Enterprise Services. "Root Cause Analysis." https://des.wa.gov/services/risk-management/about-risk-management/enterprise-risk-management/root-cause-analysis.

Chapter 7

Carnegie, Dale. 2012. *How to Win Friends and Influence People in the Digital Age*. New York: Simon and Schuster.

Mandino, Og. 1983. *The Greatest Salesman in the World*. New York: Bantam.

Schmeer, Kammi. *Stakeholder Analysis Guidelines*. https://www.who.int/workforcealliance/knowledge/toolkit/33.pdf.

Chapter 8

Heyman, Darian Rodriguez. 2016. *Nonprofit Fundraising 101: A Practical Guide with Easy to Implement Ideas and Tips from Industry Experts*. Hoboken, NJ: Wiley.

Karsch, Ellen, and Arlen Sue Fox. 2019. *The Only Grant-Writing Book You'll Ever Need*. New York: Basic Books.

Andy Robinson's fundraising webinars, http://andyrobinsononline.com/w/.

Chapter 9

Butler-Bowdon, Tom. 2017. *50 Self-Help Classics: The Greatest Books Distilled*. 2nd ed. London: Nicholas Brealey.

Appendix 5

Wessels, Tom. 1997. *Reading the Forested Landscape: A Natural History of New England*. Woodstock, VT: Countryman Press.

index